Parties and Politics
in Modern Germany

PARTIES AND POLITICS IN MODERN GERMANY

GERARD BRAUNTHAL
University of Massachusetts–Amherst

WestviewPress
A Division of HarperCollinsPublishers

Copyright © 1996 by Westview Press, Inc., A Division of HarperCollins Publishers, Inc.

Published in 1996 in the United States of America by Westview Press, Inc., 5500 Central Avenue, Boulder, Colorado 80301-2877, and in the United Kingdom by Westview Press, 12 Hid's Copse Road, Cumnor Hill, Oxford OX2 9JJ

Library of Congress Cataloging-in-Publication Data
Braunthal, Gerard, 1923–
    Parties and politics in modern Germany / Gerard Braunthal.
        p.   cm.
    Includes bibliographical references and index.
    ISBN 0-8133-2382-7 (hardcover).—ISBN 0-8133-2383-5 (pbk.)
        1. Political parties—Germany—History.   2. Germany—Politics and
government—20th century.   I. Title.
JN3972.A979B73   1996
324.243'009—dc20   95-46210
                                                                                CIP

The paper used in this publication meets the requirements of the American National Standard for Permanence of Paper for Printed Library Materials Z39.48-1984.

10   9   8   7   6   5   4   3   2   1

Contents

Illustrations

Acknowledgments

I AM DEEPLY INDEBTED to the German Academic Exchange Service and to the Friedrich Ebert Foundation (Bonn) for giving me study grants in 1990 and 1992, respectively, to interview leaders and staff of all major parties and several minor parties, journalists, and scholars in both parts of Germany and to collect party documents. I am also thankful to Inter Nationes (Bonn) for inviting me in 1990 and 1994 to participate on a team of scholars and journalists in observing the German national elections.

I offer further thanks to the ever-helpful staffs of the Federal Office for Political Education (Bonn), the Bundestag archive, Inter Nationes, the Ministry of the Interior, the Social Democratic Party press and documentation archive, Forschungsgruppe Wahlen and Allensbach public opinion institutes, the German Information Center (New York), and the University of Massachusetts–Amherst library for their kind assistance. In addition, Klaus Dammann, Dieter Dettke, Hans-Eberhard Dingels, Jürgen Faulenbach, Hannelore Koehler, Peter Munkelt, Dieter Roth, Hans-Joachim Veen, and numerous other specialists provided me with valuable information and insights. Walther Keim of the Bundestag Press and Documentation Center generously made available cartoons from his extensive collection, and several cartoonists kindly gave permission to reprint their irresistible and humorous contributions to politics. Thanks also to George C. Lane Jr. for the computer preparation of the tables and figures.

Susan McEachern, senior editor of Westview Press, suggested that the time had come for an introductory book on German political parties. Her able assistance and that of her staff in the final preparation of the book deserve special mention. In this list of acknowledgments, the unflagging support of my family should not be omitted. Of course, none of these persons bears responsibility for any errors that may still be lodged between the book's covers.

Gerard Braunthal

Acronyms

AfA	Arbeitsgemeinschaft für Arbeitnehmerfragen (Association of Workers)
A90	Alliance 90
ASF	Arbeitsgemeinschaft Sozialdemokratischer Frauen (Association of Social Democratic Women)
BBU	Bundesverband Bürgerinitiativen Umweltschutz (Federal Association of Citizens' Initiatives for Environmental Protection)
CDU/CSU	Christlich-Demokratische Union/Christlich-Soziale Union (Christian Democratic Union-Christian Social Union)
DA	Demokratischer Aufbruch (Democratic Awakening)
DBD	Demokratische Bauernpartei Deutschlands (Democratic Farmers Party of Germany)
DKP	Deutsche Kommunistische Partei (German Communist Party)
DM	deutsche mark
DRP	Deutsche Reichspartei (German Reich Party)
DSU	Deutsche Sozial Union (German Social Union)
DVU	Deutsche Volksunion (German People's Union)
FDP	Freie Demokratische Partei (Free Democratic Party)
FIS	Front Islamique du Salut (Algerian Islamic Salvation Front)
FLN	Front de Libération Nationale (National Liberation Front)
FRG	Federal Republic of Germany
GDR	German Democratic Republic
GIC	German Information Center
Jusos	Jungsozialisten in der SPD (Young Socialists in the SPD)
KPD	Kommunistische Partei Deutschlands (Communist Party of Germany)
LDP	Liberal Demokratische Partei (Liberal Democratic Party)
LDPD	Liberal-Demokratische Partei Deutschlands (Liberal Democratic Party of Germany)
NATO	North Atlantic Treaty Organization
NDPD	National-Demokratische Partei Deutschlands (National Democratic Party of Germany [GDR])

NPD   Nationaldemokratische Partei Deutschlands (National Democratic Party of Germany [FRG])

NSDAP   Nationalsozialistische Deutsche Arbeiterpartei (National Socialist German Workers Party)

PDS   Partei des Demokratischen Sozialismus (Party of Democratic Socialism)

PRD   Partido de la Revolución Democrática (Democratic Revolutionary Party)

PRI   Partido Revolucionario Institucional (Institutional Revolutionary Party)

REP   Republikaner (Republicans)

SDP   Sozialdemokratische Partei in der DDR (Social Democratic Party of the GDR)

SED   Sozialistische Einheitspartei Deutschlands (Socialist Unity Party of Germany)

SPD   Sozialdemokratische Partei Deutschlands (Social Democratic Party of Germany)

SRP   Sozialistische Reichspartei (Socialist Reich Party)

SS   Schutzstaffel (Elite Guard)

Stasi   Ministerium für Staatssicherheit (Ministry for State Security)

UFV   Unabhängiger Frauenverband (Independent Women's Association)

USPD   Unabhängige Sozialdemokratische Partei Deutschlands (Independent Social Democratic Party of Germany)

Introduction

Germany is a powerful state in the international arena, especially since the 1990 accession of the eastern German Democratic Republic (GDR) to the western Federal Republic of Germany (FRG). The country's political and economic strength has given it a visibility and influence in European and world affairs few would have predicted in 1945. Then, Adolf Hitler's Germany lay in smoldering ruins, and the victorious Allied powers dictated its uncertain future. To understand the successful revival of the prostrate country (1945–1949), the divergent developments in the two rival capitalist and communist states (1949–1990), and developments in the unified Germany (1990–present), we focus on one key segment of the political system—the political parties.

The parties, according to the first major theme of this book, were at the center of the post–1945 political systems and are at the center of the current unified system. Although in the FRG there have been strong competing interest groups and a plethora of social movements, party leaders, on assuming cabinet office, become national decisionmakers shaping the state's domestic and foreign policies.

In the GDR, the chiefs of the powerful Socialist Unity Party (SED) were the undisputed rulers of the dictatorial state. Unlike in West Germany, they could not allow countervailing forces to challenge their decisions. Opponents were jailed or forced into exile. To give the appearance of having a democratic and pluralist political system, SED leaders allowed the founding of minor parties, which, however, had no significant influence.

The parties, according to the second major theme of this book, provided the political stability underpinning the democratic FRG after 1949 and the communist GDR from 1949 to 1989. Such stability did not signify that the party systems were frozen in time and not subject to the political, economic, and social forces impinging on the development of both countries for four decades. Changes, of course, took place, but often they were glacial and came too late to appease popular dissatisfaction with the status quo. This was true especially in the GDR in 1989 when the communist regime collapsed. Since 1990, the party leaders in the unified Germany have had to confront the continuing dissatisfaction with government policies among many eastern Germans and the psychological gap between the formerly divided people.

In recent years, critics of parties have referred repeatedly to the citizens' *Parteienverdrossenheit* (disaffection with parties), a term chosen by a committee of specialists as the most favorite expression of the year 1992. Parallel with a twin term *Politikverdrossenheit* (disaffection with politics), *Parteienverdrossenheit* has become a part of the German political vocabulary. In 1992, German president Richard von Weizsäcker, supporting the critics, doubted the major parties' ability to resolve urgent political, economic, and social issues. He also claimed that parties were obsessed with holding onto power, exceeded their constitutional rights, and lacked "conceptual" leadership.[1] Other critics accused parties of lacking openness and honesty and of being prone to graft and corruption. Party leaders admitted to some of the charges but defended their organizations as the crucial variable in politics.

This introductory study of modern German parties focuses in part on the question of whether the current German party system faces the same malaise or crisis of politics many advanced industrial and developing states are experiencing. In such states, incumbent politicians have to confront the anger of voters who blame them for the grave societal problems of mass unemployment, crime, environmental pollution, cuts in the welfare system, national identity and minorities, immigration and integration, and a decline in the quality of living. Frustrated citizens, especially the young, vent their anger at the system by supporting new parties or opting out of politics. In the 1994 U.S. congressional election, only 39 percent of the electorate turned out to vote. In many parts of the world, right-wing extremist parties are gaining strength as a result of individual alienation and system breakdown.

Can we speak of a crisis of politics in Germany if its voters are identifying less with their traditional parties and in consequence switching to other parties or failing to vote? Can the party system provide political stability if a realignment of parties characterizes developments since unification in 1990? How much of a threat to the democratic system are right-wing parties and groups? What are the governing coalition combinations possible in Bonn when two equally strong party blocs, made up of center-conservative and center-left parties, might not produce a viable majority in coming national elections?

Before such questions can be answered, we must first study foreign and German parties from comparative and historical perspectives. Part 1 surveys the history of parties and party systems in various regions of the world and assesses the ways in which party systems have been categorized and analyzed. Then it examines the historical development of German parties, which operated in the authoritarian Empire, democratic Weimar, and totalitarian Nazi eras.

Part 2 deals with the array of old and new parties in western Germany from 1945 to 1949 and in the semisovereign FRG from 1949 to 1990. The parties were (and still are) the centerpiece of a pluralist system based on a democratic constitutional foundation, funded in part by public outlays, and affected by a hybrid electoral system. In this "party state," the parties' political legitimacy has been fully recognized. Chapters 4 to 8 consider each of the major and minor parties in the FRG that have had an effect on the political system. In every instance, we focus on a party's leadership, organization, membership, ideology, and electoral support to gauge its political effectiveness.

Part 3 deals first with party developments in Soviet-occupied eastern Germany from 1945 to 1949 and in the GDR from 1949 to 1989. In the authoritarian state, the Socialist Unity Party was the dominant political actor, while the vassal bloc parties played bit parts to give the system a false democratic facade. Part 3 next deals with the new democratic parties and groups that surfaced in the 1989 and 1990 collapse of the GDR.

Part 4 examines the parties in unified Germany since 1990, with particular attention to the first all-German election of 1990 and to the effect the western parties had on the emerging party system in eastern Germany. Chapter 12 dissects the 1994 national election to see whether it showed the discontent of voters with the status quo.

The concluding chapter assesses the significance of the German parties in the contrasting democratic and authoritarian systems from 1945 to 1990 and in unified Germany since 1990. In looking at the nebulous future, the chapter speculates on the strength of the leftist, centrist, and rightist parties in a democratic setting. It addresses the question of a crisis in the party system as the country approaches a probably turbulent twenty-first century.

Notes

1. *Richard von Weizsäcker im Gespräch mit Gunter Hofmann und Werner A. Perger* (Frankfurt: Eichborn, 1992).

PART ONE

An International and National Overview

• 1 •

Political Parties:
A Comparative Perspective

An assessment of the German party system will make comparisons to parties and party systems in other polities more meaningful if the diverse analytical approaches to studying parties in a supranational context are highlighted first. This chapter therefore deals with the historical origins of parties in several countries; the discord on definitions of parties; their competitiveness, or lack of it, in national political systems; their ideological or pragmatic orientation; their organizational structures; their ability to mobilize members and voters; and their functions.

Historical Origins

Parties in different forms have existed since the creation of political systems. In Roman times, circa 450 B.C., the rudimentary ancestors of parties, known as "factions" (derived from the Latin word *facere*, to do, to act), emerged. At the time, a small privileged patrician class despotically ruled Rome. It took a century for the large plebian class, through numerous struggles, to achieve political equality with the patricians.

From the twelfth to the fourteenth century, two rival political factions of notables—the Ghibellines, supporting the emperors, and the Guelphs, supporting the popes—plunged Italy into warfare. The factions, which had each controlled a few cities, disappeared with the decline of the rivalry between papacy and empire.

In the seventeenth century, the term "party" (derived from the Latin *partire,* to partition) came into use in Europe. Like the factions, the parties had no mass basis but were groups of aristocratic leaders who surrounded themselves with a coterie of loyal followers. Later these groups became parties of notables or propertied men who supported candidates for seats in parliaments.

Many political observers denounced parties and factions for undermining and endangering the governments in power. In Britain, these observers criticized the feuds between the Tories and Whigs, two governing aristocratic factions, following the restoration of the monarchy in 1660. Viscount Bolingbroke, statesman and political writer, wrote in 1738: "Governing by party . . . must always end in the government of a faction. . . . Party is a political evil, and faction is the worst of all parties."[1]

In 1770, Edmund Burke, another well-known British statesman and writer, rejected the negative image of parties. He developed a more positive meaning: "Party is a body of men united, for promoting by their joint endeavor the national interest, upon some particular principle in which they are all agreed."[2] Burke saw British parties as organizations contributing to the consensus on constitutional practices.

In France, the revolutionary ferment in 1789 accentuated the divisions in society, which led to the founding of political clubs. Representatives to the Estates General (later, National Constituent Assembly), who met in Versailles and Paris to discuss the collapse of the royal absolutist regime and the creation of a republican regime, realized that they shared common interests spanning the provinces. Girondists and Jacobins, and later Montagnards, organized, each espousing different ideologies. By the time the French Constituent Assembly met in 1848, groups of moderate republicans, Catholic monarchists, rightists, and leftists had formed, creating a system of modern parties. However, they identified themselves by the name of the place where they met rather than by their embryonic ideologies.[3]

In the United States, George Washington and John Madison warned that factions and parties were divisive and endangered the rights of citizens. But they could not halt the emergence of the class-based parties—the Federalists, led by Alexander Hamilton, and the Anti-Federalists, led by Thomas Jefferson. From the 1830s on, the parties assumed greater importance as legislatures became more representative and suffrage was extended. At the same time, party politicians, heading the successor parties, the Republicans and the Democrats, built up a system of patronage under the protection of corrupt state and city machines. As a consequence, around the turn of the twentieth century some writers again characterized the parties and their bosses as perversions of the general will.[4]

Discord on Definitions

Once modern parties had developed in many countries, scholars questioned how to define and categorize them—that is, what features and functions characterized them within various governmental systems? According to Giovanni Sartori, "A party is any political group identified by an official label that presents at elections, and is capable of placing through elections (free or nonfree), candidates for public office."[5]

Sigmund Neumann, who underlines the importance of a party as a "lifeline of modern politics," writes that it is "the articulate organization of society's active political agents, those who are concerned with the control of governmental power and who compete for popular support with another group or groups holding divergent views. As such it is the great intermediary which links social forces and ideologies to official governmental institutions and relates them to political action within the larger political community."[6]

Thomas Hodgkin broadens the definition to include parties in one-party noncompetitive states: "It is probably most convenient to consider as 'parties' all political organizations which regard themselves as parties and which are generally so regarded."[7] Sigmund Neumann disagrees, arguing that to call the Nazi Party in totalitarian Germany a party is wrong because there was no freedom to belong to another party. According to him, "The dictatorial party's monopoly, which prevents the free formation and expression of opinion, is the precise antithesis of the party system," which he characterizes as having more than one party.[8]

Classifying Parties by Competition

As the controversy over definitions indicates, scholars do not agree on how to best analyze parties and party systems. They therefore study parties from different perspectives, one of which is to classify systems by the degree of competition among parties as measured by their number and strength in any one state. However, there are a very few states, such as Saudi Arabia, the United Arab Emirates, and Iran, in which powerful monarchs, sheikhs, and clerics reign who do not allow any party to operate for fear that it could threaten their rule.

One-Party Systems

More frequently, dictatorial rulers allow only one ideological party or movement to exist as a way of legitimizing the regime and ensuring the population's loyalty to the state. In the totalitarian regimes of Nazi Germany, the former Soviet Union, and the People's Republic of China under Mao Zedong, the monolithic party in power controlled all aspects of society and the state. Similarly, in most civilian or military authoritarian regimes, such as those found on nearly all continents (e.g., in various periods, Zaire, Liberia, Portugal, Spain, Pakistan, Indonesia, Argentina, and Brazil), government leaders permitted or permit only one party to function. However, the dictatorial rule is less oppressive and the party less ideologically driven than in totalitarian systems. Opposition groups may be able to operate clandestinely until the system eventually collapses or the military hands over power to party politicians.[9]

Not all one-party states are ruled by dictators. After World War II, the charismatic leaders of newly independent Third World states, especially in Africa, converted the popular movements or parties that had battled the colonial masters into one dominant force within the new democratic political system. To some leaders, granting people the right to participate in local governing units ("people's power") was more important during the transition stage than a competitive party system, which might produce rivalries among conflicting regional interests that the country could ill afford. Unfortunately, democracy in many of these countries did not survive the eruption of fierce tribal, ethnic, or religious conflicts; the rise of personal dictatorships; or the seizure of power by military juntas.[10]

In Algeria, for instance, the National Liberation Front (FLN) battled the French colonial government from 1954 to 1962, when independence was finally achieved. Thereafter Ahmed Ben Bella, the highly popular leader of the FLN who became prime minister and president, ruled over a limited democratic and socialist system in which the FLN was the sole party but in which power soon shifted to the bureaucracy and the military. The system lasted only three years. In 1965, an army junta overthrew the government and installed Colonel Houari Boumédienne as head of a revolutionary council. As a result of military rule, opposition groups disagreeing with the policies of the government surfaced. In 1989, short-lived constitutional reforms allowed opposition parties to form legally and made the prime minister responsible to the legislature rather than to the FLN.

In 1992, the Algerian Islamic Salvation Front (FIS) won the election and, under democratic principles, should have been allowed to form a new government. The secular government refused to accept the popular verdict, claiming that the Muslim FIS, once in power, would severely restrict the rights of non-Muslims. Thereupon angry FIS militants created serious civil disturbances, leading swiftly to a government ban on the FIS. In effect, the government ruled by force, and the nascent multiparty system collapsed.

Similar regime instability is prevalent in most other African states and on other continents as well. In some Latin American countries, the ruling party is merely the tool of a powerful state regime. Rare in Latin America is the example of Mexico, in which a hegemonic party, in this instance the Institutional Revolutionary Party (PRI), has succeeded through the manipulation of power, clientelism, and bribery to remain in power since 1929. Other Mexican parties have had little chance to win even in state elections. In recent years, however, the National Democratic Front—renamed the Democratic Revolutionary Party (PRD)—has become a leftist rival. Its presidential candidate, Cuauhtémoc Cárdenas, might have won in 1988 had the PRI not committed widespread electoral fraud. In the 1994 presidential election, the PRI was challenged by two major and six minor parties. The PRI candidate, Ernesto Zedillo, won the presidency, beating Cárdenas (PRD) and Diego Fernández de Cevallos, the candidate of the conservative National Action Party. The examples (among many) of Algeria and Mexico indicate that single-party rule can last for a long time but that the fluidity of power relations between different leaders and groups within and outside the ruling party makes regime changes inevitable.

Two-Party Systems

Two-party systems, such as those in the United States and Great Britain, are more competitive than one-party systems. Normally, the two parties alternate in power over the course of time. In each national election, one of them receives an absolute majority of the vote or a majority of legislative seats. It then forms a single-party cabinet, which remains in power until the next presidential or parliamentary election.

In the United States, the Republican and Democratic Parties have monopolized seats in Congress ever since the Civil War. Their candidates have won every presidential election. However, with weak party discipline in Congress, a president finds it difficult to gain legislative support for his policy from his own party, even when the party has had a majority in Congress, which has not always been the case.

Numerous third parties and movements, occasionally strong but usually weak, operate on the fringes of the two major U.S. parties. Their candidates for Congress have virtually no chance of winning because the electoral system, in which a candidate must obtain at least a plurality of votes in a single-member district (for the House of Representatives) or in a state (for the Senate), is skewed against minor or new parties attempting to challenge the major parties. Some of these parties, such as those on the left or right of the political spectrum, are doctrinaire; others, such as the Prohibition Party in the 1920s or the Ross Perot populist movement in 1992, arise in response to widespread protest against the policies of the two major parties or their failure to act on key issues.

In Britain, from 1852 to 1924 the Liberal and Conservative Parties dominated; then Labour replaced the Liberals as the major party battling the Conservatives. The Liberals remain in Parliament, but with few members. A Labour or Conservative one-party cabinet, supported by its disciplined parliamentary group, can translate its electoral mandate into public policy without many roadblocks by the opposition parties in Parliament. The electoral single-member district system, which the United States copied, favors the major parties, one of which will normally gain a plurality of votes and a majority of seats. Yet the British electoral system does give some parliamentary representation to minor parties whose strength is concentrated in certain districts and regions where their candidates are able to beat their major party opponents. However, these parties are not often significant in national policymaking and thus do not destabilize the system.[11]

Multiparty Systems

Most states have more than two major parties competing for political power. In Australia, three parties (Australian Labour, Liberal, and National) are dominant. In Canada, two major parties (Liberals and Progressive Conservatives) are challenged by the smaller Reform and New Democratic Parties. In other states, competition is high, as in Argentina, with twenty-one parties appearing on the ballot in a recent election.

Scandinavian parties fall in the middle range numerically. Among the six to eight, however, the Social Democrats have usually gained a plurality of votes. Political stability is nearly guaranteed because party leaders, whenever coalition governments are formed, achieve compromises on major issues. With few exceptions, the cabinet manages to remain in power for the length of the legislative session.

In other countries, political stability is a dream rarely realized. Such is Italy. From 1948 on, a coalition of Christian Democrats, Socialists, Liberals, and allied parties repeatedly set up new coalition governments. Before a government was formed, parties, with little in common except the desire to govern, engaged in protracted and laborious negotiations, ending in only some minor ministerial reshuffling. The government's life span was often less than a year because of internal policy schisms that resulted in a coalition party's decision to quit the government. Communists on the left and monarchists and neofascists on the right were in perpetual opposition in Parliament.

In the early 1990s, a series of major corruption scandals implicating thousands of top government and industry officials rocked Italy. The citizens lost all faith in the establishment parties, and in March 1994 few Italians voted in the national election for the formerly powerful Christian Democrats, who in desperation had changed their name to the Popular Party, or for the Socialists. The scandal-free and reformist Communist Party, renamed the Democratic Party of the Left in 1991, did relatively well but could not beat the trio of right-wing parties that formed the government. The parties were the Forza Italia, headed by Silvio Berlusconi, the country's biggest media tycoon and owner of the champion Milan soccer team; the Northern League, a conservative regional party; and the neofascist National Alliance, one of whose officials is the granddaughter of the fascist dictator Benito Mussolini. Berlusconi, without any political experience, became prime minister. The election did not lead to a change in the multiparty system, but it produced a new set of political actors on the fragile political stage. In December 1994, Berlusconi resigned when he was implicated in a new corruption case involving one of his business firms. Lamberto Dini, a former central banker and Treasury minister, formed a new cabinet made up primarily of nonparty ministers.

When a totalitarian or authoritarian system collapses and a democratic system emerges, a multiparty system normally evolves. The swift end of communist rule in the former Soviet Union and Eastern European countries beginning in 1989 led to a blossoming of new parties. In Russia, in the December 1993 election, conducted under a replica of the German electoral system (see Chapter 3), eight parties received enough votes to gain seats in the lower house of Parliament. Russia's Choice, the party supporting President Boris N. Yeltsin and his economic reform policies, led with 94 seats. The remarkably misnamed Liberal Democratic Party was the runner-up with 78 seats. It is headed by the ardent rightist Vladimir V. Zhirinovsky, who crusaded for a new Russian empire and racial primacy and against the swift pace of Yeltsin's economic reforms. The Communists, the Agrarians, Women of Russia, and three centrist blocs captured the other parliamentary seats.[12]

In Eastern European countries, power has shifted within the new multiparty system in the course of only a few years. Centrist and rightist parties gained strength when the communist system collapsed. They dismantled the centralized command economy and, as in Russia, attempted, often through shock therapy methods, to convert it into a capitalist system. As a result, most of the population suffered severe economic hardships. Frustrated and angered by high unemployment and inflation, and by the new rich, who drove expensive cars and patronized luxury restaurants, and yearning for security in the midst of swift changes, voters in 1991 in Lithuania, 1993 in Poland, and 1994 in Ukraine and Hungary turned away from the conservative parties. Instead, they gave the Communists, by then reformists, a mandate to form new governments, which promised to proceed more cautiously toward economic reforms and to maintain a social welfare net. Despite the political shifts, the multiparty system has remained in place—no different from states having a long history of three or more competing parties.

Classifying states by their number of parties is obviously difficult. For instance, should minor parties be counted if they exist in systems with one or two dominant parties? One specialist wrote, "The upshot is that if the categories one-party, two-party, and multiparty systems are taken at face value they yield a classificatory scheme that simply does not classify."[13] Despite such limitations, however, this typology is still one of several important tools for comparing parties or party systems.

Other Classifications and Analyses

Another way to classify parties is according to whether they take a doctrinaire or a pragmatic position on public issues. In recent decades, during which ideological differences among parties have softened, some communist, socialist, religious, nationalist, and neofascist parties have maintained an official doctrinaire position. They may shed it and become pragmatic to gain the support of the large number of voters clustered in the middle of the political spectrum. If successful, these parties can be classified as mass integration, or "catchall," people's parties.[14]

Still another approach to studying parties is to look at their structures. Around the turn of the century, Robert Michels observed the hierarchical structure of socialist parties and concluded that it was based on an "iron law of oligarchy," in which leaders have tight control over members.[15] His thesis has been much contested. In the 1950s, Maurice Duverger, in a seminal book, described the variety of leadership and organizational patterns within parties. They can have mass membership or only a few leaders and followers (labeled "cadre party"). Mass parties can be centralized or decentralized, have ideological factions, and provide a choice between direct membership or indirect membership through affiliated groups.[16]

Parties can also be categorized according to their mobilization ability. In the behavioral approach, popular especially in the United States, specialists are less interested in the rules and norms of legal institutions than in the interaction and activities of party leaders and members; the voters' degree of identification with parties; and the impact of class, gender, occupation, religion, and social background on voters' preferences. Much of the behaviorists' empirical information is gleaned from periodic public opinion polls, exit polls on election day, and aggregate survey and electoral data. They consider their approach to be more scientific and less Western biased than the more institutional approaches, which have been enjoying a revival in recent years.

Yet another classification scheme, the functional-systemic approach, analyzes the functions parties perform within the political system. Parties principally express and articulate the views of interest groups and, if necessary, serve as broker among competing groups; aggregate diverse views into programmatic policy; socialize and mobilize individuals to integrate them into the organization; recruit and choose leaders (in the latest political jargon, "the political class"); and, if they gain control of the government, convert their policies into public policies or, if in opposition, criticize public policies and offer alternatives.[17]

Conclusion

The various methods for studying parties show how hard it is for scholars to design a grand theory or framework that would span diverse political systems, institutions, and cultures. How easy it would be if we could agree on how to define parties and then single out the uniformities among them. But the number of deviant cases among parties is too high for easy theory-building.

No matter what approach scholars select, a key question is how salient parties are in diverse social and political systems. In most systems, they are crucial in linking citizens and the government.[18] With this caveat in mind, we turn to the German party system to assess its salience and examine its historical development and features, with a view to discovering how typical it is in comparison with other party systems in the advanced industrialized world.

Notes

1. Viscount (Henry St. John) Bolingbroke, *The Idea of a Patriot King;* quoted in Giovanni Sartori, *Parties and Party Systems: A Framework for Analysis* (Cambridge: Cambridge University Press, 1976), p. 6.

2. Edmund Burke, "Thoughts on the Cause of the Present Discontents" (1770), in *The Works of Edmund Burke* (Boston: Little, Brown, 1839), vol. 1, pp. 425–426; quoted in Sartori, *Parties and Party Systems,* p. 9.

3. Maurice Duverger, *Political Parties: Their Organization and Activity in the Modern State,* trans. Barbara North and Robert North, 2d English ed. (London: Methuen, 1959), pp. xxiv–xxv.

4. See, e.g., James Bryce, *Modern Democracies* (New York: Macmillan, 1921), vol. 1; and Mosei Ostrogorski, *Democracy and the Origin of Parties* (Garden City, N.Y.: Doubleday, 1964 [reprint of 2 vols., 1902 ed.].).

5. Sartori, *Parties and Party Systems,* p. 63.

6. Sigmund Neumann, "Toward a Comparative Study of Political Parties," in *Modern Political Parties: Approaches to Comparative Politics,* ed. Sigmund Neumann (Chicago: University of Chicago Press, 1957), p. 396.

7. Thomas Hodgkin, *African Political Parties* (London: Penguin, 1961), p. 16.

8. Sigmund Neumann, "Germany: Changing Patterns and Lasting Problems," in *Modern Political Parties,* ed. Neumann, p. 370. Sartori also argues that a system is a whole in which parties compete. A one-party state prevents competition; hence it does not have a party system but a "party-state system" (*Parties and Party Systems,* pp. 42–46).

9. Vicky Randall, Introduction to *Political Parties in the Third World,* ed. Vicky Randall (London: Sage, 1988), pp. 2–3.

10. Basil Davidson, *Modern Africa: A Social and Political History,* 2d ed. (London: Longman, 1989), pp. 216–222.

11. Among the minor parties in Parliament are the Scottish and Welsh Nationalists, the five parties from Northern Ireland, the Liberals, and, since 1981, a right-wing defector group from the Labour Party, the Social Democratic Party. The latter allied itself and then merged with the Liberals, known now as the Liberal Democrats (George Breckenridge, "Continuity and Change in Britain," in *Parties and Party Systems in Liberal Democracies,* ed. Steven B. Wolinetz [London: Routledge, 1988], pp. 203–221).

12. *New York Times,* December 30, 1993.

13. Harry Eckstein, "Party Systems," in *International Encyclopedia of Social Sciences,* ed. David Sills (New York: Macmillan–Free Press, 1968), vol. 11, p. 441.

14. Otto Kirchheimer coined the term "catchall" (see his "The Transformation of the Western European Party Systems," in *Political Parties and Political Development,* ed. Joseph La Palombara and Seymour Weiner [Princeton: Princeton University Press, 1966], pp. 184–192).

15. Robert Michels, *Political Parties: A Sociological Study of the Oligarchical Tendencies of Modern Democracy,* trans. Eden Paul and Cedar Paul (New York: Dover, 1959; reprint of 1911 ed.).

16. Duverger, *Political Parties.*

17. See Gabriel Almond and James Coleman, *The Politics of Developing Areas* (Princeton: Princeton University Press, 1960), p. 40. For summaries of approaches, see Kay Lawson, *The Comparative Study of Political Parties* (New York: St. Martin's Press, 1976), pp. 4–19.

18. See Kay Lawson, ed., *Political Parties and Linkage: A Comparative Perspective* (New Haven: Yale University Press, 1980).

· 2 ·

German Parties:
A Historical Perspective

A SURVEY OF THE contemporary German party system must begin with its antecedents in the nineteenth and twentieth centuries. Thus, this chapter examines continuities and discontinuities in the type of party system distinguishing each political system during the successive historical eras from 1871 to 1945. The chapter looks in more detail at each of the major parties and its ideology, its appeal to social groups, its electoral performance, and its effect on shaping government policies in the context of changing political, economic, and social conditions.

The Second Reich

Before the formation of the Second Reich in 1871, Germany consisted of a number of competing dynastic states in which power was held by absolutist monarchs and an entrenched nobility. Pressed by a rising liberal bourgeoisie, the rulers gradually allowed more liberties, but only those that did not undermine their own authority. Unlike in other Western states, where individual rights were won at the expense of state power, in Germany they were linked to the state.

This linkage blocked the development of a democratic society, including the existence of political parties, because the rulers knew that opposition parties, which could threaten their rule, would quickly emerge if given the chance. Thus, in many states the rulers allowed only local groups and factions, without political power, to form. These groups consisted primarily of notables rallying around a leader but lacked organization or mass membership from the diverse groups in society.

18

In 1815, the Congress of Vienna set up the loosely linked German Confederation, in which Prussia and Bavaria held the most power among the constituent states. None of the states had any intention of creating a pluralist system, such as Britain's, within which parliaments and parties could function freely. Hence, the stage was set for the German revolution of 1848, whose leaders in the short-lived Frankfurt Parliament demanded a liberal and democratic national government. Such a government would have allowed parties to organize. However, the Parliament's liberal middle-class factions, lacking a mass following, had no chance to gain their goal against the resistance of the conservative ruling aristocracy, the army, the bureaucracy, and the Protestant church.

It was not until the late 1850s and early 1860s, culminating in 1867 when the North German Confederation was created, that national parties arose. The rulers realized that if they were to remain in power, they would have to make some concessions to the liberal bourgeoisie for more representation and influence. They allowed a parliament to function, whose deputies in the lower house were elected by direct male suffrage but who had only limited powers. The parties, organized along ideological, class, and social lines, mirrored the impact of the Industrial Revolution on society. The feudal agrarian aristocracy was gradually losing power to the rising industrial and commercial classes, which formed the German Progressive Party and the German National Association, bringing together moderate liberal constitutionalists and radical democrats. Their demand for a parliamentary system to limit the powers of the ruling aristocratic elites was blocked by the elites, which severely restricted their activities.

In 1871, an assembly of princes proclaimed Wilhelm I emperor (kaiser) and Otto von Bismarck chancellor of the Second Empire, consisting of Prussia and other northern states and the southern states of Baden, Hesse, Bavaria, and Württemberg. The kaiser appointed all imperial officials, including the chancellor, whom he could also dismiss. As king of Prussia, the kaiser presided officially, but the chancellor de facto, over the Parliament's upper house, the Bundesrat. The chamber was the organ of the states, with Prussia receiving the highest number of seats. In Parliament, the Bundesrat had sole powers to ratify foreign and defense policies made by the chancellor.

The Reichstag was the lower house; its members were directly elected by all males over twenty-five. The kaiser, the chancellor, and the ruling elite, to preserve their dominance, did not establish a cabinet, whose members, as in Western parliamentary systems, would have been responsible to the Reichstag. Moreover, the Reichstag had only limited jurisdiction over domestic policy, although it could veto the budget. In short, it was primarily a debating society, far removed from the center of power. "Iron Chancellor" Bismarck, who had been raised in an old conservative landed aristocratic Junker family, paid more attention to influential groups, such as the churches or the Pan-German League, than he did to the fragmented opposition parties. In the later years of the Second Reich, before it collapsed in 1918, the Reichstag had greater influence over national policy decisions.[1]

The National Liberal Party

Bismarck, in office until his dismissal in 1890, had the backing of the National Liberal Party up to 1878. The party was founded in 1867 as a result of a split in the Progressive Party. Championing the constitutional monarchy and national unification, its members were the conservative, Protestant, and non-Prussian segment of the middle class, especially the nascent industrial interests. This group demanded that the government support education and property, pursue a favorable fiscal policy, acquire overseas colonies as a means of expanding the German market, and impose high tariffs on the import of industrial goods to protect the new German industries. In turn, the party agreed to back high tariffs on the import of grain, as demanded by the ruling landed Junker class.

The party was split in two, with a conservative faction that harbored extreme nationalists and a liberal faction that emphasized the rule of law. Strongly anticlerical, the party supported Bismarck in his fight against Catholics but broke with him over tariff policy and his refusal in 1878 to bring more liberals into his ministry. The National Liberal Party gained a maximum strength of about 30 percent of the Reichstag vote in 1874, but its electoral support, primarily from national, rather than liberal, groups, declined swiftly thereafter. By 1912, it was receiving less than 14 percent of the votes in the Reichstag election.[2]

The Conservatives

The Conservatives were an amalgamation of the ruling feudal aristocracy, the army, and the bureaucracy and the less powerful small entrepreneurs, artisans, and peasants. The loosely organized party became a rallying point against the liberals, who had organized the middle class, and the socialists, who had organized the working class. The party stood for a powerful state backed by the military. It supported Christian ideals and the keeping of Jews out of the army, the bureaucracy, and the universities. Opposed to industrialization and mechanization within a capitalist order, the Conservative Party glorified agriculture, refusing to agree to protective tariffs until the late 1870s, when competition in the world grain market threatened to undercut the sales of grain produced by the Junker estates. The party's backing for a vanishing precapitalist order appealed, decades later in the 1920s, to many Nazis who opposed the democratic Weimar regime. In Bismarck's Germany, the party's strength was in the old Prussian provinces. The kaiser and Bismarck could rely on the loyalty of the party, even after schisms within its ranks in the early 1870s. One schism spawned the Free Conservatives, a party, supported by industrialists and large landowners from the non-Prussian states, that existed only briefly.

In 1876, the Conservative Party was reconstituted. Known as the German Conservative Party, it lasted until 1918. It worked closely with the Christian Social Party, a rightist populist mass movement led by Adolf Stöcker, an anti-Semite who blamed the ills of capitalism on the Jews. His party was one of the forerunners of the Nazi movement.

The Progressives

Three major parties—the Progressives, the Center Party, and the Social Democratic Party—opposed Bismarck's policies in Parliament, which their combined representation was too weak in 1871 to block. By 1912, they had a majority of seats in the Reichstag, yet could not form governments because the constitutional power lay with the kaiser and his appointed conservative chancellors. The Progressives consisted of the liberal segment of the middle class. Among them were the merchants and bankers of the Hanseatic cities of Hamburg, Bremen, and Lübeck and of the central German cities. The party supported a British type of parliamentary democracy, capitalism, and a free trade policy. However, lacking a mass following, it failed electorally, receiving between 12 and 17 percent of the vote cast in Reichstag elections.[3]

The Center Party

The Center Party, founded in 1870, was not based on the voters' specific social class, like other parties during the Empire period, but on the religious conviction of Catholic voters. It was formed as a reaction to the secularization sweeping Germany (and other European countries) during the nineteenth century. It appealed for support from Catholics, a minority in the Protestant Reich, who were clustered especially in Bavaria, Silesia, the Rhineland, and Westphalia. The party called for a federal greater Germany, which would have included Austria, a strongly Catholic country. Such an expansion would have ended the religious imbalance between Protestants and Catholics in Germany but would have led to war with Austria, intent on maintaining its independence. The party also demanded a decentralized state, autonomy for the Catholic Church, and freedom for religious education.

The Center Party was backed by numerous disparate social groups, ranging from the landed aristocracy to small farmers and from industrial to handicraft workers. Thus, the party's ideology spanned the political spectrum from conservatism to radical social reformism. Its members were united in opposing a Protestant- and Prussian-dominated Reich. In Bavaria, with its overwhelming Catholic majority, the Center Party formed the governments, which were closely linked to the church.

The party encouraged Christian unions to organize as a counterweight to the established socialist unions. The conservative Catholic hierarchy, still imbued with preindustrial and antistrike views but influenced by the social concerns of Bishop Wilhelm Emanuel von Ketteler, reluctantly supported the new unions because it was worried that otherwise the workers would be weaned away from the church and into the camp of the socialists.

Bismarck, a Protestant, supported by the National Liberal and Progressive Parties, waged a "cultural struggle" (*Kulturkampf*) against the Catholics and the Center Party in 1871, partly in reaction to the dogma of papal infallibility in questions of faith and morals proclaimed in Rome one year earlier. He promulgated several anti-Catholic laws, such as the dissolution of religious orders. The laws only strengthened the resolve of Center leaders to maintain and expand their party. By 1881, Bismarck, recognizing his defeat in the struggle, had ended the state-church dispute by allowing parishes to recall their priests and reopen their churches.

In addition, he needed, and received, the support of the Center Party for his protective trade policy. Agrarian interests in the party wanted their farm products protected by tariff legislation. After Bismarck's ouster in 1890, the party held the balance of power in the Reichstag but never received more than 19 percent of the vote cast in national elections.[4]

The Social Democratic Party

The harsh conditions that the laboring class had to endure in the aftermath of the Industrial Revolution, such as working long hours in dangerous surroundings at a hectic pace, led to the rise of socialist parties in Germany and other countries. Two German parties were founded in the 1860s. Because their rivalries weakened both, they merged forces in 1875 and created the

Socialist Workers' Party of Germany, renamed the Social Democratic Party of Germany (SPD) in 1890. They adopted a Marxist program calling for an end to the capitalist system.

In 1878, Bismarck, seeing another threat to his rule, launched an antisocialist campaign. Labeling SPD members "the dangerous band of brigands dwelling alongside us in our cities," he outlawed the SPD as a national organization.[5] But to keep a semblance of a constitutional state, he allowed SPD deputies to retain their parliamentary seats. The outlawed party, many of whose members ended up in jail, flourished underground. By 1890, when the antisocialist legislation had expired, the party had gained 20 percent of the vote for Reichstag candidates. During the following two decades, its strength increased considerably. On the eve of World War I, it received more than 4.2 million votes, or nearly 35 percent of the total. Its bloc of 110 deputies was the largest in the 396-member Reichstag. Yet because the SPD could not form a governing coalition with any other party, it always remained in political opposition. Nevertheless, the governments could not entirely disregard its demands for economic and social reforms.

The SPD not only had electoral strength but also was the largest membership party in Germany and the best organized in the Western world. By 1914, it had more than 1 million members, published ninety newspapers, and had an active network of youth, women's, sports, adult education, and other affiliated groups. It thereby created its own subculture within a bourgeoisie-dominated environment.

The party had electoral and organizational successes but was not spared the ideological fissures that plague so many parties. The radical left wing, led by Karl Liebknecht and Rosa Luxemburg, gained support among the unorganized urban proletariat. The leaders, espousing Marxist doctrine, believed the situation around the turn of the century was ripe for a general strike and other revolutionary tactics to transform the capitalist into a socialist system. But radical strength never surpassed one-third within the party.

The reformist wing, led by Eduard Bernstein, was supported by the socialist trade union movement. Its leaders insisted that gradual economic and political reforms, which would eventually lead to socialism, had to be made by working within the entrenched capitalist system. The centrist faction, led by August Bebel and Karl Kautsky, initially sided with the radicals, but after 1903, still using Marxist rhetoric, it increasingly supported the reformists in their demand for gradual changes.

The outbreak of World War I triggered a crisis within the party. Abandoning a pledge to promote international peace and working-class solidarity, SPD leaders supported the war effort. They were afraid the government would crush their organization if they voted against war credits. Some leaders disapproved of the prowar stance, however, and in March 1916 they broke with the party. A year later, they formed the Independent Social Democratic Party (USPD), consisting of several groups opposed to the war. In 1917 and 1918, an increasing number of war-weary and hungry workers, angry at the SPD prowar stance and the government's failure to make democratic reforms, staged massive strikes under USPD and left-wing union initiatives. By November 1918, the strikes and simultaneous military defeats had contributed to the downfall of the imperial government and its acceptance of Allied armistice terms.[6]

The Weimar Era

The SPD and USPD

At the end of the war, a left-wing revolution broke out in Kiel and swept Kaiser Wilhelm II and state rulers from their thrones. The kaiser was forced to abdicate and go into exile. The spontaneous revolutionary fervor sweeping the country thrust the SPD and USPD into a position of governance. But the cautious and moderate SPD leaders had no plan ready to head a new republican government. Indeed, afraid of a revolution, they would have been willing to serve under a democratic constitutional king. But with no such choice, Friedrich Ebert, SPD chairman, headed a six-person (three SPD and three USPD) provisional government, then known as the Council of People's Delegates. After an initial period of instability, the SPD chiefs won control of workers' and soldiers' councils established spontaneously in different localities and modeled partly on the soviets in the Soviet Union.

The USPD left wing included the Spartacists, who were the forerunners of the Communist Party of Germany (KPD) established in December 1918. The left wing demanded the swift nationalization of industry, expropriation of Junker agricultural estates in East Prussia, and purges of conservative army officers, civil servants, and judges. The SPD did not dare endorse these bold demands because it opposed a radical change of the old order, fearing that a dictatorship of the proletariat might arise. The party was traumatized by the attempt of left forces in late 1918 and early 1919 to overthrow the transitional SPD-controlled government through strikes, riots, and an uprising. Reluctantly, the SPD chiefs ordered the conservative Reichswehr (army) and the antirepublican Free Corps paramilitary units to put down the widespread disturbances. In their aftermath, rightists murdered former SPD radical, and later Spartacist, leaders Liebknecht and Luxemburg while the two were being taken to prison. Their bodies were thrown unceremoniously into a nearby canal. Outraged left-wing leaders in the USPD and the KPD never forgave the SPD for cooperating with the conservative forces to crush the Left, thereby blocking profound political, economic, and social reforms.[7]

The Parliamentary System

During this period of major civil disturbances, the SPD and the bourgeois parties insisted that a parliamentary system be established. The result was that in January 1919 Germans elected delegates to a national assembly in Weimar, whose task it was to draft a constitution. In the election, the SPD received 37.9 percent of the vote; the USPD, 7.6 percent; and the bourgeois parties, the balance. The delegates enacted a constitution, at the time the first democratic one in German history and one of the most democratic in the world. Among its many provisions were an array of civil liberties, not listed separately like the amendments to the U.S. constitution but incorporated in basic social rights. The constitution also gave women the right to vote and equal rights with men.

The constitution did not mention parties specifically, but in effect the parliamentary system revolved around them. Because the constitution provided for the direct election of the president, each party had the right to nominate a candidate. In turn, the president had the right to select a nominee for chancellor, who often was the leader of the strongest party in Parliament or could muster the support of parties for a coalition cabinet. The chancellor was responsible to Parliament and, together with the cabinet, had the power to shape policy. In case of a national emergency, the president had the right to govern by decree. The position of the parties was thereby weakened, although they had the right to reject a decree in Parliament. The first president, Friedrich Ebert, who originally had learned the saddle trade and held offices in the union and SPD, rarely used the decree power. However, conservative Field Marshal Paul von Hindenburg, elected to the presidency in 1925, used it frequently between 1930 and 1932, when the Great Depression led to severe political, economic, and social unrest.[8]

The Electoral System

Reichstag deputies were elected by universal suffrage after women gained the vote. The Social Democrats got enough support from the other parties to scrap the Empire's electoral system, in which deputies had been elected by a simple majority in single-member constituencies. The failure of imperial authorities to redistrict the constituencies when the population moved increasingly from rural to urban areas had often given the conservative parties, whose strength was in rural areas, an edge over the SPD, whose strength lay in urban workers' districts.

Under the new Weimar system, deputies were elected according to a scheme of proportional representation. The parties put up lists of candidates for each of the thirty-five large electoral districts. The number of votes cast for a party in a district determined the number of deputies elected. For every sixty thousand votes, the party received one seat. Its surplus votes were pooled to elect extra members from a national list that each party had compiled.

The new system had its critics, especially after the downfall of the Weimar Republic and Hitler's triumph. They argued that proportional representation had fragmented the party system by enabling many small parties to win seats in the Reichstag. Thus, it was hard for the major parties to form stable coalition governments, which could have solved the country's pressing problems.

The critics also argued that the system did not allow voters to choose their party's candidates. Rather, the voters merely ratified the choices made by the party's district organization. The candidates' ranking on the list that it drew up was crucial for victory or defeat. Thus, if officials put a candidate high on a list in a district where the party traditionally gained seats, that candidate was nearly assured of election. In effect, the list system gave party officials, rather than voters, the power to determine which candidates of each party would win seats in the Reichstag.

The defenders of the system argued that it gave minor parties a chance to be represented in the Reichstag rather than being shut out, as in the U.S. or British simple majority, single-member constituencies. They also claimed, justifiably, that it was not because small parties predominated in the Reichstag that the Weimar Republic fell. On the contrary, in the late 1920s, when their number was greatest, small parties never gained more than 15 percent of the vote in the national elections. The Nazis benefited from the electoral system in the 1930 election, but in the 1932 election they would have gained an absolute majority if Germany had had the U.S. or British system. As it was, they never gained such a majority of seats, even in the last "free" election of March 1933, when Hitler was chancellor.[9]

The constitution introduced not only a representative form of democratic government but also an element of direct democracy, the plebiscite. If a minimum of 10 percent of the electorate petitioned for the introduction of legislation and the Reichstag refused to enact it, the proposal could be put to popular vote in a plebiscite. Usually the governments tried to suppress such initiatives because political unrest might result, but several parties backed controversial proposals only to see them go down to defeat.

Once the constitution was adopted in 1919 and the parliamentary system was in place, the parties were crucial in shaping the destiny of the nation. As the largest party that year, the SPD sought the USPD's support to form a coalition cabinet, but the USPD declined, unwilling to join a cabinet that would have to include members of the bourgeois parties (Catholic and liberal) to gain majority backing from the Reichstag. Thus, the SPD had to look for allies among the bourgeois parties to produce viable governments. From February 1919 to June 1920 and from June 1928 to March 1930, SPD leaders headed coalition cabinets, but in other periods, as SPD electoral strength declined, nonsocialist chancellors governed, with occasional SPD representation.

In the meantime, the USPD received almost as many votes (17.9 percent) as the SPD (21.7 percent) in the June 1920 Reichstag election, but the USPD split internally over the issue of backing the parliamentary system. At an October 1920 convention, the left-wing majority, preferring a workers' council system, voted to join the KPD and the communist Third International. The right-wing minority tried to keep the rump party alive, but by September 1922 it had rejoined the SPD. From then on, it constituted the left wing of the SPD.[10]

Conservative and Liberal Parties

Parties, once in existence, have an instinct for survival. They build up a leadership corps and an organization that will not necessarily disappear when the political system of which they are a part vanishes. This was the case with the parties of the Empire era, although from 1919 on several adopted new names, in some instances including the term "people," in the spirit of the new democratic system. The Conservatives became the German National People's Party. Its leaders announced their support for the new republican government as long as stability, law, and order were maintained, but these leaders did not hide their preference for a monarchical system. They also emphasized German national identity, Christian teaching, private property, and equal treatment for Germany in international relations. Many of the leaders no longer came from the discredited Junker caste but from the old imperial civil service. They soon realized that they had to cooperate with other bourgeois parties if they were going to have any influence in the state. Hence, they participated in two cabinets, in 1925 and 1927. In the 1924 election, the party gained 20.5 percent of the vote but slipped to 5.9 and 8.3 percent in the two 1932 elections.

The National Liberal Party of the Empire era became the German People's Party. Its officials also hedged their support for the new system unless it supported capitalism, individual initiatives, and nationalism in domestic and foreign policies. They appealed especially to the interests of small entrepreneurs, professionals, and artisans, who, however, did not constitute a mass following.[11]

The most progressive bourgeois party was the newly formed German Democratic Party. It consisted of the old Progressives, left-wing members of the National Liberals, and liberal intellectuals who, in the spirit of the revolution that had swept the monarchy away, were no longer sympathetic to a monarchical system. The party staunchly supported the new Republic, appealed to voters with democratic and nationalist but nonsocialist views, and backed social justice and social welfare measures under a modified capitalist system. When liberalism as an ideology came to have less attraction to voters than conservatism or socialism, the combined strength of the two liberal parties (German People's Party and German Democratic Party) declined steeply, from 23 percent in 1919 to 2 percent in 1933.

The Center Party

After the 1918 revolution, the Center Party changed its name briefly to the Christian People's Party but soon reverted to the original name. Many of its leaders would have been satisfied if the old system, with reforms, had been maintained. They assailed the Social Democrats as a danger to the social and educational interests of the Catholic population. As in the Empire period, the party was supported chiefly by Catholics, including a trade union federation, but since they were only one-third of the German population, the party had no chance of gaining a majority. A separatist and conservative Bavarian People's Party was founded in 1919 to ensure that the state's interests would be safeguarded. Unlike the Center Party, the Bavarian party opposed any coalition with the SPD. The combined electoral strength of the two Catholic parties hovered around 15 percent of the total vote throughout the Weimar era.[12]

The Communist Party

The Weimar Republic began to collapse during the Great Depression of 1929. Massive unemployment and economic hardships affecting millions of people caused much dissatisfaction with the democratic parties that had governed the Republic since 1919. The parties, lacking solutions to overcome the crisis, could not form governments capable of resolving their differences and establishing a stable majority. Consequently, the president and chancellor governed by issuing a series of emergency decrees, thereby further undermining the democratic system. Many voters, in their desperate quest for a solution to the crisis, turned to the extremist parties on the Left and Right.

On the Left, the Communist Party of Germany (KPD), already involved in revolutionary class struggles against the Republic during its infancy, gained many adherents in 1931 and 1932. The party sought to mobilize both unemployed workers and unskilled workers in its expanding network of factory-based revolutionary trade union cells. The KPD gained in industrial areas, but not enough to produce a revolutionary situation that would have enabled it to seize power. On several occasions, the KPD made common cause with the Nazis (NSDAP, or the National Socialist German Workers Party) against the SPD, which it labeled "social fascists." This shortsighted policy was based on a historical split between the two leftist parties, dating back to the founding of the KPD, over how to achieve socialism. The SPD wanted to do it through evolutionary, reformist means; the KPD, through revolution. If the rift between them could have been healed, Hitler's rise to power might have been averted.[13]

The Nazi Party

On the right, the NSDAP, led by Hitler, made the most spectacular electoral gains during the Republic's waning years. The party was founded in 1920 as the successor to the short-lived German Workers' Party. In 1921, Hitler captured control and became its undisputed leader. In November 1923, he carried out an unsuccessful putsch in Munich against the Bavarian government. A court sentenced him to five years in jail, of which he served only nine months, a testimonial to the conservative judiciary's leniency with right-wingers. While in jail, he wrote *Mein Kampf* (My Struggle), which became the official ideological source of the movement. Filled with nationalistic, imperialistic, racist, and anti-Semitic passages, it devoted much space to mass persuasion and propaganda techniques for winning over the masses. In the 1920s, the party attracted numerous marginalized citizens, including unskilled workers and soldiers, because it protested against developments that embittered them—the 1918 revolution, the regime's perceived sellout of Germany's interests in the Versailles Treaty, the democratic system, rationalism, and materialism.[14]

The Great Depression led to the party's swift growth. Hitler, with demagogic oratorical skill, gained support from a variety of groups: desperate
workers, many of whom had voted earlier for leftist parties; salaried employees threatened with unemployment; and industrialists and bankers, who
sympathized with his virulent anticommunism and opposition to the socialist trade unions. Hitler could also count on support from the civil service, judiciary, and the army, which had shown greater attachment to the Empire
than to the Weimar Republic.

In July 1932, the Nazis became the largest party in the Reichstag.
President Hindenburg, by then nearly senile, offered Hitler a cabinet post,
but the Nazi leader held out for the chancellorship. Hindenburg thereupon
appointed in succession Franz von Papen and Kurt von Schleicher, neither of
whom had a party following, as chancellors. During the following months,
the parliamentary system collapsed as the Reichstag lost its power to legislate
under the authoritarian leadership of the two chancellors. Schleicher, realiz-
ing too late that the Republic was threatened from the Right, tried to
broaden the base of the cabinet. His effort failed; the democratic parties dis-
trusted the sly Schleicher, who had spun a web of intrigue against them.
Lacking enough support, he resigned in late January 1933. Thereupon
Hindenburg appointed Hitler chancellor but refused him the extraordinary
powers that he had demanded. This appointment sealed the fate of the
Weimar Republic. Hitler had no intention of governing democratically, although on January 30, the day of his appointment, he swore allegiance to the
Weimar constitution.[15]

The Third Reich

Hitler's assumption of power had been legal. His initial cabinet appoint-
ments to the "Government of National Concentration" gave no clue to the
totalitarian system that he was ready to inaugurate. His eleven-person coalition cabinet consisted of eight conservatives and only three National
Socialists. The conservatives held the key posts of Defense, Economics, and
Foreign Affairs, but the Nazis held that of Interior, indirectly controlling the
police. The conservatives were confident that within two months they would
be able to rein in Hitler. But his steamroller tactics eventually wiped out all
opposition, some of which had not taken seriously his intentions to set up a
totalitarian system. In February, Hitler dissolved the Reichstag and issued a
set of emergency decrees, approved by Hindenburg, that laid the foundations for total power. One decree gave his top lieutenant, Hermann Göring,

an air force hero in World War I, virtual control over the key state of Prussia. Other decrees limited freedom of the press and assembly.

The failure of the president, the army, the courts, the unions, and most parties to vigorously protest such limitations on democratic rights gave Hitler the facade of legality that he was seeking. He proclaimed a "national revolution" that stood above parties. Yet despite a terror and propaganda campaign against the non-Nazi parties, Hitler could not muster a majority of votes for the NSDAP on March 5, 1933, the last nominally free election during the period he was in power. Once again, he had to fall back on an electoral alliance with the conservative German National People's Party.

On March 23, all parties, except for the SPD, voted for the Enabling Act, drafted by the Nazi-controlled cabinet. KPD deputies would have voted against it, but as part of the terror campaign against leftist parties, they had been prevented from entering the chamber. The act handed all legislative powers to the government and allowed it to restore "public safety and order" wherever a threat was perceived. Center and liberal deputies supported the act in the mistaken impression that legislative rule would soon be restored. But the act was never rescinded during the Hitler era. It was the pseudolegal basis for Hitler's maintenance of control over the country.

In a systematic campaign of *Gleichschaltung* (enforced conformity), the government forbade all non-Nazi organizations to continue functioning and made sure that in the years to come all remaining centers of power, including the Foreign Office and the Reichswehr, would be under Hitler's tight control. As early as May 1933, Hitler eliminated the trade unions; in the weeks thereafter he outlawed or forced the liquidation of all non-Nazi parties, leaving only the NSDAP to exist legally. Some of the banned parties went underground and participated in heroic but futile resistance against Hitler's regime. In subsequent elections to the Reichstag, now stripped of all powers, the NSDAP was the sole party on the election slates. The only reason for retaining the legislature was to give a facade of legality to the system and to provide well-paid jobs to faithful Nazi deputies.[16]

The NSDAP, led by Hitler in his capacity as Führer, had its tentacles in all state and private institutions to ensure conformity and to suppress any potential resistance to the regime. The state was not an independent entity but a tool of the party. The NSDAP had an authoritarian, semimilitary structure in which policy decisions made at the top were not discussed by the rank and file. From 1933 on, the party admitted new members only after the most rigorous screening. Most were young and had risen through the ranks of the Hitler Youth, one of the many party or party-affiliated organizations. Other organizations included the paramilitary Storm Troopers and Elite Guard

(SS), women, workers, and teachers. By 1943, the party had 6.5 million members.

The totalitarian one-party system collapsed only when Hitler sought to expand the Third Reich by conquering neighboring European states. Germany's defeat in 1945, after nearly six years of cataclysmic war, marked the end of the short-lived Hitler regime and the NSDAP.[17]

The Postwar Years

In 1945, the Allied powers (the United States, Britain, France, and the Soviet Union) carved up Germany, which had lost its sovereignty, into four occupation zones. The Soviets ruled over the eastern zone and the Americans, British, and French over the western zones. Berlin, surrounded by the Russian zone, had a special status and was divided into four sectors, each governed by one of the Allied military commanders. The German citizens' hope that their country would be reunited was dashed in the immediate postwar period when the Allied powers could not concur on its future. The Allies did agree that the defeated state had to be "denazified," demilitarized, and democratized. Thus, the NSDAP and all its affiliated organizations were liquidated immediately. The Western Allies allowed parties and other democratic organizations to form first on the local level and eventually on the zonal level (see Chapter 3). The Soviets granted the leftist and centrist parties permission to organize on a zonal level immediately (see Chapter 9).

By 1949, the Allies considered the Germans ready to assume governing powers, but with limited sovereignty, in the two newly created states. In the western zones, the Americans, British, and French ceded powers to the newly elected government of the Federal Republic of Germany; in the Soviet zone, the Russians empowered the communist government of the German Democratic Republic. Berlin remained a separate entity under special Allied status.

Conclusion

German political parties were formed much later than those of Britain and the United States because the Second Reich was not founded until 1871. In the relatively brief life span of the German parties, they operated under several divergent political systems, which meant that a kaleidoscope of parties emerged during the Empire and Weimar eras. The sharp class, social, ideological, and religious cleavages in society produced a multiparty system in which each party mirrored the interests of one or more segments of the population. From 1871 to 1918, these parties, having only limited power under an autocratic government, had little effect on executive policymaking.

The parties had more powers during the Weimar period. But the lack of a democratic tradition had fateful consequences for the socialist- and bourgeois-led democratic governments, which had to cope with catastrophic conditions from 1918 to 1923 and from 1929 to 1933. In the latter years, the governments' inability to solve the economic problems meant that the extremist parties—the KPD and NSDAP—gained significant popular support, which was not the case in Britain or the United States that had been exposed to a similar Great Depression. The appointment of Hitler as chancellor in early 1933 signaled the rise of a totalitarian system in which all parties, except for the NSDAP, were outlawed. The brief experiment in democracy during the Weimar period had come to a tragic end.

Notes

1. Gordon Craig, *From Bismarck to Adenauer: Aspects of German Statecraft,* rev. ed. (New York: Harper and Row, 1965), pp. 3–28.

2. Koppel S. Pinson, *Modern Germany: Its History and Civilization* (New York: Macmillan, 1954), pp. 168–169.

3. Ibid., pp. 169–172.

4. Sigmund Neumann, "Germany: Changing Patterns and Lasting Problems," in *Modern Political Parties: Approaches to Comparative Politics,* ed. Sigmund Neumann (Chicago: University of Chicago Press, 1957), pp. 357–359.

5. Heinrich Potthoff, "Social Democracy from Its Beginnings Until 1945," in *A History of German Social Democracy: From 1848 to the Present,* by Susanne Miller and Heinrich Potthoff (Leamington Spa, England: Berg, 1986), p. 33.

6. Gerard Braunthal, *The German Social Democrats Since 1969: A Party in Power and Opposition,* 2d ed. (Boulder: Westview Press, 1994), pp. 10–13; Potthoff, "Social Democracy from Its Beginnings Until 1945," pp. 7–63.

7. Braunthal, *The German Social Democrats Since 1969,* p. 13.

8. For details, see Gordon Craig, *Germany, 1866–1945* (New York: Oxford University Press, 1978), pp. 498–568.

9. A. J. Nicholls, *Weimar and the Rise of Hitler* (London: Macmillan, 1968), pp. 36–38.

10. Braunthal, *The German Social Democrats Since 1969,* p. 14.

11. In 1919, the Business Party was founded, supported by conservative property and small business owners. From 1924 until 1933, it was represented in the

Reichstag by a few deputies (Heino Kaack, *Geschichte und Struktur des deutschen Parteiensystems* [Opladen: Westdeutscher Verlag, 1971], pp. 100, 103).

12. For details of the democratic parties, see Sigmund Neumann, *Die Parteien der Weimarer Republik* (Stuttgart: Kohlhammer, 1970), pp. 27–72; Alfred Milatz, *Wähler und Wahlen in der Weimarer Republik* (Bonn: Bundeszentrale für politische Bildung, 1968), pp. 86–106.

13. Neumann, *Die Parteien der Weimarer Republik,* pp. 87–95.

14. Karl Dietrich Bracher, *The German Dictatorship: The Origins, Structure, and Effects of National Socialism* (New York: Praeger, 1970), pp. 79–102; Dietrich Orlow, *The History of the Nazi Party, 1919–1933,* 2 vols. (Pittsburgh: University of Pittsburgh Press, 1969, 1973).

15. Nicholls, *Weimar and the Rise of Hitler,* pp. 144–171.

16. To make certain that no rival arose to challenge him, Hitler, on Hindenburg's death in 1934, abolished the office of president and proclaimed himself Führer and Reich chancellor.

17. Thomas L. Jarmon, *The Rise and Fall of Nazi Germany* (London: Cresset Press, 1955).

PART TWO

West German Parties Since World War II

· 3 ·

The Party State:
Political Legitimacy

T HE POLITICAL LEGITIMACY of parties in various political systems varies considerably. In Germany, as we have seen, parties were fully accepted during the Weimar era, only partly during the Empire era, and not at all, except for the NSDAP, during the Nazi era. The end of Nazism gave Germans in the three western occupation zones a new chance, under the tutelage of the Western Allies, to build sound democratic institutions that would lay the foundations for a "party state." In a party state, strong democratic parties are an integral part of the political system. They compete against each other to gain political power and guide the nation's destiny. They also seek to dominate other key institutions, such as the bureaucracy, the judiciary, and the media, to maximize power.[1] However, when parties fail to address crucial economic and social problems affecting citizens or become involved in financial scandals, disenchantment with them sets in, which has been the case in Germany since the late 1980s.

This chapter examines key factors of the party state: the rebirth of the pluralist party system in western Germany in 1945, the constitutional foundation of the West German parties, the funds given the parties, and the electoral system that affected the party configuration. A survey of these factors should help determine whether the rise of the party state contributed to the development of a stable democratic system and a political culture that made citizens more tolerant of and sympathetic to parties than in earlier periods of German history.

Rebirth of a Pluralist Party System

May 1945 marked the collapse of the Nazi regime. In western Germany, Allied representatives insisted that a democratic system be created, initially at the local level. To work with them in the three occupation zones, these representatives chose both German anti-Nazi leaders and officials who had served under the Hitler regime but had been denazified. The latter were imbued with the values of democracy that had already flourished during the Weimar period.

As part of the democratization, in summer 1945 at the Potsdam Conference U.S., British, and Soviet top leaders agreed that only democratic parties would be permitted to operate in their respective zones. (The French were not invited but were given a zone carved out of the U.S. zone.) Western Allied officials allowed political parties to form initially in districts and only thereafter in the newly formed Länder (states). The Americans were the first to grant licenses to parties in August 1945, followed by the British in September and the more hesitant French in December.[2] The Western Allies believed that it was best to allow four parties—the Communist Party of Germany, the Social Democratic Party of Germany, the Christian Democratic Union (CDU), and the Free Democratic Party (FDP), or the Liberals—to form rather than the multitude that had existed during Weimar, which had contributed to the political instability of the governments. The Western Allies envisaged a balance between the SPD and KPD, representing the workers' movement, and the CDU and FDP, the bourgeois movement. In view of Germany's past, the Western Allies forbade right-radical and monarchist parties to organize, although they made some exceptions in licensing regional or separatist parties, such as the CDU's Bavarian-affiliated party, the Christian Social Union (CSU).

In summer and fall 1945, Western Allied officials appointed Germans to govern the Länder in the three zones, but under Allied supervision and with limited freedom to make policy. All the licensed parties at one time or another formed Länder governments. In 1946 and 1947, as another step in democratization, the governments were allowed to schedule elections for each newly established parliament (Landtag). Of the four licensed parties that competed in all Länder elections, the CDU and SPD received nearly 73 percent of the votes, while the KPD and the Liberals had a loyal but small following.

Thus, a two-party system emerged, with minor parties on its periphery. In the parliaments, the parties that made up the cabinets were pitted against the opposition parties, typical of a parliamentary system in which the minister-president (governor) of a Land usually was one of the leaders of the party that had received the most votes in the previous election. The minister-president then formed either a coalition cabinet or, if the party had received an absolute majority of more than 50 percent of the vote, a one-party cabinet.

The system has not changed since then, except that some minor parties have fallen by the wayside and others have taken their place.

In June 1947, the Americans and the British created an economic council for their two zones, another step in the projected foundation of a West German state. The Allies appointed to the council fifty-two deputies, twenty of whom belonged to the SPD, twenty to the CDU and CSU, and twelve to five minor and regional parties.

Constitutional Foundation

In July 1948, the Western Allies pressed German officials to convene a constituent assembly to draft a constitution for the projected West German state. The Germans were reluctant to write a final constitution, which would have given the impression that Germany's pending division into two hostile states—a result of the cold war—was permanent. The Western Allies and the Germans reached a compromise. They would convene a parliamentary council, which would draft a basic law, the equivalent of a constitution. That Basic Law for West Germany was to remain in effect for more than four decades and is still in effect, with amendments, for the united Germany.

The Parliamentary Council began its deliberations on September 1, 1948, in Bonn, under the presidency of Konrad Adenauer (CDU), a former mayor of Cologne and future chancellor of the Federal Republic. A majority of its sixty-five members, who were also deputies in Länder parliaments, belonged to the CDU/CSU or the SPD; a minority belonged to the Liberals, KPD, the revived Center Party, or the new German Party. After nine months of discussions, the members agreed on the formation of a West German state founded on the Basic Law. As is usual in a parliamentary system, the chancellor and the cabinet must have the backing of the majority of deputies in the legislature. Within this institutional setting, the political parties are important in theory, if not always in practice, in articulating and reconciling the voters' interests.

The Basic Law went into effect on May 23, 1949, after ten of eleven Länder parliaments gave their approval. The Bavarian Landtag, yearning for more Land autonomy, did not ratify the Basic Law because it objected to the excessive power given the central executive and legislative institutions. Nevertheless, Bavaria recognized the Basic Law as binding. On the day it was approved, the Federal Republic was founded as a semisovereign state, with the Allies reserving key powers in defense and foreign affairs.

Because of the historic antipathy of many Germans to political parties, seen as quarreling and unable to compromise on major policies, the architects of the Basic Law emphasized the importance of parties in the new state. According to Article 21:

Section 1. The parties shall help form the political will of the people. They may be freely established. Their internal organization shall conform to democratic principles. They shall publicly account for the sources and use of their funds and for their assets.
Section 2. Parties which by reason of their aims or the conduct of their adherents seek to impair or do away with the free democratic basic order or threaten the existence of the Federal Republic of Germany shall be unconstitutional. The Federal Constitutional Court shall rule on the question of unconstitutionality.
Section 3. Details shall be the subject of federal laws.[3]

The founders wrote Section 2 into the Basic Law to prevent a repetition of the NSDAP's subversion and destruction of the Weimar democratic government. Having witnessed the end of Weimar, they rejected the possibility of a democracy committing suicide by allowing parties to form that would endanger the democratic system. The Federal Constitutional Court has made sparse use of Section 2, having banned only two parties (but several extremist groups): in 1952, the rightist Socialist Reich Party; in 1956, the KPD. Ironically, the bans had little long-range effect; new rightist and leftist parties arose to replace those banned.

Since 1956, the governing authorities, which must initiate a legal suit for the court to deal with the issue, have been reluctant to drive an extremist party into illegality, where it may become more dangerous to the free basic order. The authorities prefer that no ban be imposed so long as they can keep the party under observation. Moreover, they are aware of most civil libertarians' belief that Section 2 limits free expression. However, when right-wing parties achieved some electoral successes in the late 1980s, the discussion on banning was revived.[4]

Parliament did not approve a law regulating the details of parties, as stipulated by Article 21, until July 1967, after an eighteen-year delay and much debate, especially on party financing. The Law on Parties recognizes their necessity in a free and democratic order and includes a remarkable and detailed catalog of functions that they should perform:

The parties shall participate in the formation of the political will of the people in all fields of public life, in particular by: bringing their influence to bear on the shaping of public opinion; inspiring and furthering political education; promoting an active participation by citizens in political life; training talented people to assume public responsibilities; participating in Federal, Land and Local Government elections by nominating candidates; exercising an influence on political trends in parliament and the government; initiating their defined political aims in the national decision-making processes; and ensuring continuous, vital links between the people and the public authorities.[5]

Such a listing of party functions is an exception in democratic states, which normally do not emphasize the existence or the role of parties in a legislative act. Other sections of the West German law grant parties the right to undertake political education and influence political development. They are also expected to be internally democratic. However, that provision has often been violated as the chiefs try to crush factions, make policy from the top down, and, with few exceptions, impose voting discipline on their party's deputies in the Bundestag. This last practice runs counter to Article 38 of the Basic Law, which states that deputies "shall be representatives of the whole people; they shall not be bound by any instructions, only by their conscience."[6]

Parenthetically, in the United States the Democratic and Republican Party leaders rarely gain support from all their congressional members on a bill. In parliamentary systems, however, parties customarily expect their deputies to support the decisions arrived at by their officials in the executive branch. Because prime ministers or chancellors, unlike the U.S. president, are not elected separately by the voters in parliamentary systems, the two branches work closely together. The cabinet can be expected to carry out its electoral mandate and government program without many roadblocks in Parliament.

Party Finance

The 1967 law also deals with party financing. Parties, which must account for the sources of their funds, receive a part of their income from membership dues but not enough to cover their considerable outlays. Therefore, rank-and-file members are also asked to contribute to special fund-raising drives for campaigns, but with limited response. In addition, the candidates of several parties are expected to pay from their own income a share of the campaign expenses. The amount varies, depending on the candidate's wealth and the party's financial strength.

Private Donations

More lucrative have been appeals, especially by conservative and liberal parties, to business associations to help pay for the parties' high operating and campaign costs. Beginning in 1952, the business community set up sponsors' associations to collect funds primarily from the larger firms in industry, trade, banking, and insurance. The amount collected from each participating firm was calculated on the basis of payroll figures or sales turnover. The pooled funds were then distributed to the bourgeois parties all at once, thus eliminating frequent appeals by rival parties for funds from the major firms. Until 1958, such funds were partly or fully tax deductible. The SPD, which at the time received almost no support from the business community, asked the Federal Constitutional Court to strike down the legal provision of tax deductibility. The court voided it in 1958 on the basis, in part, that some parties benefited from it more than others. According to the court, the provision was incompatible with the equality clause in the Basic Law.

To bypass the court's ruling, trade associations took over the task formerly performed by the sponsors' associations in national campaigns. The trade associations were able to give political parties up to 25 percent of their tax-exempt dues received from member firms. In a spirit of selective largesse, they did not give funds to the SPD, fearing that it would pursue an antibusiness policy should it get into power.[7]

To provide the public with more information about party financing, the 1967 law stipulated that parties reveal the names of individuals and companies contributing more than DM 20,000 ($8,000) and DM 200,000 ($80,000), respectively. Thus, for example, in 1991 the public found out, in a Bundestag report on party finances, that Daimler-Benz, the giant automobile and technology firm, generously gave DM 1.62 million ($982,000) to four parties. As in the United States, where many companies, for insurance, allocate money to both major parties during a campaign year, Daimler-Benz did not hesitate to give funds to the archrivals CDU/CSU and SPD.[8] Not surprisingly, the Greens, the party that had emerged from the environment and peace movements, received no donations from firms but only from private individuals.

Private donations by firms and, especially, wealthy individuals can lead parties to grant favors to the donors, which in turn can give rise to well-publicized scandals and corruption. As a result, a growing segment of the public loses confidence in the parties and challenges the legitimacy of the system.

One of the most glaring instances of corruption in Germany occurred in 1982 and 1983. According to the news weekly *Der Spiegel,* the powerful

Werdegang eines Politikers:

POLITIK
KARRIERE
MACHT
GELD
AFFÄRE
RÜCKTRITT
MACHT NIX

"The trajectory of a politician: politics, career, power, money, affairs, resignation, makes no difference." No wonder that the public has relegated politicians to the lower end of the prestige scale. *Source:* Walther Keim, ed., *Ohne Moos nix los: Karikaturisten sehen Geld und Macht in Deutschland* (Munich: List, 1993), p. 60. Reprinted by permission.

Flick firm had transferred large sums of money for many years to the three major parties, expecting to reap bountiful dividends. More specifically, Flick wanted to avoid paying DM 437.5 million ($175 million) in taxes and expected the Ministry of Economics, headed by Otto von Lambsdorff (FDP), to rule in its favor. When the ministry so ruled, a court indicted Lambsdorff for having misused his office and illegally accepted campaign funds. He subsequently resigned his post. The FDP, CDU/CSU, and SPD lost public confidence for having accepted Flick money, which obviously had strings attached.[9]

Tax deductibility remains controversial. In 1993, lawmakers decided, after critical court rulings and citizens' complaints about the wealth of the parties, that corporations could no longer take tax deductions for financial donations to parties. Individuals could, but not more than DM 6,000 DM ($3,500), or DM 12,000 for couples. The new limits were only 10 percent of the previous maximum.[10]

Public Funding

The parties' operational, public relations, personnel, and campaign expenditures climb from decade to decade.[11] The income from membership dues, business donations, and other private sources has not been sufficient to cover the escalating costs, which rise partly because public funding is available. In a few other Western democracies, governments have subsidized parties' expenses, but none so much as in Germany.

The initial purpose of public subsidies, begun in 1959, was to help finance the parties' "political education." The CDU, FDP, SPD, and CSU received funds, totaling a modest DM 5 million ($1.25 million), based on their strength in the Bundestag. Minor parties that had not received enough votes to qualify for seats, and therefore could not get any public funds, asked the Constitutional Court to declare the restrictions on funding unconstitutional. In 1966, the court concurred that the principle of equality of opportunity for all parties had been infringed on.

The court also ruled that public funds had to be restricted to electoral campaigns and could not cover expenses for operations and publicity. It reasoned that government support was the most equitable way to give all parties at least minimum assistance in their campaigns to gain legislative seats. The SPD welcomed public funds to offset the advantage accruing to conservative parties, which were receiving substantial support from the private business sector.

The 1967 party law, conforming to the court's ruling, specified that each party receive DM 2.50 (about $1.00) for each of its voters, as long as it had mustered at least 2.5 percent of the vote in the preceding election. Thus, several minor parties received public funds, often sufficient to cover their campaign costs. Subsequent changes in the law raised the amount per vote, largely to keep up with inflation, to DM 3.50 and, in 1983, to DM 5.00. That year, the threshold for receiving funds was lowered from 2.5 percent of the total vote in the previous election to 0.5 percent, thereby giving all but the most minuscule parties at least some government funds.

Once government funding to parties had become part of the political culture, the parties jockeyed constantly to maximize that source of revenue. Thus, in the 1980s the government gave additional sums to some parties, allegedly to offset inequities in the existing system. After German unification, the Alliance 90/Greens, a leftist party then based only in eastern Germany, petitioned the Constitutional Court to declare the system unconstitutional because it created new inequities.[12] In April 1992, the court ruled against the existing financing laws and ordered the government to draw up a revised law.

The revised law, enacted in 1993, scrapped the inequities and reinstated the grant of funds to parties based solely on votes received in the previous election. However, primarily because of pressure by the Alliance 90/Greens Fraktion (parliamentary group), new tightened provisions were introduced. Each party would no longer receive DM 5.00 per vote but only DM 1.30 for the first 5 million votes. For every subsequent vote, the party would receive DM 1.00. In addition, the government would match up to 50 percent of funds received by each party from membership dues and private donations. The maximum annual subsidies for all parties could not exceed DM 230 million ($135 million), which could be adjusted for inflation in subsequent years. The new subsidies were a sharp cut from the earlier total of DM 500 million ($294 million) per year, which had substantially enriched party coffers.[13]

Thus, in the election year 1994, the national government disbursed a total of DM 228 million ($141 million) to the qualified parties. The CDU/CSU received DM 92 million ($57 million); the SPD, DM 89 million ($55 million); Alliance 90/Greens, DM 15.5 million ($9.6 million); the FDP, DM 14.4 million ($8.9 million); and the Party of Democratic Socialism (PDS), DM 10.6 million ($6.5 million).[14] After every election, the government gives these funds to the parties proportionately each year until the next election, normally scheduled every four years.

However, public funding for campaigns is but one source of government support for the parties. With little public awareness, the parties also receive funds for expenses incurred by their Fraktionen and their semiofficial foundations. The foundations carry out political research, issue publications, and train party and interest group officials and staff members from foreign countries that have weak democratic traditions. The foundations' work mirrors the sponsoring party's ideology.[15]

A 1993 report by a commission of experts on party financing appointed by the federal president estimated total direct and indirect revenue from the

national and Länder governments for all parties in 1992 at about DM 1.4
trillion ($848 million).[16] This munificent sum should be more than ade-
quate for the parties' expenses, despite their numerous complaints.

Parties and Politicians

Through media publicity about scandals and corruption arising from the
funds received by parties, the public has become aware of the comfortable
salaries, pensions, severance pay, and other benefits that politicians have
given themselves. It is also aware of politicians who, while holding well-paid
elective office, sit on several equally well-paid governing boards of public-
sector enterprises, and of lower-level politicians who benefit from the widespread patronage system that rewards them, as faithful party members, with
jobs in the public sector.[17]

The public is less aware of the great influence that officials of parties have
when they serve on the governing boards of Länder-controlled public television and radio. Their number is determined by the proportionate strength of
their party in the Land. There are obvious dangers of politicization, patronage, and favoritism when these officials make allegedly nonpartisan decisions.[18]

Electoral System

Bonn policymakers created a mixed electoral system based partly on single-
majority districts, as in the United States and Great Britain, in which a candidate must gain a plurality of votes to win, and partly on proportional representation, which gives all parties a fair chance to gain some representation
in the legislature based on their electoral strength. These policymakers, however, wanted to avoid a repetition of the Weimar proportional representation
system (see Chapter 1), which encouraged a multiplicity of parties to run
candidates for the Reichstag, thereby contributing to political instability and
to the rise of Hitler. (In the early 1990s, Russia, Mexico, and Japan adopted
a similar mixed electoral system.)

In Germany, to reduce the number of splinter parties in the Bundestag,
the law stipulates that a party must gain at least 5 percent of the vote on the
second ballot or three seats in the districts. Similar laws apply in Länder legislative elections. Although many minor parties run candidates for election,
few have a chance of jumping the 5 percent or the minimum three seat hurdle. They nominate candidates to gain visibility and to indirectly influence
public policy. Despite the multiplicity of parties, the law really does restrict

"5% hurdle." Minor parties have had difficulty in mustering the 5 percent of total votes necessary to gain seats in the Bundestag since the first election in 1949. *Source: Informationen zur politischen Bildung* 119/124: *Das parlamentarische System der Bundesrepublik Deutschland* (Bonn: Bundeszentrale für Politische Bildung, 1980), p. 19. Reprinted by permission.

the number of parties in the Bundestag and the Länder parliaments and thereby ensures political stability.

Until German unification in 1990, each Bundestag had at least 496 deputies, half of them elected directly by plurality in the 248 single-member districts and the other half elected on a system of proportional representation by party lists in the Länder. Since unification, the deputies number at least 656, and the districts 328, to provide sufficient representation to eastern German voters. Each voter casts two ballots: the first, for one of the competing party candidates in the district; the second, for one of the lists of candidates drawn up by each party. The number of seats received by the party is based on its percentage of votes in the entire country. The seats are then distributed to the parties according to their strength in each Land. Of the two ballots, the second is the more important because it will determine the number of Bundestag seats that each party gains. If a party receives more direct seats than it would be entitled to under proportional representation, then it receives additional, or "overhang," seats. For instance, the 1994 Bundestag has 16 overhang mandates (12 CDU, 4 SPD), giving the parties 672 seats.

Voters are allowed to split their ballots by voting for a candidate of one party and the list of another. Ticket splitting is frequent among adherents of governing coalition partners to ensure that the minor party in the coalition surpasses the 5 percent hurdle needed to secure a seat in the Bundestag. Thus, during the period of CDU/CSU-FDP governance many CDU or CSU voters cast their first ballot for the Christian Democrats but their second ballot for the Free Democrats. They wanted to make sure that the FDP survived in the Bundestag to provide the necessary support for a new CDU/CSU-FDP coalition.[19]

The election law stipulates that parties choose candidates for the Bundestag by democratic procedure. In nominating candidates under proportional representation, the party's Land organization, pursuant to the delegates' wishes at nominating conventions, will put its senior officials with name recognition at the top of the list to gain a maximum of votes and to ensure their winning seats. Similarly, the organization will give important policy experts, who may not have the personal appeal to win in the districts, a high place on the list. The organization must also, to gain the maximum number of votes, give women and various groups and interests adequate representation. The candidate running for the party's district seat must be chosen by secret vote of the party members of that district or by a district selection committee elected by the members.

Conclusion

From 1945 on, Allied and German officials reestablished a pluralist party system, legitimized by constitutional and legislative provisions and enriched by private and public funds. It was shaped to some extent by a mixed electoral system that combined the features of the single-member district and proportional representation.

Required to adapt to new laws and institutions, but with only the flawed Weimar system to build on, German leaders developed a modified two-party system in which minor parties competed with the powerful CDU/CSU and SPD for seats in the legislatures. This democratic system has produced remarkable and unprecedented political stability. Most national governments have stayed in office throughout the legislative term of four years. Such stability helped move the political culture toward more tolerance and sympathy for parties than before 1945. However, public confidence in the established parties began to erode in the late 1980s and early 1990s because of their increasing involvement in scandals and their inability to solve pressing economic and social problems.

For a more detailed understanding of the West German parties, Chapters 4 to 7 examine each major and minor party that has been in the Bundestag and shown some continuity in existence. Chapter 8 examines the left and right radical parties that mostly failed in their quest for parliamentary representation but contributed to the nation's political dialogue.

Notes

1. Kenneth Dyson, "Party Government and Party State," in *Party Government and Political Culture in Western Germany*, ed. Herbert Döring and Gordon Smith (London: Macmillan, 1982), pp. 77–100.

2. French officials were fearful that a powerful Germany would arise once again and be a threat to France.

3. "Basic Law for the Federal Republic of Germany," in *Documents on Democracy in the Federal Republic of Germany*, 2d ed. (Bonn: Press and Information Office, 1994), p. 22.

4. *Der Spiegel*, May 2, 1994, pp. 41, 44, 48.

5. Article 1, Section 2, "The Law on Political Parties," in *Documents on Democracy in the Federal Republic of Germany*, p. 13.

6. "Basic Law for the Federal Republic," in *Documents on Democracy in the Federal Republic of Germany*, p. 30.

7. Ulrich Duebber and Gerard Braunthal, "Germany," in "Comparative Political Finance: A Symposium," special issue of *Journal of Politics* 25 (1963):776–779.

8. Daimler-Benz gave the CDU DM 600,000 ($364,000); the SPD, DM 420,000 ($255,000); the CSU, DM 400,000 ($242,000); and the FDP, DM 200,000 ($121,000). The country's largest bank, Deutsche Bank, another major contributor, gave the then governing party, the CDU, DM 516,000 ($313,000) and substantially less to the FDP and the CSU, but none to the SPD (GIC, *The Week in Germany*, January 22, 1993). The pattern of donations may also be determined by the political sympathies of the top management. (Currency exchange rates vary constantly; thus the 1967 rate of DM 2.50 for $1.00 had changed to DM 1.65 for $1.00 by 1991.)

9. David P. Conradt, *The German Polity*, 5th ed. (New York: Longman, 1993), p. 119; Andrei S. Markovits and Philip S. Gorski, *The German Left: Red, Green, and Beyond* (New York: Oxford University Press, 1993), p. 198.

10. German Information Center (GIC), New York, *The Week in Germany*, November 19, 1993.

11. For instance, in 1991 SPD expenditures totaled DM 272.7 million ($170.4 million); CDU, DM 216.7 million ($135.4 million); CSU, DM 48.4 million ($30.2 million); FDP, DM 50.6 million ($31.6 million); and Greens (western Germany), DM 54.5 million ($34 million) (GIC, *The Week in Germany*, January 22, 1993).

12. At issue were provisions granting parties that gained at least 2 percent of the vote DM 5 per voter and an additional yearly sum (*Sockelbetrag*) and parties that obtained at least 0.5 percent of the vote an additional yearly sum based on party mem-

bership, membership dues, donations, and the number of votes received in the previous election (the "equal opportunity" [*Chancenausgleich*] provision) (GIC, *The Week in Germany,* November 19, 1993).

13. The subsidies have constituted a substantial portion of the parties' annual income. In 1990, for instance, the CDU got nearly 42 percent of its total revenue from government reimbursement, 25 percent from dues, and 21 percent from donations. The SPD got close to 40 percent of its revenue from government funds, 37.5 percent from dues, and about 10 percent from donations (Gerard Braunthal, *The German Social Democrats Since 1969: A Party in Power and Opposition,* 2d ed. [Boulder: Westview Press, 1994], pp. 61–62; GIC, *The Week in Germany,* November 19, 1993).

14. Minor parties received a total of DM 6.5 million ($4 million) (GIC, *The Week in Germany,* January 20, 1995). The Länder governments also disburse funds to the parties for their state campaigns.

15. The CDU has the Konrad Adenauer Foundation; the CSU, Hans Seidel; the SPD, Friedrich Ebert; the FDP, Friedrich Naumann; and the Greens, Heinrich Böll. Among the host of activities, the Friedrich Ebert Foundation, for instance, trains unionists in developing countries, and the Heinrich Böll Foundation supports environmental, women's, and peace organizations. In 1991, the government gave foundations about DM 553 million ($325 million), the bulk of their income, for their activities (Conradt, *The German Polity,* p. 85). For a critical appraisal, see Hans Herbert von Arnim, *Staatliche Fraktionsfinanzierung ohne Kontrolle?* (Wiesbaden: Karl-Bräuer-Institut des Bundes der Steuerzahler, 1987).

16. Deutscher Bundestag, 12th election period, Drucksache 12/5777, September 29, 1993, p. 4.

17. For details, see Erwin K. and Ute Scheuch, *Cliquen, Klüngel, und Karrieren: Über den Verfall der politischen Parteien—eine Studie* (Reinbek: Rowohlt, 1992); Hans Herbert von Arnim, *Der Staat als Beute: Wie Politiker in eigener Sache Gesetze machen* (Munich: Knaur, 1993).

18. Hans Rattinger, "Abkehr von den Parteien? Dimensionen der Parteienverdrossenheit," *Aus Politik und Zeitgeschichte,* supplement to *Das Parlament,* B 11/93 (March 12, 1993):25.

19. For details, see Tony Burkett, *Parties and Elections in West Germany: The Search for Stability* (New York: St. Martin's Press, 1975), pp. 131–135.

· 4 ·

The Christian Democrats:
Right of Center

THE CHRISTIAN DEMOCRATIC UNION is the political heir of the prewar Center Party, which gained the support of Catholics during the Empire and Weimar periods. When parties were allowed to form during the immediate post–World War II era, CDU officials did not restrict their appeal for votes to Catholics but also wooed conservative and liberal Protestants. Eager to bridge the two religious communities' differences, which had surfaced repeatedly and often catastrophically in German history, CDU officials established a Christian party designed to appeal to all social classes and regions. The Catholic Church gave its blessing because it expected thereby to increase its political influence. The church knew the risks of watering down its social goals but believed that an interdenominational party, even if not a strictly religious one, would gain benefits for its mission.

The CDU officials' strategy paid off when the party embarked on a pragmatic course that took advantage of the secularization within the Federal Republic. Conservative secular voters had no qualms in voting for the CDU. The CDU also capitalized on the loss of the eastern German territories, Protestant bastions whose population would have been less sympathetic to an interdenominational party with strong Catholic influence.[1]

These diverse factors led to the CDU and its Bavarian affiliate, the Christian Social Union, becoming one of the two dominant mass, or catchall, parties in West Germany and the governing party for twenty-eight of the country's forty-one years of existence. The Christian Democratic movement was not restricted to West Germany. In France, Italy, and other European states, similar parties, although supported primarily by Catholic voters, played a key role in postwar politics. Their deputies in the European Parliament in Strasbourg have formed a Christian Democratic bloc, second in strength to that of the Social Democrats.

This chapter focuses first on the CDU's and CSU's crucial formative years from 1945 to 1949 and second on their role during West Germany's existence as a state from 1949 to 1990. The current shape of the party was determined by pre-1990 leadership changes, organizational rebuilding, membership growth, and ideological retooling. The story of the party since German unification in 1990 is told in Chapters 11 and 12.

The Occupation Years: 1945–1949

The Christian Democratic Union

In late 1945, ad hoc Christian political groups were formed in many western German cities, especially in Catholic regions. They were rivals to socialists and communists establishing their own parties at the local level. In chiefly Protestant regions, at first mostly Catholics joined the groups, but later Protestants joined as well. Although there were many differences between these groups, they agreed that Christian values would be the core of the fledgling movement's philosophy. Unlike some of the Center Party leaders during the Empire and Weimar eras, these group leaders emphasized their commitment to democracy, the rule of law, and individual freedoms—essential ingredients in the post-Nazi years. In December 1945, with Allied, and especially U.S., blessings, the groups met in Bad Godesberg to form a new organization, the Christian Democratic Union. The word "union," instead of "party," signaled their determination to create a loosely federated structure, which would consider different regional interests and not be controlled by national party bureaucrats.

The CDU leaders knew that Allied approval of their nominations to party offices would hinge on the nominees having clean anti-Nazi records. The logical choice to head the CDU was Konrad Adenauer, a former mayor of Cologne from 1917 to 1933, whom the Nazis had dismissed and subsequently imprisoned on a few occasions. During the Nazi years, he retired from public life. At the end of the war, U.S. officials reinstated him as mayor of Cologne. In October 1945, the British authorities, by then controlling the city, dismissed him and banned his involvement in political activities, accusing him of obstructionism and noncooperation with them. They lifted the ban two months later but did not reinstate him as mayor.

By February 1946, Adenauer was heading the CDU in the British zone and in his native Rhineland. As an eldest statesman (he was seventy at the time), he took over the party's reign and had no difficulty in squelching the ambitions of rival leaders. His authoritarian governance did not endear him to everyone but did ensure his climb to the top. A British journalist wrote that Adenauer "does not get his way by pounding the table; he uses men by flattering them, charming them with silky good humour or freezing them with quiet contempt."[2]

Despite Adenauer's success in establishing himself as party boss in the British zone, he was challenged for national leadership by Jakob Kaiser. One of the founders of the CDU in Berlin and in the Soviet zone, Kaiser had been chairman of the Catholic trade unions during the Weimar period and believed strongly in the Christian socialist movement. He wanted to establish a CDU for all four zones, with headquarters in Berlin. But Adenauer's view prevailed that with Germany divided into zones, a national CDU would play into the hands of the Soviets, eager to gain influence over parties in the western zones. Instead, the CDU opened an understaffed coordinating office for the four zones in Frankfurt. By 1948, the Soviets were forbidding the Berlin and the eastern zone CDU representatives to attend western CDU meetings.

During the first postwar years, the western CDU was fervently anti-Nazi for moral reasons. It blamed many Germans for supporting Nazism because of their "avaricious materialism." Succumbing to Nazi demagogy, they had expected the Nazis to bring them "paradise on earth."[3] In 1947, the CDU British zonal council met at Ahlen to draft a basic program. The delegates, who believed that Nazism had misused the capitalist system to commit many abuses, wanted the program to affirm the party's commitment to Christian ethics rather than materialism. Hence the powers of the state would be limited and the rights of individuals protected. The program opted for a middle course between private enterprise and state socialism. It called for nationalization of the coal industry and reorganization of chemical, steel, and other basic industries within a mixed economy. The industries would be controlled by government agencies, cooperatives, and workers to prevent an undue concentration of power in the hands of the owners. The economic planks were backed reluctantly by Adenauer and the party's conservatives, who were aware that many voters at the time rejected discredited rightist values and were attracted to a progressive Christian social but not socialist movement. However, Adenauer was successful in expunging the concept of Christian socialism, propagated by former leftist members of the Center Party, from the draft of the program.[4]

From 1947 on, disregarding the Ahlen program, the CDU supported the capitalist system that had begun to take root. Adenauer fully backed the efforts of Ludwig Erhard, director of economics in the Bizonal Administration (U.S. and British), to abolish all economic controls, introduce a currency reform in 1948 to stop postwar inflation and the black market, and establish a social market economy—a mixture of the free enterprise system and social protection for the underprivileged. His economic system was responsible for the "economic miracle" that brought prosperity to West Germany.

The CDU's turn toward conservatism established its enduring ideological orientation. Adenauer frequently voiced strong procapitalist, pro-West, and anticommunist views, which were supported by the approximately four hundred thousand members of the loosely organized party.[5] From 1946 to 1949, CDU strength was evident also in five of the eleven states that had elected CDU-led governments and in the Parliamentary Council, established in 1948 to draft a constitution for the nascent Federal Republic. Adenauer, who by then had made himself head of the Conference of CDU Land Chairpersons, also became president of the Parliamentary Council. He had swiftly put his imprint on western zonal politics.

The Christian Social Union

The CSU, the Bavarian semiautonomous branch of the CDU, has its antecedents in the Bavarian People's Party, established as the regional offshoot of the Center Party during the Weimar period. During 1945, Josef Müller, a member of the German underground movement during the Nazi terror years, hoped to establish a left-wing counterpart of the CDU in Bavaria. He wanted the new party to be interdenominational and to adhere to the tenets of Christian socialism, which has been one of the underpinnings of the British Labour Party. He failed to get support from either Social Democrats, who were busy reconstructing their own party and in no mood to dilute its identity, or from ultraconservative leaders of the former Bavarian People's Party, who wanted to rebuild the Catholic party.

Thereupon Müller, after receiving crucial backing from Adam Stegerwald, who had headed the Catholic trade unions during Weimar, and from Protestant North Bavarian leaders, founded in January 1946 a more conservative CSU than he had envisaged. Not surprisingly, given the Bavarian striving for a decentralized and federal, rather than a central, German government, the party accentuated state rights. It had the strong support of the Catholic Church, whose Bavarian leaders resented northern German politicians' lack of interest in guaranteeing state support for confessional schools. The CSU was also supported by conservative farmers, who were unhappy about the Bizonal Administration's edicts on food price controls, cattle quotas, and grain deliveries, all of which affected them adversely.

During the occupation period, relations between the CSU and CDU were not always friendly. Adenauer had been interested in a close interzonal link, but the CSU agreed to form only a working partnership. The CSU could stand up to the CDU because it had received over 52 percent of the votes in the Bavarian Landtag election of December 1946. However, its leaders were worried about internal dissension and competition from the smaller Bavarian Party, which had received an Allied license in 1948. In May 1949, Bavarian minister-president Hans Ehard (CSU), sympathetic to the conservative CSU faction, headed by Alois Hundhammer, a former leader of the Bavarian People's Party, won the CSU chairmanship against Müller, leader of the liberal wing.[6] Adenauer was satisfied with Müller's fall.

The CDU: 1949–1990

The CDU/CSU won the first national election in 1949, narrowly out-polling the SPD by 31.0 to 29.2 percent (see Table 4.1 and Figure 4.1). Adenauer, with a cliffhanger, one-vote majority in the Bundestag, became chancellor of the fledgling Federal Republic. *Der Alte* (The Old One), as he was nicknamed affectionately by many, thereupon sought to become the first chairperson of the loosely knit CDU. In 1950, at the first West German convention of the CDU, he gained his objective after having skill-

TABLE 4.1 Bundestag Election Results, 1949–1994 (in percentages)

Election Year	Voter Turnout	CDU/ CSU	SPD	FDP	Greens[a]	PDS	Others
1949	78.5	31.0	29.2	11.9	–	–	27.8
1953	85.8	45.2	28.8	9.5	–	–	16.5
1957	87.8	50.2	31.8	7.7	–	–	10.3
1961	87.7	45.3	36.2	12.8	–	–	5.7
1965	86.8	47.6	39.3	9.5	–	–	3.6
1969	86.7	46.1	42.7	5.8	–	–	5.5
1972	91.1	44.9	45.8	8.4	–	–	0.9
1976	90.7	48.6	42.6	7.9	–	–	0.9
1980	88.6	44.5	42.9	10.6	1.5	–	0.5
1983	89.1	48.8	38.2	7.0	5.6	–	0.5
1987	84.3	44.3	37.0	9.1	8.3	–	1.4
1990	77.8	43.8	33.5	11.0	5.1	2.4	4.2
1994	79.1	41.4	36.4	6.9	7.3	4.4	3.6

[a] In 1990, Greens in western Germany; Alliance 90/Greens in eastern Germany. In 1994, Alliance 90/Greens.

SOURCE: *Die Bundestagswahl vom 16. Oktober 1994* (Sankt Augustin: Konrad-Adenauer-Stiftung, 1994).

FIGURE 4.1   Bundestag Election Results, 1949–1994

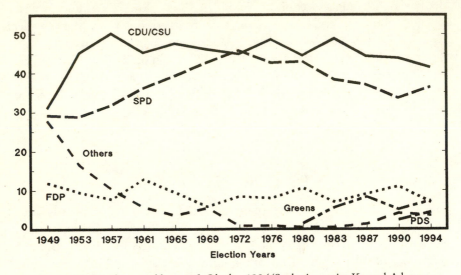

SOURCE: *Die Bundestagswahl vom 16. Oktober 1994* (Sankt Augustin: Konrad-Adenauer-Stiftung, 1994).

fully eliminated his rivals or after they themselves had lost power in their Länder. Paradoxically, the CDU governed in Bonn and had the strongest Fraktion in the Bundestag during the first years without having established a central party organization. A national headquarters could not be established until 1952 because the Länder associations (Landesverbände) wanted to maintain as much autonomy and freedom from orders from above as possible. Thus, in the first two decades the associations were satisfied to have a purely electoral organization, led by Adenauer and his successor, Ludwig Erhard, operating out of the Chancellor's Office. Notwithstanding the lack of a centralized organization, the party won the 1953, 1957, 1961, and 1965 elections (see Table 4.2). The SPD assumed governing responsibility only in 1969, after the CDU/CSU had been in office for twenty years.

Organization

The CDU has always been based on the principles of federalism and decentralization, although since the 1960s the party has become more centralized. The organization consists of a periodically held (annual or biennial) convention, whose delegates from the Länder associations approve broad policy and

TABLE 4.2 Distribution of Seats in the Bundestag, 1949–1994

Election Year	CDU/ CSU	SPD	FDP	Greens	PDS	Others	Total
1949	139	131	52	–	–	80	402
1953	243	151	48	–	–	45	487
1957	270	169	41	–	–	17	497
1961	242	190	67	–	–	–	499
1965	245	202	49	–	–	–	496
1969	242	224	30	–	–	–	496
1972	225	230	41	–	–	–	496
1976	243	214	39	–	–	–	496
1980	226	218	53	–	–	–	497
1983	244	193	34	27	–	–	498
1987	223	186	46	42	–	–	497
1990	319	239	79	8	17	–	662
1994	294	252	47	49	30	–	672

SOURCE: *Die Bundestagswahl vom 16. Oktober 1994* (Sankt Augustin: Konrad-Adenauer-Stiftung, 1994).

programmatic goals and elect members to the Federal Executive Board (Bundesvorstand). The Federal Executive has thirty members, many of whom are cabinet ministers (when the party is in power), Länder officeholders, and officials of affiliated organizations. It has primarily coordinating, rather than political, powers. Because of the large size of the Federal Executive, a smaller ten-member Presidium, whose members belong to the inner circle of elected CDU leaders, meets frequently to determine the party's position on pressing policy issues. The Federal Committee (Bundesausschuss), nicknamed the "small party convention," is made up mostly of delegates from Länder associations who meet two or three times a year to handle political and organizational matters not dealt with by the previous convention.[7]

Until the late 1960s, the CDU's national headquarters, headed by a federal business manager (*Bundesgeschäftsführer*), had only a few administrative functions, such as distributing information and publicity material to the Länder and district associations. Local notables selected candidates for public office but had little interest in making the CDU a mass party and enrolling dues-paying members. The Federal Committee did not decide until 1964 on obligatory dues scaled according to income, as in the SPD. The new policy found little favor among those members who were eager to maintain maximum freedom in their lives, an attitude that coincided with the party's ideology.[8]

As long as CDU chancellors Adenauer (1949–1963), Erhard (1963–1966), and Kurt-Georg Kiesinger (1966–1969) headed national governments, political decisions were made by CDU leaders in the cabinet, the Bundestag Fraktion, and the Land associations. However, once in opposition, some CDU officials, appalled by the lack of an effective organization, demanded that the party be modernized. For instance, the chairman of the CDU's youth branch said: "The CDU should not take its opposition role as an undeserved blow of fortune and show whining self-pity, but must seize the change in role as an opportunity. . . . At present it appears predominately as a disorganised, loosely united reservoir of heterogeneous associations and autonomous regional branches."[9]

Their pleas for action finally bore fruit. In 1970, the senior leaders reorganized national headquarters in Bonn into seven departments, including internal administration, organization, policy, publicity, and media. In 1971, the party's numerous scattered and crowded offices of the departments and working groups were moved to the new miniskyscraper Konrad Adenauer Haus.

After some dispute about the primary functions of national headquarters, the business manager became the principal administrative officer in charge of personnel, and the secretary-general, a post newly created in 1967, became the principal political officer and head of the organization. Party activists were required to take training courses, personnel planning was instituted, and communication and coordination among the party's national, regional, and local units were developed. Kurt Biedenkopf, secretary-general from 1973 to 1976, insisted that the secretary-general coordinate the party's organizational activities at all levels, promote intraparty discussions, and gear up the party for national and state elections. He set up a speakers' service, enhanced contacts with the media, and professionalized the district offices by ensuring well-paid and competent staff.

Biedenkopf's headquarters largely made policy from 1972 to 1976, but at other times when the CDU was in opposition (from 1969 until 1982), the Bundestag Fraktion set the political direction. This was especially true when party chairman Helmut Kohl headed the Fraktion from 1976 until he became chancellor in 1982. Before rising to national prominence, Kohl had been minister-president of Rhineland-Palatinate for seven years. As chancellor and party chairman, Kohl became the dominant figure within the CDU. Even though critics called him a "bumbling dilettante" and pointed to his lack of popular appeal, he has had an uncanny ability to fend off rivals, integrate a heterogeneous party, and continue in office.[10]

In 1982, Kohl became chancellor. He is sitting on a chair painfully reflecting the political intrigues facing him. The original caption read, "It's got to be wonderful." *Source:* Walther Keim, ed., *Das waren Zeiten: Achtzehn Karikaturisten sehen vierzig Jahre Bundesrepublik* (Munich: Süddeutscher Verlag, 1989), p. 145. Reprinted by permission.

Membership

The party's membership has fluctuated considerably over the decades. It had close to 400,000 members in 1949, perhaps a testimonial to Allied efforts to democratize Germany and the voters' eagerness not to identify themselves with the Nazi past. But the number dipped after the economic recovery to a low of just over 200,000 in 1953 because politically apathetic citizens were reluctant to join any party and CDU notables did not encourage sympathizers to become members. Membership remained stagnant at below 300,000 until 1968. Between 1970 and 1977, when the party was in opposition and eager to recapture power, officials tried hard to recruit new members. By 1983, membership had peaked at 735,000. Later it dropped again (as did

SPD membership) because of the CDU's involvement in scandals and corruption, popular dissatisfaction with the establishment parties, and political apathy among youths.

The social composition of the membership is typically middle class. Among overrepresented occupational categories in the party have been the self-employed, including many farmers, who made up 24.8 percent of the membership in 1982; salaried employees, 28 percent; and civil servants, 12.4 percent. Underrepresented blue-collar workers totaled 10.4 percent; pensioners, 4.9 percent; and homemakers, 11 percent.[11]

During the first postwar decades, middle- and older-aged groups and males predominated, partly because many surviving pre-1933 party activists had joined and partly because the notables were not eager to recruit young members. By the late 1960s, however, more young people, including women, had joined, increasing the female membership from 13 to 21 percent.[12]

As CDU membership expanded, the proportion of Catholics, who have been its most staunch supporters, declined from about 75 percent in 1971 to 59 percent in 1982. Despite this decline, the party still has more Catholics among its members compared with their 50 percent in the West German population. Protestants have been reluctant to join the party, even though millions vote for it. CDU leaders, to ensure maximum Protestant support, have introduced informal proportional quotas for all offices.

The party's strength varies from Land to Land. Its greatest membership support comes from the Rhineland, Westphalia, and Baden-Württemberg, with large Catholic populations, and its lowest support from the SPD Protestant strongholds of Berlin, Hamburg, and Bremen.

Ancillary Organizations

Like many mass parties throughout the world, the CDU has created ancillary organizations to gain more members and voters. There are eight social organizations (*Vereinigungen*) that serve as centers for those with common interests, links to society, and vehicles for political socialization. The organizations, which make programmatic demands on the party, are the youth division, Young Union; an association for municipal politics; a women's association; the Christian Democratic Workers' Social Committees, with close ties to Catholic unionists; two employers' groups; a group of refugees and expellees from former German settlements in Eastern Europe; and (more recently) a senior citizens' group. Other auxiliary organizations, such as the Christian Democratic Students and the Secondary School Union, the Economic Council, Catholic lay groups, and the Protestant Working Group, have loose ties to the party. Members of the ancillary and auxiliary organizations do not need to join the party.

The diverse interests of members produce tensions within the heterogeneous party, especially between the workers' and employers' groups, that reflect similar tensions within society. Although both groups are represented in the top party organs, the employers wield more power within the CDU and have greater influence on its policy goals than has labor.[13]

Ideological Foundations

Political parties, no matter how pragmatic, need programmatic directions. Otherwise they cannot be distinguished from one another, attract members and voters, and provide guidelines for government policy should they attain power. Even the pragmatic U.S. parties adopt election platforms, vague as the platforms may be on many issues.

German parties, the CDU included, have issued a host of basic programs and election platforms. As noted, in 1947 the CDU adopted the Ahlen left-wing program, which was soon supplanted by more conservative documents. In the 1950s, when Adenauer was chancellor, the party dispensed with a basic program because it identified closely with its own government policies, which were based on the social market economy and West Germany's close links with the West. In 1968, in the post-Adenauer era, the party adopted the conservative Berlin program, which was revised three years later when the party was out of power in Bonn. The program contained few new departures, but a commission on basic principles worked during the following years on specific issues, such as vocational education and codetermination (workers' right to sit on corporate boards).

In 1975, the convention accepted the Mannheim Declaration dealing with urgent social issues. In 1978, after years of internal discussions, the CDU finally approved a basic program at its Ludwigshafen convention. The program assailed the SPD-FDP–led government's reform policies, defended the free market economy, underlined the state's obligation to maintain law and order, and insisted on limited welfare budgets. In the 1980s, CDU delegates at several conventions approved new basic guidelines regarding technological, scientific, and ecological developments.[14]

The CDU's ideological foundations gave it, whether in power or in opposition, strategies for electoral campaigns and policy guidelines. With a conservative profile, it was easy for the CDU/CSU in 1982 to regain the support of the increasingly conservative FDP and persuade it to renew their pre-1966 governing coalition.[15] Thus, the CDU/CSU again became the senior governing party in West Germany until reunification in 1990 and since then in the reunited Germany. Chancellor Kohl, buoyed by 1983 and 1987 electoral victories, pursued a moderately conservative domestic policy, less conservative, however, than that of Ronald Reagan in the United States or Margaret Thatcher in Britain.

The CSU: 1949–1990

The CSU, the Bavarian affiliate of the CDU, has its own leaders, organization, and membership, whose social composition is akin to that of the CDU membership.[16] The CSU's numbers have gradually risen, from 35,000 in 1955 to over 180,000 in the 1980s. With a preponderance of votes in conservative Catholic rural areas and in newly industrialized regions, the CSU has consistently outpolled the SPD in nearly all elections. Since 1957, it has mustered more than 50 percent of the Bavarian vote in the Bundestag elections and since 1966 has formed every Bavarian government—without even a coalition partner.

In the Bundestag, CSU deputies are integrated into the joint CDU/CSU Fraktion. When the CDU/CSU controls the executive branch in Bonn, the CSU is always represented in the cabinets, where CDU and CSU ministers make joint decisions. Regardless of whether the linked party is in power, CDU and CSU have always concurred on a joint candidate for chancellor, normally chosen by the CDU. They have also agreed not to encroach on each other's territory to recruit members and voters. Thus, there is no CDU in Bavaria and no CSU in the other Länder.

The pooled arrangements have not always led to peaceful coexistence. Ideological differences, with the CSU standing to the right of the CDU, have arisen on some policy issues. Franz Josef Strauss made life difficult for many CDU officials, including Kohl, especially when they balked at putting him up as the CDU/CSU's candidate for chancellor in 1976. They worried that the CSU leader's controversial ultraconservative and nationalist views would repel many CDU supporters and cause a CDU/CSU defeat. Kohl was nominated instead, but despite his less controversial views, he could not defeat Helmut Schmidt, the incumbent SPD chancellor.

Thereupon Strauss tried to take revenge. At a CSU meeting in November 1976, the party announced that it would not remain in the joint CDU/CSU Bundestag Fraktion. In response, Kohl, fearful that the CSU would become a rival national party, threatened to establish a CDU in Bavaria. Strauss backed down, afraid of a schism within his party, poor electoral prospects for the

CSU throughout Germany, and a weakening of both parties. A crisis was averted. However, Strauss did not give up his ambition to become chancellor. In 1980, the CDU/CSU nominated him, but he, like Kohl, lost to Schmidt. He then withdrew from national politics and in 1988 died, a controversial but respected politician. His head now adorns the back of the DM 2 coin.

Conclusion

The CDU's and CSU's leadership of every postwar West German government since 1949, with the exception of the period from 1969 to 1982, attests to their combined strength and electoral appeal. The two parties' conservative policies found resonance among a voting population satisfied with the status quo. Nevertheless, the CDU/CSU has, with one exception, always needed the cooperation of another Bundestag party, normally the FDP, to form cabinets and gain support from a majority of deputies.[17]

The CDU's organizational buildup and flexible policy choices contributed to its electoral appeal. Yet it faced difficulties, especially in the post-Adenauer period. It often lacked unity and a sense of purpose. It experienced a turnover of leaders until Kohl established himself as party chairman in 1973. His longevity in party office, not to speak of his chancellorship, is quite remarkable, but he has shown a lack of charisma and an intolerance of dissenting leaders, has failed to promote intraparty democracy, and has committed occasional domestic and foreign policy blunders. Despite the CDU's weaknesses, it has remained, along with the affiliated CSU, a major force in West German politics and one of the pillars of political stability in the nascent and pluralist Federal Republic.

Notes

1. William M. Chandler, "The Christian Democrats," in *The Federal Republic of Germany at Forty,* ed. Peter H. Merkl (New York: New York University Press, 1989), p. 293.

2. Brian Connell; quoted in Terence Prittie, *Konrad Adenauer: 1876–1967* (Chicago: Cowles Book Company, 1971), p. 121. See also Arnold Heidenheimer, *Adenauer and the CDU: The Rise of the Leader and the Integration of the Party* (The Hague: Martinus Nijhoff, 1960).

3. Geoffrey Pridham, *Christian Democracy in Western Germany: The CDU/CSU in Government and Opposition, 1945–1976* (London: Croom Helm, 1977), p. 25. See

also Tony Burkett, *Parties and Elections in West Germany: The Search for Stability* (New York: St. Martin's Press, 1975), pp. 31–35.

4. Hans-Otto Kleinmann, *Geschichte der CDU, 1945–1982* (Stuttgart: Deutsche Verlags–Anstalt, 1993), pp. 89–92.

5. Heino Kaack, *Geschichte und Struktur des deutschen Parteiensystems* (Opladen: Westdeutscher Verlag, 1971), p. 495.

6. Alf Mintzel, *Geschichte der CSU: Ein Überblick* (Opladen: Westdeutscher Verlag, 1977), pp. 78–110.

7. Karl G. Tempel, *Die Parteien in der Bundesrepublik Deutschland und die Rolle der Parteien in der DDR* (Opladen: Leske und Budrich, 1987), pp. 101–102.

8. In 1971, the party treasurer, Walther Leisler Kiep, faced with deficits stemming from reduced business contributions (the party was no longer in power), increased the membership dues, which, along with an influx of members, led to an appreciable rise in the percentage of income from dues.

9. Jürgen Echternach; cited in Pridham, *Christian Democracy in Western Germany*, p. 261; see also pp. 241–260.

10. Gordon Smith, *Democracy in Western Germany: Parties and Politics in the Federal Republic*, 3d ed. (Aldershot, England: Gower, 1986), p. 154; Clay Clemens, "Power in Moderation: Helmut Kohl and Political Leadership in Germany, 1973–89" (Paper presented at the German Studies Association conference, Minneapolis, Minnesota, October 1–4, 1992), p. 5.

11. Peter Haungs, "Die CDU: Prototyp einer Volkspartei," in *Parteien in der Bundesrepublik Deutschland*, ed. Alf Mintzel and Heinrich Oberreuter (Opladen: Leske und Budrich, 1992), pp. 191–192; William E. Paterson, "The Christian Union Parties," in *West German Politics in the Mid-Eighties: Crisis and Continuity*, ed. H. G. Peter Wallach and George K. Romoser (New York: Praeger, 1985), p. 71.

12. Chandler, "The Christian Democrats," p. 303.

13. Pridham, *Christian Democracy in Western Germany*, pp. 291–302; Chandler, "The Christian Democrats," pp. 304–306.

14. Haungs, "Die CDU," pp. 182–190.

15. From 1969 to 1982, the FDP had been the SPD's junior governing partner, but because their policy dispute on how to meet the economic crisis proved unbridgeable, the coalition fell apart.

16. For details of the CSU organization, see Mintzel, *Geschichte der CSU*, pp. 113–142.

17. In 1957, the CDU/CSU gained an absolute majority of votes and Bundestag seats but still preferred to form a coalition with the FDP as a guarantee that the FDP would remain on the CDU/CSU's side.

· 5 ·

The Social Democrats:
Left of Center

THE SOCIAL DEMOCRATIC PARTY and the Christian Democratic Union/Christian Social Union have been the dominant people's parties in West Germany. Unlike the CDU/CSU, whose only direct link to the Weimar parties was as the Center Party's political heir, the SPD could look back to its formation in the nineteenth century and its almost uninterrupted existence since then (see Chapter 2). In the post-1945 era, the SPD governed West Germany for only thirteen years of the country's forty-one years of existence, but it co-governed with the CDU/CSU for three years and had a limited influence on Bonn politics as the chief opposition party during the other years. This chapter tells of its rebirth after World War II, its changing leadership and membership, its factionalism, its ideology, and its experience as government party under Chancellors Willy Brandt and Helmut Schmidt. This brief survey attempts to show why the party suffered so many defeats in national elections (but not in many Länder and municipal elections) and assesses its ability to change the direction of policies toward the left when in power in Bonn.

The Occupation Years: 1945–1949

Soon after the Nazi regime collapsed in May 1945, former SPD officials received permission from Allied authorities to rebuild their party. But schisms within party ranks and differences among the occupation powers complicated the task. Three SPD centers emerged: one in Hannover, led by Kurt Schumacher, a veteran SPD leader whom the Nazis had imprisoned for years; a second in London, headed by Erich Ollenhauer and consisting of an exile group isolated by its distance and not permitted to move back to Germany until February 1946; and a third in Berlin, a "Central Committee" led by Otto Grotewohl, which claimed to be the legal heir of the party suppressed in 1933.[1]

The Berlin Central Committee soon became the focus of an intense intraparty dispute. As had been the case with Adenauer and the CDU, Schumacher refused to recognize the committee's claim to represent the SPD in all of Germany, accepting it only in the Soviet zone of occupation. He won this struggle. In April 1946, however, the SPD vanished in the Soviet zone when Grotewohl agreed to a merger of the SPD and the Communist Party of Germany (see Chapter 9).

Schumacher did not want to see the eastern German merger repeated in the western zones. He was sympathetic to a united workers' party, but not based on unity with the KPD, considered a tool of the Soviet Union. Some unity committees were started in western German cities, but they withered away once SPD members heard about developments in eastern Germany. In a western Berlin referendum (forbidden by the Soviets in their Berlin sector), 82 percent of the SPD members voted against a merger. Hence, the SPD in western Berlin survived.

In the meantime, Schumacher became undisputed party leader in western Germany. At the first convention in Hannover in May 1946, he was elected chairman, and Ollenhauer, who by then had returned from London, was elected deputy chairman. The party was rebuilt on the foundations set before 1933. A statute was accepted; ancillary organizations serving various groups, such as youths, women, and sports, resurfaced; and a party press appeared again. By 1947, more than 875,000 members had signed up; three years later, however, membership dipped to 683,000, partly because many idealistic members hoping for a new socialist age had become disillusioned and left the party.[2]

The party, as before 1933, adopted a mixture of Marxist doctrine and reformist practice. Schumacher advocated an economy based on planning rather than private profit. He warned that monopoly capital had helped Hitler gain power and said that democracy could be guaranteed only if the state owned the major means of production. In his speeches he called for support not only from the working class but also from all those who "share a concern for the free development of the individual."[3] Thus, Schumacher set the stage for the transformation of the SPD into a people's party.[4]

Schumacher's foreign policy goals included reunification of the divided country to maintain peace in Europe (as well as to ensure that the party regain its many former supporters in eastern Germany). The SPD leader's emphasis on nationalism was designed to counter the image disseminated during Weimar by conservative parties, which had accused the SPD of stabbing Germany in the back by accepting the 1919 Versailles Treaty calling for major German reparations to the victorious Allied powers. Ironically, the emphasis on nationalism at a time when supranationalism was popular among German youths cost the party some support.

The Federal Republic: 1949–1990

The SPD's hopes of becoming the governing party once the FRG was created in 1949 were dashed when it narrowly lost the first federal election to the CDU/CSU. Adenauer assumed the chancellorship, and the SPD became and remained the major opposition party until 1966. The SPD defeat had several causes: the western zones' successful economic revival credited to Ludwig Erhard (then CDU head of the Economic Council), Adenauer's strong anticommunist and pro-West position in the face of tight Soviet control in the eastern zone, the SPD's loss of its Protestant bastion in eastern Germany, and the voters' rejection of the SPD leaders' neo-Marxist rhetoric in campaign speeches.

In the next four federal elections (1953, 1957, 1961, and 1965), the SPD gradually gained voter support but could not reach 40 percent of the total to secure a chance to form a coalition government. The party faced numerous problems in the quadrennial elections. An opposition party must present realistic alternatives to government policy that will appeal to the electorate, but Schumacher's foreign policy alternatives to Adenauer's lacked broad support. The SPD chairman opposed West Germany's joining the Council of Europe and the European Coal and Steel Community because he feared that capitalist countries would dominate them and that reunification of the two Germanys, needing Soviet consent, would be doomed.

In the 1950s, the SPD opposed the Adenauer policy of rearming the FRG within the Western alliance, fearing rearmament would make German reunification impossible. At the 1954 convention, the party agreed to support a small West German volunteer army if several conditions were met, but when these conditions were rejected by the Adenauer government, the SPD maintained its opposition. In 1959, it proclaimed a "Germany Plan" advocating fewer troops in central Europe and a political and economic rapprochement of the two Germanys in advance of free elections in both states, but this plan did not gain popular support.

The SPD and CDU/CSU differed sharply on foreign policy but less on domestic policy. The SPD accepted many government bills, subject to only minor changes.[5] Even though the SPD publicized its legislative contributions, the public could not easily perceive the nuances of which party was responsible for which policy revisions. It was hard for the SPD to shed its image of being always on the negative side or even disloyal to the state.

In short, although the party contributed its share to policy input and output during its initial years of opposition in Bonn, the governing parties shaped the contours of domestic and foreign policies. In many Länder and cities, SPD officials were in policymaking positions, but their achievements did not get the same publicity as did those of the CDU/CSU-dominated federal government, which took credit for achieving economic prosperity and for putting the country solidly in the Western camp.

Organization

As already observed in regard to the CDU/CSU, the organization of a party, as specified in its periodically revised statute, tells little about the capability of its policymakers, the amount of membership activity, and the cleavages among its factions. Such organizational dynamics can affect the political fortunes of the party as it seeks to become the governing party or, having succeeded, to maintain itself in power.

SPD policy is made in the Presidium, an "inner cabinet" of eleven top leaders (thirteen since 1990). It consists of the party chairperson, the deputy chairpersons, the secretary, the treasurer, the Fraktion chairperson, and several members-at-large. When the SPD was the government party, the chancellor and some SPD cabinet members also held Presidium seats, thus facilitating joint policymaking in respect to key domestic and foreign policy issues. In practice, the SPD chancellor first made policy decisions in the cabinet and then informed the Presidium. The Presidium, meeting weekly, might not concur with a decision, but there was little chance of reversal once the chancellor had argued that national interests transcended party interests. Normally, there was some identity of interests because the left-wing SPD faction, which often criticized party or government policy, was almost unrepresented on the Presidium.[6]

The party's Executive (Vorstand), meeting monthly, is its second most important decisionmaking body. Its members are elected at the convention, at times from rival left and right slates of candidates for the coveted posts. The factions normally win seats in proportion to their strength at the conventions. The left faction at its peak captured about one-third of the seats, giving it a chance for policy input. The Executive receives reports from the Presidium and deals with basic policies, organization, and personnel. The convention, usually meeting biennially, is in theory the highest policymaking organ, but in practice it is limited to approving decisions made in the Presidium and Executive.

Besides these top bodies, the organization has a secretary heading the staff at national headquarters and supervising the regional associations in the Länder, districts, and subdistricts. The ten thousand local branches in cities and small communities give members a chance to discuss party and government policies; to assist in local, state, and national campaigns; and to recruit new members.

The Associations

The SPD has established a host of commissions, committees, ad hoc working groups, and associations. The three most important associations are those of the Young Socialists (Jusos), the manual and salaried workers, and the women.[7] Others comprise the self-employed, health sector staff, teachers, lawyers, and municipal officials.

The Jusos' strength peaked in the late 1960s and 1970s. The association included all SPD members under thirty five and made up much of the party's left faction. The Jusos were highly critical of SPD policies and the oligarchical rule of their elders. They urged the senior officials to move the party to the left and accentuate its socialist goals rather than strengthen the capitalist system. They asked for more democratization within the party, the political system, and the economy. Senior centrist and rightist chiefs disagreed with most of the Jusos' objectives and worried about their capturing control of many local branches. The Jusos partially succeeded in democratizing the party but, rent with factionalism, could not gain enough support among party colleagues to have much effect on national policies.

The major resistance came from the bloc of union leaders and blue-collar workers, making up much of the SPD's right wing, who blocked Juso attempts to "march through the institutions" of the party and the state in an effort to capture them. Although the unionists backed progressive social legislation, they had in effect abandoned the socialist goals in which earlier generations of workers had believed. Union leaders formed the Association of Workers (AfA) within the party, partly to offset Juso influence and partly to recruit more workers into the SPD. AfA leaders maintained close ties to the German Trade Union Federation, the leading labor organization, with seventeen national unions and a membership in the 1980s of 8 million.

In addition to the Jusos and the AfA, the Association of Social Democratic Women (ASF) has represented an important constituency within the male-dominated SPD. Founded in 1972, the ASF demanded a greater voice for women within the party, sought to attract more women as members, and asked the party to put a priority on the political, economic, and social concerns of women. In the late 1980s, the ASF gained approval for a quota system within the party to ensure that by 1994 at least 40 percent of all SPD policymaking organs would be occupied by women and that by 1998 at least 40 percent of the SPD candidates for public office would be women.

A Shift in Membership

The SPD underwent an important social shift in membership, which in turn affected its electoral fortunes and its programmatic goals. After 1945, the percentage of blue-collar workers in the labor force began to decline. By 1980, this traditional core group of the party constituted only 28 percent of the SPD membership (compared with 45 percent in 1952). Despite these waning numbers, the party could not disregard the workers' demand that bread-and-butter issues be put high on its agenda. The workers' traditional social, religious, sexual, and ideological values were bound, however, to clash with those of the new, young members who streamed into the party when Brandt became chancellor in 1969. Many of them were left-wing students; others were salaried employees and civil servants (especially teachers), making up the "new middle class." The employees and civil servants had relatively high incomes, were well educated, and held modern, secular, and progressive ("postmaterialist"), rather than traditional, views. They wanted the party to emphasize quality-of-life issues, such as protection of the environment and democratization of institutions, instead of bread-and-butter issues, which they deemed important but less urgent.

The changed character of the membership paralleled the secularization, social mobility, and economic prosperity within society. As in other advanced industrial states, the occupational shift was the result of the shift from a manufacturing to a service-oriented economy. The new SPD members, making up much of the left and center wings in the party, supported Brandt's reformist domestic policies. The SPD's public attractiveness peaked, however, during the mid-1970s, when it numbered more than 1 million members. Primarily because many left-wing youths thereafter dropped out of politics or joined the Greens, membership had fallen to 920,000 by 1990. The resulting increase in the average age of members caused great concern among officials as to how the party could be rejuvenated. The gender inequality, with male members predominating (73 percent male to 27 percent female in 1990), also worried them, especially since new female members came primarily from the middle class, thus representing only one stratum of society. Secularization in Germany redressed the imbalance of Protestants and Catholics in the SPD, as more of the less devout Catholics joined the party. By 1977, the membership was 53 percent Protestant, 28 percent Catholic, and 19 percent mostly unaffiliated.

It was hard for the party to recruit new members in the conservative strongholds of Bavaria and Baden-Württemberg, where the CSU and CDU had the support of many farmers and self-employed persons. In other regions, where recruitment was a smaller problem, the party could not overcome the difficulty of activating members, whose only contribution to the party was to pay dues.[8]

Marxism Out, Reformism In

A party program that corresponds to the zeitgeist permeating society facilitates membership recruitment—and electoral success. From 1949 on, the SPD had to design policies alternative to those of the CDU/CSU-led governments and expand its electoral base if it meant to surpass the CDU/CSU's national vote. This issue became more pressing as the socioeconomic composition of the population changed. In the early 1950s, when even blue-collar workers no longer considered themselves an exploited class in the Marxist sense but, increasingly, part of the middle class, a group of reformist and pragmatic mayors in the party's strongholds of Hamburg, Bremen, and West Berlin, later joined by many SPD Bundestag deputies, called for a change in the direction of policy. Chairman Ollenhauer, who had succeeded Schumacher on his death in 1952, was somewhat receptive, unlike most functionaries, who clung to past traditions and doctrine.

More electoral defeats convinced Ollenhauer that changes had to be made. After years of preparatory work by a program commission, the 1959 Bad Godesberg convention approved the new program, with only a few dissenting votes from a neo-Marxist group.[9] The program abandoned Marxist determinism and affirmed the religious and philosophical roots of democratic socialism. It emphasized freedom, justice, and solidarity in a parliamentary, democratic system. It no longer viewed nationalization as the major principle of a socialist economy but only one of several (and then only the last) means of controlling economic concentration and power. The program assented to as much free competition as possible, with only as much planning as necessary. It also committed the party to defending the country and supporting the army. It asked respect for and cooperation with churches, based on a free partnership with them.

The program reflected the political views of many former émigré leaders, who admired the British and Scandinavian pluralist and social welfare systems. It also reflected the leaders' conviction that West Germans were hostile to any "experiments" that might undermine the neocapitalist, social welfare system. Although the Godesberg program seemed to mark a sudden change to reformism, it was the culmination of a slow decline in ideology within the party. The SPD was not alone in accepting a reformist doctrine; other European socialist parties and the Socialist International had already taken or were adopting similar positions. Hoping to widen their voter base, these parties evolved from workers' parties to people's parties, gaining support from most groups in society.

The SPD basic programs last about a generation, then are revised. During the intervals, electoral and government programs are agreed on to deal with current issues. Party leaders decided in the mid-1980s to replace the partly outdated Godesberg program with a new basic program that would deal with the contemporary economic, ecological, social, and international problems facing German society. After years of intraparty discussions, the Berlin convention adopted the final program in December 1989.

It emphasizes a reduction of inequalities in income, a granting of some power to the state to intervene in the economy, an expansion of economic democracy and participatory democracy, an ecological restructuring of industrial society, and gender equality. According to SPD officials, the ideological position and the economic and social reforms defined in the program were the only viable alternatives to a crisis-ridden capitalism. They acknowledged that the program was also designed to integrate the party and distinguish it from competing parties (which also claim commitment to individual freedoms, social justice, and the social market economy).

Passage of the program, intended to give the party a modern image and to appeal to a broad segment of the electorate, came just when SPD members and the public were focusing their attention on the crumbling GDR regime. Partly because of the timing, the program did not achieve the fame of its Godesberg predecessor. Nevertheless, it pointed the way for the party to move in a nondogmatic progressive direction during the 1990s. It paralleled the programs of other northern European social democratic parties but not those of southern European parties, which still clung to some Marxist rhetoric.[10]

The SPD in Power: 1966–1982

The SPD's doctrinal shift to pragmatic reformism, as enunciated in the 1959 program and reaffirmed in 1989, enabled it to join the CDU/CSU in 1966 as the junior governing party in a "grand" coalition. Periodically from 1961 to 1966, Herbert Wehner, a leading SPD official, had discreetly probed the possibilities for such a grand coalition as the best way for the SPD to gain respectability and demonstrate to the voters its capacity to govern West

Germany.[11] The party's left wing opposed in principle a coalition with a conservative party.

The SPD's opportunity came in late 1966 when Chancellor Ludwig Erhard (CDU) suddenly resigned, primarily because of a national economic recession. The CDU/CSU chose Kurt-Georg Kiesinger, minister-president of Baden-Württemberg, as its candidate for chancellor. When he could not gain the support of the FDP, he formed a grand coalition with the SPD. The small FDP occupied the opposition benches.[12]

On December 1, 1966, the new government took office, with the first SPD participation in a national government since 1930. The nine SPD cabinet members (the CDU/CSU had ten) included Willy Brandt, vice chancellor and foreign minister, and Karl Schiller, minister of economic affairs. The SPD was eager, within the limitations of a coalition, to affect domestic and foreign policies. Brandt desired to establish closer relations with Eastern bloc states (*Ostpolitik*), and Schiller pushed hard for a Keynesian pump-priming program to reinvigorate the economy. Both had partial success in their efforts.[13]

In 1969, the grand coalition neared the end of the parliamentary four-year term. The CDU/CSU gained an electoral plurality but could get neither SPD nor FDP support for another coalition. Instead, the SPD and the FDP formed a coalition, headed by Brandt as chancellor. In the government declaration, Brandt emphasized "continuity and renewal," indicating that modest social-liberal policy changes were in the offing. During the next three years, such reforms were initiated but were limited by discords between the SPD and FDP, budgetary constraints, and the complexity of some of the issues.

Paradoxically, the successful pace of *Ostpolitik* caused a major governmental crisis in 1972. A few conservative SPD and FDP deputies, criticizing *Ostpolitik* as a sellout to the communists, crossed over to the CDU/CSU. As a result, the coalition lost its governing majority and was forced prematurely to call a national election.

The SPD and FDP gained a clear-cut victory. For the first time since 1949, the SPD outpolled the CDU/CSU (by less than 1 percent) (see Table 4.1 and Figure 4.1). With a comfortable forty-six-seat majority, the governing coalition had a popular mandate to accelerate its reform policies (see Table 4.2). SPD and FDP chiefs agreed on a government program and on the distribution of cabinet seats.

But one year later, the chancellor ran into roadblocks. Within the SPD, the Young Socialists were dissatisfied with the lack of any radical government policies. Wehner, head of the SPD Fraktion, publicly criticized Brandt's stand on one aspect of *Ostpolitik*, thereby showing that the SPD troika of

Brandt, Wehner, and Helmut Schmidt (then minister of finance) had its differences. New economic and financial problems arose from the international oil crisis, and some public service workers went on strike. To compound Brandt's difficulties, in April 1974 a spy scandal broke in the Chancellor's Office. Günter Guillaume, one of Brandt's personal assistants, was arrested when it was revealed that he had been a secret agent of the GDR. His arrest also stimulated news stories about the chancellor's personal life. Brandt chose to resign on May 5. After consulting SPD chiefs, he urged the appointment of Schmidt as successor.

On May 16, Schmidt was sworn in as chancellor and formed another SPD-FDP cabinet. It contained a few new members, who were technocrats and pragmatists. In the government policy statement, the chancellor pledged to abide by Brandt's social-liberal coalition program. Brandt remained party chairman and was reelected to this post at succeeding conventions. The dual leadership of Brandt and Schmidt was unusual; normally in the FRG the chancellor is simultaneously head of the party. But Schmidt claimed that to hold both jobs was too demanding and that Brandt's political strength, personal attractiveness, and skill in integrating feuding factions made him the best chairman. The two leaders worked fairly well together, although they had no close personal ties.

In the 1976 federal election, the SPD and FDP won only a slim majority because of continuing national economic problems (high unemployment and rising welfare costs) and SPD intraparty squabbles and corruption scandals. The CDU/CSU once again received the most votes, but its inability to find a coalition partner left it in opposition. Schmidt was reelected chancellor.

Within the SPD, some leftist and centrist leaders criticized Schmidt's leadership style, his failure to accept enough party recommendations, and his repeated compromises with the FDP. In 1977, the SPD suffered a series of damaging reverses from which it recovered only slowly. Factional disputes in the Munich and Frankfurt SPD locals continued, Brandt and Wehner feuded openly, and dissidents in the SPD Fraktion voted against or abstained from voting on some government bills. On the positive side, Schmidt and cabinet members won popular support for their cool response to terrorist acts. The chancellor's increased prestige at home and abroad enhanced that of the party.

From 1978 to 1980, the ideological clashes within the party were beginning to subside, although important differences remained on the construction of more nuclear power stations and on the 1979 North Atlantic Treaty Organization (NATO) decision to deploy medium-range missiles in the FRG. In the 1980 election, the two parties again received a majority, partly because the CDU/CSU nominated the controversial Franz Josef Strauss as its candidate. Despite the electoral victory, frustration arose within the SPD over its inability to emerge from the shadow of the chancellor, who did not want to be too closely identified with a party lacking his own appeal within the nation.

From 1980 to 1982, Schmidt's coalition cabinet faced growing problems. SPD and FDP ministers disagreed sharply on how to combat the recession, with unemployment at its highest level in thirty years. FDP ministers insisted on cuts in social programs and lower corporate taxes to spur more business investments. To save the coalition, Schmidt made some concessions to them, which aroused anger within SPD ranks. But FDP leaders decided that the concessions were insufficient and in September 1982 withdrew from the Bonn coalition to cast their lot with the CDU/CSU. Helmut Kohl became chancellor of a CDU/CSU-FDP cabinet, and the SPD was forced into opposition in the Bundestag.[14]

The SPD in Opposition: 1982–1990

The SPD attempted to regain power in the 1983 and 1987 West German national elections but failed to outpoll the CDU/CSU each time. In 1983, Hans-Jochen Vogel, a former mayor of Munich and West Berlin, was the SPD candidate for chancellor. The party campaigned vigorously but could not gain enough support from voters to oust the governing coalition.

After the election, Wehner retired from the SPD Fraktion chairmanship, and Schmidt resigned his deputy chairmanship. The new leaders were Brandt, who continued as chairman, and the two deputy chairmen, Johannes Rau, minister-president of North Rhine–Westphalia, and Vogel, also head of the SPD Fraktion. The leaders pledged to work for greater party unity and to present constructive policies alternative to those introduced by the Kohl government.

During the legislative session from 1983 to 1987, the SPD introduced bills in the Bundestag designed to appeal to three core groups—the technical intelligentsia, youths, and blue-collar workers—whose support was crucial in future elections. The SPD knew that its minority position in the Bundestag gave its bills little chance for passage, but for electoral purposes the party needed to present alternatives to the government's program.

Rau was the candidate for chancellor in the 1987 election. Although popular in North Rhine–Westphalia and among trade unionists, he lacked enough support among floating voters, many of them civil servants and salaried employees, and among former leftist supporters, who voted for the

Greens. The SPD gained only 37 percent of the vote, its worst showing since 1961.

In March 1987, Brandt resigned from the party chairmanship after twenty-three years in office, to be succeeded by Vogel. Rau remained deputy chairman, and Oskar Lafontaine, minister-president of the Saar, became the other deputy chairman. One year later, Herta Däubler-Gmelin, a leader of the Fraktion, was elected deputy chairwoman, a new post reserved for women to give them more leadership positions within the party.

During the late 1980s, the SPD found it difficult to recruit many new members, especially among apolitical youths. Its factions were still divided on several policy issues, although Vogel was a skillful conciliator. Among the contested issues was which party should be considered a potential coalition partner in an SPD-led government should the SPD gain a plurality in a coming national election. The party left supported and the right rejected a coalition with the Greens. Senior officials considered the fratricidal discussion premature.[15]

Conclusion

The SPD successfully reconstituted itself after 1945 to become one of the two dominant parties in the FRG. It was not spared the leadership, factional, and ideological schisms that seem to mark any large organization. Such schisms arise partly because of power struggles and differences among leaders over the direction the party should take. Undoubtedly, the SPD suffered so many electoral defeats before cosharing political power in 1966 because Schumacher and his followers were out of tune with the political views of a slim majority of voters and because Adenauer was backed by U.S. policymakers opposed to any leftist programs.

When the SPD became the senior governing party in Bonn from 1969 to 1982, it had a chance, within the constraints of a coalition with the more conservative FDP and budgetary limitations, to make some leftist reforms of the neocapitalist system. After 1982, when the SPD was again in opposition, the political climate had turned conservative, and the SPD had trouble maintaining itself in power even in its traditional municipal and Länder bastions.

Notes

1. See Lewis J. Edinger, *Kurt Schumacher: A Study in Personality and Political Behavior* (Stanford: Stanford University Press, 1965).

2. For the post-1945 period, see Douglas A. Chalmers, *The Social Democratic Party of Germany* (New Haven: Yale University Press, 1964); David Childs, *From Schumacher to Brandt: The Story of German Socialism, 1945–1965* (Oxford: Pergamon Press, 1966); Susanne Miller, "The SPD from 1945 to the Present," in *A History of German Social Democracy: From 1848 to the Present,* by Susanne Miller and Heinrich Potthoff (Leamington Spa, England: Berg, 1986), pp. 149–235.

3. Cited in Harold K. Schellenger Jr., *The SPD in the Bonn Republic: A Socialist Party Modernizes* (The Hague: Martinus Nijhoff, 1968), p. 34.

4. Hesse and Bremen, two SPD strongholds, and North Rhine–Westphalia incorporated the SPD program for limited nationalization into their constitutions but because of Allied opposition could not implement it.

5. For the role of the SPD in opposition, see Otto Kirchheimer, "Germany: The Vanishing Opposition," in *Political Oppositions in Western Democracies,* ed. Robert A. Dahl (New Haven: Yale University Press, 1966), pp. 237–259.

6. For details on the SPD organization, see Gerard Braunthal, *The German Social Democrats Since 1969: A Party in Power and Opposition,* 2d ed. (Boulder: Westview Press, 1994), pp. 45–68.

7. Ibid., pp. 121–192.

8. Ibid., pp. 69–94.

9. For the full text, see SPD, *Basic Programme of the Social Democratic Party of Germany* (Bonn: SPD, n.d. [1959]).

10. Gerard Braunthal, "The 1989 Basic Program of the German Social Democratic Party," *Polity* 25, no. 3 (Spring 1993):375–400.

11. For a biography of Wehner, see Wayne C. Thompson, *The Political Odyssey of Herbert Wehner* (Boulder: Westview Press, 1993).

12. Gerhard Lehmbruch, "The Ambiguous Coalition in West Germany," *Government and Opposition* 3, no. 2 (Spring 1968):181–204.

13. SPD, Bundestagsfraktion, *Soll und Haben: Bilanz sozialdemokratischer Bundespolitik in Regierung und Parlament von 1966 bis 1969* (Bonn: SPD, 1969). Among the many biographies of Brandt, see David Binder, *The Other German: Willy Brandt's Life and Times* (Washington, D.C.: New Republic Book Company, 1975); Terence Prittie, *Willy Brandt: Portrait of a Statesman* (New York: Schocken, 1974).

14. Gerard Braunthal, "The Social Democratic Party," in *West German Politics in the Mid-Eighties: Crisis and Continuity,* ed. H. G. Peter Wallach and George K. Romoser (New York: Praeger, 1985), pp. 91–100.

15. Braunthal, *The German Social Democrats Since 1969,* pp. 23–24, 249–251.

· 6 ·

The Free Democrats:
Keeping the Balance

T HE CDU/CSU AND SPD dominance in the FRG should not suggest that smaller parties were frozen out of the parliamentary system and had no chance to gain representation in the Bundestag. In the 1949 Bundestag, seven small extremist, regional, and interest group parties held seats, in addition to the national Free Democratic Party. But by 1961, all except the FDP had fallen under the 5 percent barrier. Without the ability to attract voters and gain support from the major coalition ally (CDU/CSU or SPD), the FDP would have suffered the same fate as its minor party rivals. But the FDP's ability to hold seats in the Bundestag throughout West Germany's existence from 1949 to 1990 meant that it blocked the emergence of a two-party system in which the CDU/CSU and SPD would have been the only parties in the Bundestag. From 1961 until 1983, when the Greens joined the parliamentary club, the country in effect had a hybrid "two-and-one-half" party system (two dominant parties and one minor party) rather than a two-party or multiparty system.

This chapter examines the reasons for the remarkable staying power of the FDP and its participation in most postwar coalition governments in Bonn and in many Länder. When the trend was away from ideologically committed parties to pragmatic people's parties, how could the FDP, as the heir to the legacy of liberalism, stem the decline in popularity of this doctrine and still survive, notwithstanding the greater electoral appeal of the two major parties? How could the FDP have remained significant in West German politics, despite its disputes between liberals and conservatives, its low membership, and its weak organizational structure? Focusing on these questions, we analyze the party's development, organization, ideology, and electoral performance.

Historical and Ideological Development

Unlike Britain, Germany never had a united liberal party. As discussed in Chapter 2, German liberalism had two persistent strands during the Empire and Weimar eras. The conservative National Liberal Party (renamed the German People's Party in Weimar) was pitted against the liberal Progressives (renamed the German Democratic Party). The movement's weakness resulting from this rivalry was compounded by voters' declining interest in liberalism as an ideology. They turned to conservatism or socialism, as had British voters after the turn of the century.

In 1945, the liberals' lack of homogeneity in the western occupation zones reflected the heritage of the Empire and of Weimar. The Democratic People's Party of Württemberg-Baden, long the home of liberal democracy, headed the liberal wing, while the Free Democrats and the Liberal Democrats of several British-occupied Länder and of Hesse constituted the conservative, nationalist wing.[1]

The two wings did not merge into a united party until December 1948. In June 1949, the new party held its first convention under the tutelage of Theodor Heuss, the liberal leader who would soon become the first president of the FRG. In the meantime, Liberals had organized in the Soviet zone, but an all-zonal working committee failed to bridge the gap between West and East.[2]

The new party in the western zones has had to compete with the CDU/CSU for the nonsocialist vote. As a party of the middle class, the FDP has been committed to a free enterprise system in which the individual has maximum civil rights and the state minimum powers to interfere in the economy. The FDP rejects all forms of state planning, favoring individual economic freedoms as the route to accumulating wealth. Yet the party acknowledges the state's responsibility for the underclass. Thus, it champions the social market economy, started by Ludwig Erhard, the former Liberal who joined the CDU and became chancellor in 1963. The FDP, even though supporting a minimal government, has not hesitated to ask it to grant tax concessions to business and to provide subsidies to farmers, two social groups whose support is crucial. The FDP has little sympathy for the unions, which backed mainly the SPD and, less, the Catholic workers' wing of the CDU.

Conservative on economic issues and pro-West in foreign affairs, the FDP could and did join most CDU/CSU-led governments from 1949 to 1966 and thereby received substantial financial support from the business community. But to present a distinct profile at election time, the FDP emphasizes its differences with the CDU/CSU. These differences, including the relation of parties to the Catholic Church, the role of the state, and the emphasis on individual rights, enabled the FDP to join a coalition cabinet with the SPD almost as easily as with the CDU/CSU, especially when the FDP's liberal wing was dominant. The anticlerical FDP has insisted on the separation of church and state. Thus, in the 1950s the party criticized the Catholic clergy's support of the CDU/CSU and the reestablishment of Catholic denominational schools in many parts of the FRG.

Organization

Liberal parties in many countries are committed to decentralizing their structure and diffusing power. In the FDP, power resided in the eleven semi-autonomous Land associations, which have roots in local politics and supply candidates for state and federal offices. The party established local party organizations, but most have been inactive or have been too scattered and small to be effective. The locals in turn created "working groups," which deal especially with municipal politics but also with national economic and social issues. Party officials, more interested in state and national politics, were surprised by the members' interest in local politics but supported the grassroots initiatives. For instance, the officials issued a brochure on the British Liberals' successful efforts to help shape the politics of Liverpool. They pointed to the "sidewalk politics," the informal chats with citizens about their grievances, and the Liverpool Liberals' electoral canvassing as worthy of emulation.[3]

Initially, the FDP Land organizations were more powerful than the small national party organization. But in the 1950s, the latter gained more power in order to increase party unity and cohesion. The eleven-member Presidium and the approximately fifty-member Federal Executive Committee (Bundesvorstand) are the key decisionmaking organs. They determine the party's policies, although in theory they are supposed to receive advice from the larger Federal General Council (Bundeshauptausschuss), which serves as a permanent committee of the convention. In theory, the convention is the highest body, but in practice it ratifies decisions made by the smaller units, assuming that an agreement has been reached by the often feuding liberal and conservative officials. As in other parties, the Executive Committee has created specialized committees and working groups to prepare position papers on current issues.

It is the Land chairpersons, especially those heading the party's strongholds in North Rhine–Westphalia and Baden-Württemberg, who select the party chairperson. At convention time, they caucus behind the scenes to find an acceptable candidate who will also gain the support of the delegates. Unlike in the CDU/CSU and SPD, chairpersons in the FDP emerge who are not dominant figures. Yet they exert some influence on internal affairs and Länder and national politics wherever the FDP is in coalition governments.

As in other parties, the FDP's linkage to its parliamentary group has varied from distant to close. Normally leaders, who are also Bundestag deputies, want to ensure Fraktion support for the party's policies, but often the Fraktion is the key policymaking and integrative unit of the party.

Among the party's few semiautonomous associations, the Young Democrats challenged the more conservative policies of senior officials. The Young Democrats quit the party in 1982 after it switched from a coalition with the SPD to one with the CDU/CSU. Officials swiftly created a more compliant youth organization, the Young Liberals, with a membership of about twenty-three hundred.[4]

Membership and Voter Profile

The FDP has always had few members in comparison with the CDU/CSU and SPD. Imbued with a spirit of individualism, many sympathizers do not enroll as members. Thus, membership has ranged from only about forty-eight thousand to eighty-seven thousand, with more than twice as many conservative than liberal members.[5] The small size of the social groups that support the FDP rules out the possibility that it will ever become a mass party.

Most members belong either to the "old" middle class of professionals, owners of small and medium-sized businesses, and the self-employed or to the "new" middle class of upper civil servants, salaried employees, and teachers. Lower-income groups, such as workers, are underrepresented (only 5 percent), and higher-income groups are overrepresented.

Members are more highly educated than average citizens. The gender imbalance found in the CDU/CSU and SPD also applies to the FDP. In 1971, only 15 percent of its members were women. By the 1980s, the total had risen to nearly 25 percent. Yet few women have held policymaking posts within the party, partly because they have been less educated and younger than their male colleagues. Until 1971, FDP members were slightly older than the average population. Since 1977, nearly half have been under forty, but the party still has had difficulty in attracting members under twenty-five.

It is also hard for the party to keep its members once they have joined. For instance, between 1968 and 1972, when the FDP switched from opposition in the Bundestag to a governing coalition with the SPD, 17,000 individuals joined the party, but 16,300 left it. According to questionnaires sent to members and former members, the high turnover rate was caused by the unpopularity of FDP policies and of the coalition accords with the SPD in Bonn and in some Länder, the inability of members to contribute to the party, poor internal communication, and the proliferation of cliques competing for party posts. Young members especially were dissatisfied with older members holding onto their posts. Of all members, at least 40 percent were mere dues payers (colloquially known as "cadavers"), who did not actively participate in the organization. When members were asked why they had joined the FDP, about 40 percent emphasized their commitment to strengthening the ideology of liberalism. Others obviously joined for career advancement, hoping to gain positions within the party or the community.[6]

Surveys probing the social substructure of German parties have shown that FDP voters and members have more in common with one another than those in other parties. Before 1966, a typical FDP voter was a Protestant, old-middle-class male who lived in a community with a population under fifty thousand. More specifically, FDP male voters outnumbered women voters by 52 to 48 percent, and Protestants outnumbered Catholics by three to one (primarily because of the party's anticlericalism). However, with modernization from 1966 to 1972, the FDP gained more voter support from the new middle class living in urban areas and lost support in rural areas.

Schisms and Coalition Switches

In 1949, the CDU/CSU did not gain a majority and sought coalition partners. As a reward for joining the government, alongside other minor parties, the FDP received the vice chancellorship and three cabinet posts and remained a loyal partner in the CDU/CSU-led governments from 1949 until 1956.

However, in 1956 the FDP quit the Adenauer government over disagreements with the chancellor on foreign policy. Like the SPD, then in parliamentary opposition, the FDP lashed out at his slack German reunification attempts and at his failure to initiate direct negotiations with the Soviet Union. Adenauer, afraid to bypass the West, had rejected several FDP proposals in the early 1950s for negotiating directly with Moscow and for establishing a reunited, neutral Germany free of foreign troops as part of an all-Europe collective security system. The FDP was also unhappy about Adenauer's authoritarian governing style; the CDU's left-wing economic and social policy proposals, including its backing of a codetermination law (workers and managers sharing seats on the supervisory boards of coal and iron companies); the few administrative posts that the FDP had been allocated; and, most important, the chancellor's proposal to change the electoral law, which would have eliminated minor parties in the Bundestag.

These interparty discords were accompanied by the FDP's intraparty schisms. In the early 1950s, the conservative wing, concentrated in Hesse, Lower Saxony, and North Rhine–Westphalia, had visions of forming a new German Right. It bitterly opposed the left wing's alliance with the SPD and the All-German Bloc of Expellees in a Baden-Württemberg governing coalition just when the wing's own Hesse branch was fighting the SPD in a Land election.

Each FDP wing drafted its own program. The conservatives issued the "German Program," which lauded nationalism, the middle class, peasants, and the family and demanded restitution for persons prosecuted by the authorities as former Nazis. The liberals in Baden-Württemberg, Hamburg, and Bremen published the "Liberal Manifesto," which called for economic deconcentration and more cultural freedom and denounced extreme nationalism.

The two antagonistic wings, having equal strength at party conventions, were forced to compromise and allow the party to pursue a middle course. Later, however, the conservative bloc was weakened when one of its leaders was arrested by the British, who discovered documents in which he had urged former Nazis to join the FDP and capture its leadership. In 1956, in North Rhine–Westphalia, a rebellion broke out against the conservative leadership. The young, pragmatic leaders, forcing the FDP ministers in the CDU-FDP coalition to resign, successfully engineered the formation of an SPD-FDP cabinet. The rebels reasoned correctly that this marriage of convenience would stymie some of the more radical SPD policy proposals.

Many conservative FDP members criticized the revolt in the Ruhr and the break with the CDU in Bonn, viewing the CDU as their natural coalition ally. The leaders, however, continued to oppose Adenauer's course, partly to give the party its own profile as a third force in German politics. They said that German democracy would be endangered if any party, especially one with an authoritarian leader, gained 50 percent of the electoral vote and forced through a single-member district electoral system, thereby in effect narrowing the voters' choice to two parties. The FDP leaders had cause to worry. In 1957, the CDU/CSU had gained a 50 percent majority, while the FDP's total in federal elections had slipped from nearly 12 percent in 1949 to less than 8 percent. The slippage was caused partly by the switch of conservative FDP members to the CDU.[7]

The Christian Democrats could not repeat their electoral triumph in 1961 and so were forced to renew their coalition with the FDP to have a governing majority. The FDP, in turn, wrested some concessions from the Christian Democrats in the makeup of the cabinet and in its demand for more sympathy toward a détente between West and East.

In 1966, the FDP played kingmaker in coalition politics when it withdrew support from CDU chancellor Erhard, who could not pull Germany out of its economic crisis. The FDP may not have realized that when Erhard resigned, his successor, Kiesinger (CDU), would choose the SPD, rather than the FDP, as the junior coalition partner. The grand coalition of the two major parties forced the FDP into unaccustomed opposition in the Bundestag.

From 1969 to 1982, the FDP served in coalition governments again, now with the SPD. The FDP's willingness to ally itself with the SPD in 1969 was the result of earlier secret negotiations between SPD leader Brandt and FDP leader Walter Scheel, both of whom favored such a coalition should the election results give the two parties a majority. The FDP top organs, after the party's conservatives lost and the liberals triumphed, endorsed the coalition. Most officials sympathized with Brandt's *Ostpolitik* plans for a rapprochement between East and West. Even the FDP's conservative businesspeople, who were strongly anticommunist, had few objections to a policy that would mean increased trade and profits.

As in all coalition talks that follow national elections, SPD and FDP negotiating teams met frequently for more than two weeks in 1969 to determine the distribution of cabinet seats to each party and to agree on a government program for the coming legislative session (which normally lasts four years). Needless to say, each party had to be willing to make compromises to reach such an accord.

In 1969, Chancellor Brandt appointed Scheel foreign minister, giving the FDP a key ministry, which it has held since then. Subsequently the two parties succeeded in reaching their *Ostpolitik* goals. In domestic affairs, the FDP took a more liberal position than in earlier decades because it was no longer beholden primarily to the conservative business community for financial support, its conservative supporters had become fewer, and the post-1968 political climate had become more liberal. In accord with the SPD, the FDP backed reform legislation on the judiciary, individual rights, pensions, educational opportunities, environmental planning, and capital accumulation and shop democracy for workers. These positions had been agreed on by FDP policymakers in the important basic program, the Freiburg Theses of 1971, which also called for equality of opportunity, democratization of social institutions, and removal of social injustices within the capitalist system.[8]

The FDP's opening to the left did not last. When Helmut Schmidt (SPD) became chancellor in 1974, the reform mood had already dissipated, and the

FDP supported his stringent crisis management approach to economic problems. Minister of Economics Count Otto von Lambsdorff, an FDP conservative, was appointed to the SPD-FDP cabinets from 1974 to 1982. When the SPD's left wing and the unions pushed for changes in taxation, investment, and property policies, Lambsdorff, supporting Schmidt, blocked them. Hans-Dietrich Genscher, who had succeeded Scheel as FDP chairman and foreign minister in 1974 (on Scheel's election to the federal presidency), also backed Lambsdorff's economic policies. In the cabinets, the influence of Minister of the Interior Gerhart Baum, an FDP liberal, was more restricted, except on matters pertaining to his ministry.

Despite ideological affinities between Schmidt and most FDP leaders, the FDP forced the breakup of the ailing coalition in 1982 for a number of reasons. The two parties disagreed strongly in the cabinet on how to deal with the mounting economic problems facing Germany, which was beset by sharp increases in unemployment and business failures. The FDP ministers wanted cuts in the social budget to decrease the spiraling national deficit. The SPD ministers wanted instead to overcome the crisis by public borrowing and higher taxes (see Chapter 5). Schmidt tried to compromise with the FDP, but Lambsdorff viewed a switch to the CDU/CSU as less threatening to the FDP's economic and social interests.

The FDP leaders gambled that their party's entrance into a CDU/CSU coalition would not result in a split in their party and a voter backlash at the next election. There was no major split, but national secretary Günter Verheugen and two liberal FDP leaders quit the party in protest and joined the SPD, and fewer than two thousand members formed a short-lived dissident liberal party. However, in an electoral backlash the FDP received only 6.9 percent of the vote in the 1983 election compared with 10.6 percent in 1980.

The FDP hoped to recover from this setback in succeeding years but was thwarted by the involvement of some of its officials in financial scandals. For instance, Lambsdorff had to resign from his ministerial post in 1984 after being indicted of accepting bribes from the giant Flick holding company in return for granting lucrative tax waivers. In 1987, when he was finally convicted and fined only $100,000 (DM 284,000) for tax evasion, one Green Party leader remarked that Lambsdorff and others involved received mild punishments considering the "finesse and criminal intensity" with which the defendants had robbed the state of "millions."[9]

There was also a turnover in leadership. In 1985, Genscher resigned from the party chairmanship, partly because he felt responsible for the FDP's inability to gain 5 percent of the national vote in the European Parliament election in 1984. His replacement, Minister of Economics Martin Bange-mann, held the office for three years, whereupon Lambsdorff, undamaged within his own party by the earlier government scandal, took over.

By the time German unification appeared imminent in 1990, the centrist-conservative CDU/CSU-FDP coalition under Helmut Kohl's chancellorship was working well. In the cabinets, the FDP retained the key ministries of Foreign Affairs, Economics, and Justice but had lost Interior to a CSU appointee. Thus, FDP policies filtered through the executive branch and influenced cabinet decisions.

Conclusion

The FDP's small size belies its importance within the FRG's political system. Each of the two major parties, the CDU/CSU and SPD, failed to gain 50 percent of the national vote in nearly all national elections and thus govern alone, which made coalition government the only viable alternative. As the leading third party, the FDP was the perennial coalition partner of either the Christian Democrats or the Social Democrats (except for the years in parliamentary opposition, 1956–1961 and 1966–1969). Its payoff was key ministerial posts and political visibility.

Pivotal within the party system, the FDP contributed to the decisions of Chancellors Adenauer and Erhard to step down prematurely from their office. It also facilitated a change from CDU/CSU to SPD governance in 1969 and back again in 1982. The FDP's radical twist from one political side to the other exposed it to accusations of not being a loyal coalition partner. But most FDP leaders dismissed such accusations as not corresponding to political realities. They insisted that their party served not only as a loyal partner to either major party but also as a moderating influence on legislation.

For instance, if the CDU/CSU was the senior governing party, the FDP would try to block ultraconservative proposals, especially those stemming from the CSU, on social affairs and law-and-order issues. Conversely, if the SPD was in power, the FDP would try to block leftist proposals on economic affairs. The FDP could exert this power because its assent to policy proposals was normally needed in the cabinets.

Whether in coalition with the CDU/CSU or the SPD, the FDP's commonality of views with the CDU/CSU on many key issues and with the SPD on others guaranteed some political stability with either party as a coalition partner. Indeed, the narrowing of differences between the CDU/CSU and SPD on foreign and domestic issues made it that much easier for the

FDP to ally itself with either party during the 1949–1990 period. One observer writes, "It might be fair to conclude that the German electorate does not determine the government, the FDP does."[10]

Despite the party's importance in Bonn and continuity in policies, the FDP lacked the mass appeal of the major parties. Therefore, its vote in some national elections hovered close to the 5 percent barrier to parliamentary representation. This spurred the FDP to develop strategies of survival, which in turn led its opponents to say that the party was unreliable and had no identity of its own. To ensure that the FDP would survive and remain a viable coalition partner, officials of whichever major party in power urged their supporters to split their vote by casting the first (district) ballot for their own party and the second (list) ballot for the FDP. In many Land elections, less important to the FDP's national image, the party was shut out of parliament because it did not receive the 5 percent minimum and fewer voters split their ballots.[11]

Notwithstanding the party's mixed electoral record, the decline of liberalism as an ideology, internal schisms, weak leadership, and organizational problems, West German voters gave the national FDP a mandate to check the political power and moderate the policies of the CDU/CSU and SPD. Consequently, the FDP was in power longer in Bonn than either of them, thereby providing continuity in co-governing the nation.

Notes

1. In 1951, voters in a plebiscite approved the merger of the three smaller Länder Württemberg-Baden, Württemberg-Hohenzollern, and Baden into the newly created Land Baden-Württemberg.

2. For details, see Gerard Braunthal, "The Free Democratic Party in West German Politics," *Western Political Quarterly* 13, no. 2 (June 1960):332–348; Christian Søe, "The Free Democratic Party," in *West German Politics in the Mid-Eighties: Crisis and Continuity*, ed. H. G. Peter Wallach and George K. Romoser (New York: Praeger, 1985), p. 124.

3. Eva Kolinsky, *Parties, Opposition, and Society in West Germany* (New York: St. Martin's Press, 1984), pp. 114–115.

4. Søe, "The Free Democratic Party," pp. 172–173; Jürgen Dittberner, *FDP—Partei der zweiten Wahl* (Opladen: Westdeutscher Verlag, 1987), pp. 86–96.

5. Hans Vorländer, "Die Freie Demokratische Partei," in *Parteien in der Bundesrepublik Deutschland*, ed. Alf Mintzel and Heinrich Oberreuter (Opladen: Leske und Budrich, 1992), pp. 306–308; personal interview with Klaus Pfnorr, FDP staff official, Bonn, June 25, 1992.

6. Kolinsky, *Parties, Opposition, and Society in West Germany,* pp. 102–112.

7. Braunthal, "The Free Democratic Party in West German Politics," pp. 340–345.

8. Søe, "The Free Democratic Party," pp. 132–138.

9. *New York Times,* February 17, 1987.

10. Russell J. Dalton, *Politics in Germany,* 2d ed. (New York: HarperCollins, 1993), p. 297.

11. Gordon Smith, *Democracy in Western Germany: Parties and Politics in the Federal Republic,* 3d ed. (Aldershot, England: Gower, 1986), pp. 154–157.

• 7 •

The Greens:
Challenging the Establishment

T HE WEST GERMAN PARTY system's stability was shattered in the late 1970s when an environmental movement emerged, which coalesced numerous citizens' initiative groups *(Bürgerinitiativen)*. Local activists had established them in the late 1960s to protest the parties' failure to deal with ecological and other urgent issues. The movement leaders decided that their goals could be reached more easily if direct protest actions and parliamentary actions were linked. Thereupon they formed environmental parties in the Länder and ran slates of candidates in local and regional elections. In 1980, a national coalition of environmental parties founded a new party, the Greens, to run candidates in municipal, Länder, and national elections.

Few predicted then that the party would become a new political force seriously challenging the troika establishment—the CDU/CSU, SPD, and FDP. This chapter traces the trajectory of the Green Party in its first decade of existence. Despite numerous intraparty factional and programmatic cleavages, organizational problems, and ebbing social movements, the Greens became a fourth national party, which gained seats in most municipal, Länder, and national elections. What are the reasons for the Greens' success? Would they have done as well if the establishment parties had addressed ecological and other problems in time? Have the Greens produced instability in the party and political system, or have they shown the necessity for flexibility in politics?

The Antecedents of the Greens

The social protest movements that arose in West Germany in the late 1960s and the 1970s had their antecedents in the Empire era when autocratic governments were forced to relinquish some of their powers to social groups demanding a share in governing the nation. In the post-1945 period, protests in 1968 against the establishment swept from the United States to Europe and other continents. In France, Italy, and the Netherlands, small New Left parties became the rallying point for students and others dissatisfied with the "conservatism" of communist and socialist parties. A decade later, Green parties arose in other northern and central European countries, including West Germany, Iceland, Sweden, and Austria. However, in the United States, Canada, Australia, the United Kingdom, France, Spain, and Japan, Green parties either did not form or were too weak to have any effect on politics. According to two specialists, the emergence of Greens in northern and central European countries was the result of a political climate that enabled social democratic parties to gain power and provided space for New Left protest parties. The latter were able to muster citizen support when the social democrats, faced by financial constraints, had to scuttle reformist programs. But in those countries with weak Green parties, either the electoral system favoring major parties was an obstacle to the founding of new parties, or strong communist parties syphoned off the support of leftist protest voters.[1]

In West Germany, social movements were the precursors of the Greens. In the 1950s, a peace movement arose in opposition to rearmament and the stationing of U.S. nuclear weapons on German territory. From the late 1970s on, new nationwide social movements mushroomed, including antinuclear power and women's rights. In the early 1970s, citizens' initiative groups were founded in municipalities to deal with single issues, such as housing shortages, high rents, and the dangers of air and water pollution. Some of the groups, intent on gaining more participatory rights, accused the government and the major parties of not solving local environmental problems. A coordinating group, the Federal Association of Citizens' Initiatives for Environmental Protection (BBU), was established in 1972 to act as a national pressure organization. By 1977, it comprised nine hundred affiliated groups with about two hundred thousand members. The BBU supported groups that staged local demonstrations, gathered petitions, and engaged in other protest actions. The groups had as a model the widespread popular opposition to the Emergency Laws, which gave the government special powers to deal with national crises. One observer wrote that the groups "are to some extent the adult version of the student protest movement."[2]

The nonpartisan peace, antinuclear, and women's movements, which were supported by millions of citizens, had no official ties to the Greens because they wanted to maintain their organizational independence. Yet many movement adherents became supporters of the Green Party, which saw itself, perhaps too hopefully, as the political arm of all social movements.[3]

The rise of the Greens can also be attributed to changing social structures and value priorities among West Germans. The growth of a new middle class meant that for its members postmaterialist quality-of-life issues, such as a safe and healthy environment, became a top priority. Some of them joined self-help groups, communes, cooperatives, and small alternative service shops. Many joined the citizens' groups and the Greens, partly because of the Greens' prediction of a worldwide ecological disaster unless citizens took immediate countermeasures, a call resisted by the establishment parties.[4]

The Launching of the Party

The Greens established regional groups before creating a nationwide organization. In 1977, they participated in local elections in Lower Saxony, in the aftermath of an unpopular state cabinet decision to build a nuclear waste disposal center in the Land. In 1978, in response to further ecological threats, environmental groups, espousing views ranging across the political spectrum, sprouted throughout the FRG. Left-wing groups, known colloquially as the "red" Greens because they stemmed from neo-Marxist and radical leftist groups, called for major social changes. Centrist groups, known as the "green" Greens, demanded, above all, that public bodies conserve nature and protect the environment. Rightist groups, known as the "brown" Greens, warned that environmental problems were a threat to global human survival and to racial and national preservation. Leftist critics charged that the rightists did not address themselves to the question of social change.[5]

In January 1980 at Karlsruhe, the Greens held their founding conference. The one thousand "rainbow" delegates, representing the rival factions, and including Christian pacifists, environmental activists, and liberal bourgeois adherents, clashed over organizational control and the agenda but then voted to create the national Greens organization. Two months later, Green delegates met in Saarbrücken to formulate a party program. Once again, political factions were pitted against each other. Center-leftist and leftist leaders, Petra Kelly among them, gained control of the executive bodies after rightist leaders Herbert Gruhl and Baldur Springmann, dissatisfied by the program and especially its proabortion plank, withdrew their candidacies.

Kelly, one of the founders of the party, became its best-known personality, both in Germany and abroad, as a result of her quick wit, sharp tongue, and fluency in English. Born in Germany, she was raised in the United States after her mother married a U.S. officer. Disillusioned by U.S. policies, including the Vietnam War, she eventually returned to Germany, where a similar disillusionment with the SPD-led government's defense policies led her to join other critics to form the Greens. Although originally supporting the left faction, she moved toward the center in later years.

The Saarbrücken program reflected the dominance of the left-center and left factions. Partly as a result of Kelly's urging, the program ranged far beyond the single issue of ecology. As a party seeking to draw support from an array of voters, the program touched on most domestic and foreign policy issues. The introductory section emphasized the party's key ecological, social, nonviolent, and grassroots democratic principles. The economic demands included a just distribution of income in a noncapitalist system, where production would be based on need rather than on profit; the breakup of large enterprises into smaller worker-administered units; the introduction of a thirty-five-hour work week, without a loss of pay or increased production; a ban on the export of nuclear technology; an end to the operation and construction of nuclear power plants; and greater use of solar and wind power. The foreign policy demands included dissolution of the rival NATO and Warsaw military pacts, unilateral nuclear disarmament in the FRG, an end to industrial countries exploiting Third World countries' raw materials, and Third World countries' right to self-determination and to an ecological safeguarded economy.[6] In one of her writings, Kelly justified the Greens' interest in focusing on a broad range of issues rather than just on environmental questions: "We can no longer rely on the established parties and we can no longer depend entirely on the extra-parliamentary road. The system is bankrupt, but a new force has to be created both inside and outside parliament. . . . In West Germany, it is becoming increasingly important to vote for what we consider right and not just for the lesser evil."[7]

The Electoral Balance Sheet

The SPD saw in the Greens a new rival for the leftist vote because the Greens' programmatic direction was to the left. The rivalry began in 1977 when the Greens participated in local elections in many Länder. Two years later, they ran a slate of candidates, under the catchy slogan "The Greens: Another Political Association," for the European Parliament election. Although the slate mustered only 3.2 percent of the West German vote, it was a respectable showing for the Greens' first nationwide attempt to gain the support of a potentially large protest vote. The German government reimbursed the Greens DM 4.5 million ($2.4 million) for having received the minimum number of votes, which the party plowed back into the 1980 national campaign.

The Greens fared poorly in the 1980 election, garnering only 1.5 percent of the vote. Many voters were disillusioned by the Greens' internal squabbles; others did not want to "waste" their vote on a party that had no chance of being a coalition partner in Bonn. Most protest voters cast their ballot instead for the SPD, which was battling the conservative CDU/CSU candidate, Franz Josef Strauss. However, in 1981 and 1982 the Greens captured seats in six Landtag elections and made significant gains in local elections. Their opposition to nuclear energy; their support for women's, youth, and minority rights; and their criticism of patronage among the established parties brought them support from an array of voters, especially in communities near nuclear power plants, in university towns, and in large cities where environmental concerns overshadowed the issue of economic growth. Thus, when Frankfurt authorities planned to expand the mammoth international airport by encroaching on nearby forests, many voters, including conservative farmers, supported the Greens. For instance, in 1981 in the small town of Moerfelden (near Frankfurt), which was adversely affected by the airport expansion, the Greens won nearly 26 percent of the vote. Yet when antinuclear protests escalated into violence, most conservatives voted once again in subsequent elections for the CDU/CSU.

Except for such defections, the Greens reaped electoral dividends not only from their local activities but also from their positions on national issues. In their eclectic and innovative election manifesto for the 1983 national election, they called for a dismantling of nuclear power plants; a conversion of the war industry to peaceful uses; an outlawing of pesticide and herbicide use on agricultural products; a ban on assembly-line work and night shifts; an end to the sale of war toys and to television and radio advertisements featuring cigarettes, liquor, and candy; a requirement that home economics and child-rearing classes be made obligatory for male and female students; and an introduction of legislation banning discrimination against homosexuals.

During the campaign, the Greens assailed the stationing of U.S. nuclear weapons on German soil and called on Western and Eastern states to begin nuclear disarmament. The Greens also accused the other German parties of having done little to stem ecological disasters, such as acid rain's heavy damage to the nation's forests.[8] As a result of their positions, the Greens, surmounting for the first time the 5 percent hurdle, gained 5.6 percent of the vote and twenty-seven Bundestag seats, mostly at the SPD's expense. To reaffirm their antiestablishment position, the new deputies joyfully entered the Bundestag en masse, wearing jeans and sweaters, scattering flowers, and singing peace songs. They shocked older and staid deputies in their business suits, who wondered whether the system could survive such shenanigans.[9]

In succeeding years, the Greens consolidated their position further. They mustered a respectable 8.2 percent in the 1984 election for the European Parliament, gained strength in most Länder parliaments, and increased their vote in the 1987 national election to 8.3 percent. Their Bundestag Fraktion of forty-two deputies included twenty-four women, a ratio that no other party could match. However, the Greens lost their momentum in West Germany after the collapse of the Berlin Wall in 1989 and, lacking a minimum 5 percent vote, were frozen out of the Bundestag in the 1990 election (see Chapter 11).

Organization

The Greens emerged out of groups and social movements that eschewed centralized bureaucracies and hierarchical organizations. The motto of the Green groups, variously called the Greens, the "multicolored," and the "alternative lists," was "Democracy at the base" (*Basisdemokratie*). Their leaders hoped that grassroots activists would have a strong input into the nontraditional organization, making it a truly "antiparty" party.

However, to abide by the Party Law of 1967, the Greens had to create an organization hardly different from that of the established parties. It consists of a federal delegate assembly, comparable to the convention or congress of the major parties; the Federal Steering Committee (Bundeshauptausschuss) meeting more frequently; and the smaller Federal Executive Board (Bundesvorstand), consisting of eleven members, including the three party speakers. The speakers, forming a collective leadership, represent party views and coordinate national activities but are not policymakers. Members can contribute their expertise in numerous working groups, which advise the party and its Bundestag Fraktion. National headquarters is the coordinating center of the Länder and of subsidiary organizations. It has a small staff, working in shabby quarters because of a commitment to spending funds for more pressing matters. Thus, the Green deputies have also been expected to plow back most of their generous salaries into an ecofund, created to assist local alternative projects, and to live on the same salary as a skilled laborer. The Länder have their own organizations, with considerable autonomy to shape programs, hire staff, and disburse funds.

Consonant with the participatory democratic organization, in which many decisions are arrived at by consensus and in which the elite is discouraged from becoming oligarchical, leaders must choose between a position in the party or in the legislature. Federal Executive Board members cannot be elected more than twice to the two-year terms. Deputies who do not abide by party resolutions must resign their position. In addition, 50 percent of staff and nominees for party office and the legislature must be women to assure gender equality.

The Greens' most publicized practice was the requirement that their Bundestag deputies and, in most Länder, their Landtag deputies not serve a full term. Instead, the deputies were expected to resign their seats after two years, when the legislature had reached its midway point, and make way for the next candidate on the list. The rationale for this unusual practice was to limit the power of the Fraktion within the party and to curb the rise of a professional elite.[10] But the practice damaged the party when its deputies, who had gained valuable legislative and specialized experience, were rotated out before they could make their full mark in the Fraktion.

Several well-known Green leaders did not want to abide by the rotation practice. Otto Schily, a brilliant lawyer and deputy, assailed it and was rebuked by other party officials. Eventually he quit the Greens and joined the SPD. General Gert Bastian, a well-respected former army officer, retained his Bundestag seat when rotation was due. But he resigned from the party, primarily because he believed the Greens had come under the unacceptable influence of radical left and communist groups and because the Fraktion lacked harmony and solidarity. In 1985, Petra Kelly, whose relationship to the party had become strained, refused to give up her seat. She bitterly charged the Greens with attempting to establish a dictatorship of incompetence.[11]

Membership and Voter Profile

The Greens cannot expect to become a mass party comparable to the CDU/CSU and SPD because of limited support from diverse social strata. Indeed, some Green leaders prefer a small party that can maintain a close link between members and officeholders. During the 1980s, party membership increased from eighteen thousand to forty-two thousand but by 1989 had shrunk to thirty-eight thousand. Most members had participated in the peace and student movements of the 1960s or were adherents of left-wing splinter groups. Many remained activists within and outside the party. Thus, every sixth member held either a party office or a legislative seat.

Official data on the social profile of Green members are sparse, primarily because the party views such information as an invasion of privacy. Most members belong to the middle class; in 1987 about one-third were women, an amount which is still below the party's desired goal of parity.[12] Among voters in the early 1980s, the Greens received up to three-quarters of their core support from persons under thirty-five whose parents had been primarily middle-and upper-level civil servants and salaried employees. In subsequent years, as these voters became older, most of them retained their loyalty to the party, thereby giving it a less youthful image. The Greens have gained above-average support from students and academic staff in university towns. One survey showed that 22 percent of Green voters have an advanced education, as compared to 10 percent of the population. Another survey showed that during the 1980s one-third of the Green voters were studying and not yet employed. The Greens also have done well among young professionals employed in health, education, and social service, but not among blue-collar workers, the self-employed, retired persons, and homemakers.[13] Green attempts to forge closer ties to the trade unions have failed.

Factional Disputes

Since the beginning of the party, it has not been able to eschew the factional schisms that have weakened its appeal to the electorate. Many schisms have arisen over the question of strategy, especially whether to participate in local, state, and national elections. Two chief wings competed for internal power from the mid-1980s on. The first, the "fundamentalists" (known as "Fundis"), was a loose group headed at one time by Petra Kelly, radical ecologist Jutta Ditfurth, and ecologist-socialist Rainer Trampert. The group consisted of Marxists, utopians, and activists who favored extraparliamentary actions and opposed any coalition, even a red-green one with the SPD, which they felt had betrayed socialist principles. Most of the Fundis wanted the Greens to remain critics of the capitalist system rather than to share power in a coalition with the procapitalist establishment parties. Even though the SPD, the most logical coalition partner, was left of center, the Fundis assailed its acceptance of the military, economic, and nuclear status quo and its faint-hearted support of environmental, peace, women's, and Third World issues. The Fundis insisted that the Greens work for societal changes from the bottom up by mobilizing the public to join social movements opposing the existing order.

The second wing competing for power comprised the pragmatic "realists" ("Realos"). Its leaders, among them Otto Schily and former bookseller and taxi driver Joschka Fischer, denounced the Fundis for their utopian views, which would not attract new voters to the Greens. Instead, Realo leaders called on the party to form coalitions, especially with the SPD, because the Greens' goals could be achieved only through incremental governmental reforms. The Realos gained the support of enough delegates at several Länder and national conventions to commit the party to enter governing coalitions should the occasion arise. This happened, for example, in Hesse in 1985 following an earlier Land election in which the SPD had failed to receive 50 percent of the vote and needed a partner to ensure support for mutually acceptable legislative proposals. Fischer became minister of the environment in Hesse, the first Green cabinet member in Germany. The coalition's formation, even though it broke up after sixteen months, was the precursor to SPD-Green coalitions in other Länder, indicating that differences between the two parties could be bridged through compromises.[14] In the 1987 national election, an SPD-Green coalition might have emerged if the two parties had gained a majority of votes, which proved not be the case with a renewed CDU/CSU-FDP victory.

In late 1988, the Fundis lost their long-held majority on the Greens' Executive Committee because of financial scandals, tactical mistakes, and the decline of social movements, whose members had given them considerable support in the past. Thereafter many small libertarian, moderate, and radical Green groups, opposed to state bureaucracy and central controls, called on the dominant Realos to emphasize once again direct actions in towns and cities.[15] The factional disputes on tactics contributed to the debacle of the 1990 all-German election, when the West German Greens lost their Bundestag seats (see Chapter 11). Observers recalled a statement made by a Green leader: The party gave the impression of "desolation without political contours, and grim trench warfare."[16]

Conclusion

Cultural changes in Western societies since the late 1960s produced the rise of the Greens. In many countries, a highly educated, mobile, and affluent New Left generation, suspicious of bureaucratic and oligarchic organizations, challenged its elders to make the system more participatory and to concern themselves more with the environment, alternatives to nuclear energy, and peace. In West Germany, the younger generation's political allegiance had been to the SPD, but disillusionment set in when the party tried in vain to balance youths' values with those held by the Old Left workers' generation. Consequently, many youths left the SPD and founded the Greens.

Despite the Greens' many problems—factionalism, programmatic cleavages, organizational weaknesses, and ebbing social movements in the late 1980s—they have often been on the cutting edge of politics. They have put ecological, weapons exports, and other controversial issues on the political agenda, forcing the establishment parties to take a position. They have challenged the political mores and customs imbedded in the West German system, contributed to the democratization of society, and enlivened the tradition-laden political scene. Their creative actions have gained them a loyal group of members and voters, which has led to electoral success and participation in Länder coalition governments. Despite occasional electoral defeats, they hold a firm place in the more flexible party system. The Greens have also served as a safety valve in the political system. They have offered an electoral home to those who are disillusioned with the establishment's failure to promote social justice, group solidarity, and equal opportunities for women and minorities.

The pioneering German Greens have also been in the vanguard of the European Green movement, thereby making them arguably the most influential antiestablishment party in Europe. Their program and structure have been widely adopted elsewhere.[17] Their Bundestag representation did not remain unique; in the late 1980s Green parties had seats in the national parliaments of Austria, Belgium, Finland, Italy, Luxembourg, Sweden, and Switzerland. The multinational Green bloc in the European Parliament has left an imprint on legislative deliberations. In short, the West German Greens have made a mark in subnational, national, and supranational politics in Europe.

Notes

1. Andrei S. Markovits and Philip S. Gorski, *The German Left: Red, Green, and Beyond* (New York: Oxford University Press, 1993), pp. 14–18.

2. David P. Conradt, *The German Polity,* 5th ed. (New York: Longman, 1993), p. 65.

3. Eva Kolinsky, *Parties, Opposition, and Society in West Germany* (New York: St. Martin's Press, 1984), pp. 297–300.

4. E. Gene Frankland and Donald Schoonmaker, *Between Protest and Power: The Green Party in Germany* (Boulder: Westview Press, 1992), pp. 3–4.

5. The rightists were led by former CDU member Herbert Gruhl and "ecological" farmer Baldur Springmann. Gruhl, dissatisfied with the Greens' leftist course, quit the party in 1981 and established the rival Green Action Future, which foundered soon thereafter (Kolinsky, *Parties, Opposition, and Society in West Germany,* pp. 301–304).

6. Elim Papadakis, *The Green Movement in West Germany* (London: Croom Helm, 1984), pp. 161–163.

7. Petra Kelly, *Um Hoffnung kämpfen,* p. 204; quoted in Werner Hülsberg, *The German Greens: A Social and Political Profile* (London: Verso, 1988), p. 78.

8. Papadakis, *The Green Movement in West Germany,* pp. 172–173; Russell J. Dalton, *Politics in Germany,* 2d ed. (New York: HarperCollins, 1993), p. 299.

9. Ibid.

10. Frankland and Schoonmaker, *Between Protest and Power,* pp. 104–109.

11. For details, see Rudolf van Hüllen, *Ideologie und Machtkampf bei den Grünen* (Bonn: Bouvier, 1990), pp. 415–417. In 1992, Bastian, according to a still-disputed government version, fatally shot his companion Petra Kelly and then himself, perhaps because of their despondency over the faction-riddled party and their fear for Germany's future in the face of right-wing terror against foreigners (GIC, *The Week in Germany,* October 23, 1992; *New York Times,* October 21, 1992).

12. Ferdinand Müller-Rommel and Thomas Poguntke, "Die Grünen," in *Parteien in der Bundesrepublik Deutschland,* ed. Alf Mintzel and Heinrich Oberreuter (Opladen: Leske und Budrich, 1992), pp. 349–350.

13. Frankland and Schoonmaker, *Between Protest and Power,* pp. 85–87.

14. Markovits and Gorski, *The German Left,* pp. 117–125; Gerard Braunthal, "Social Democratic–Green Coalitions in West Germany: Prospects for a New Alliance," *German Studies Review* 9, no. 3 (October 1986):571–597.

15. For comparative overviews, see Herbert Kitschelt, *The Logic of Party Formation: Ecological Politics in Belgium and West Germany* (Ithaca: Cornell University Press, 1989); Ferdinand Müller-Rommel, ed., *New Politics in Western Europe: The Rise and Success of Green Parties and Alternative Lists* (Boulder: Westview Press, 1989).

16. GIC, *The Week in Germany,* September 25, 1987.

17. Frankland and Schoonmaker, *Between Protest and Power,* p. 211.

· 8 ·

Left and Right
Radical Parties:
Protesting the System

CITIZENS' POLITICAL VIEWS in a democratic polity span the spectrum from left to right, with a strong cluster in the middle. Those on the left and right extremes are dissatisfied with the status quo and yearn for different radical or utopian solutions to their economic and social problems. In the United States, Britain, France, Italy, and elsewhere, communist, ultraconservative, and neofascist groups and parties have surfaced since World War I. They have served as agents of protest against the existing systems and have gained occasional policy concessions from the governments in power. At times, as in France and Italy, they have even participated in coalition cabinets.

In western Germany after 1945, radical parties emerged, but their appeal was limited once the CDU/CSU, SPD, and FDP captured most votes. In this chapter, we look first at the left and then at the right radical parties, with particular attention to right-wing Republicans, whose sudden electoral successes in the late 1980s created fear in Germany and other states of a reemerging Nazism. We must ask how the radical parties were able to gain a measure of support from disaffected voters and how effective the federal government was in weathering the challenges to its authority.

The chapter does not deal with the numerous radical action or terrorist groups, which sought through spectacular media-gaining actions to undermine the system. The groups were not formally organized as political parties and thus fall outside the scope of this book.

Left Radical Parties

The Communist Party of Germany

The Communist Party of Germany was founded after World War I but was banned by Hitler in 1933 (see Chapter 2). Western Allied powers permitted it to regroup in their territory after World War II, primarily because they had agreed with the Soviets in Berlin that the four traditional German groups of parties (communist, social democrats, liberals, and conservatives) be licensed in all zones. In June 1945, east Berlin party officials sent Max Reimann to the Ruhr and another leader to Hamburg to rebuild the party in two western areas where the KPD had had its strongholds before 1933. Thereafter the party was organized throughout the western zones (in addition to its formation in the Soviet zone). In April 1948, west German zonal delegates elected Reimann, a former miner and inmate of a concentration camp, as KPD (West) chairman. Until then, he and other leaders had hoped to form a united front with the SPD, but all such efforts failed in the western zones. SPD chairman Schumacher strongly opposed cooperation or fusion with a party that had bitterly fought the SPD during the Weimar years.

The KPD (West) grew from 75,000 members in 1945 to 324,000 in 1947 and received up to 14 percent of the vote in Länder elections held before the West German state's formation in 1949. The party attracted a sizable following because many former KPD members rejoined it after the Nazi interregnum and because the party distinguished itself as part of the small but heroic underground resistance movement against the Hitler tyranny.

The KPD's electoral strength meant that its deputies in Länder legislatures and ministers in coalition cabinets participated in western German politics. However, as the cold war between the Soviet Union and the West erupted and as anticommunism became a potent ideology among other parties, the KPD was forced into a defensive posture. In the 1949 Bundestag election, it still won 5.7 percent of the vote and received fifteen seats, but thereafter it lost seats in most Länder legislatures. Its membership had dropped to 148,000 by 1951 and to 78,000 by 1956. Its unswerving fealty to the Soviet Union and to the East German SED regime and its undiluted Marxist program cost the party substantial support. Conservative critics stigmatized its leaders and members as disloyal.

The death warrant came in 1956 when the Constitutional Court ruled, on the basis of a government request made nearly five years earlier, that the KPD be banned for advocating the overthrow of the democratic order and the setting up of a proletarian dictatorship. The ban became controversial because civil libertarians argued that as a small party the KPD posed no threat to democracy and should be allowed to function. Others argued that the state, by driving the party underground, would have more difficulty controlling it. The KPD charged, with some credibility, that it was the victim of state political repression. As a result, many of its members went underground or joined KPD front organizations.[1]

The German Communist Party

West German communist leaders established in 1968, at a time of worldwide ferment in leftist circles, the German Communist Party (DKP). The successor to the West German KPD, it advanced less revolutionary goals, at least in its basic program, to survive any possible new challenge to its constitutionality. The leaders had the assurance of Minister of Justice Gustav Heinemann (later federal president) that they could proceed as long as the party endorsed the Basic Law. Three years later, in 1971, the SED Central Committee in East Berlin gave its belated blessing to the DKP. The SED action precipitated the dissolution of the illegal KPD, which had kept up a precarious existence since its ban in 1956.

DKP leaders established a national organization, which included grassroots groups set up in residences, shops, and universities to deal with community, work, or educational issues. The party engaged in extensive propaganda, publishing numerous newspapers and pamphlets. However, DKP chief Herbert Mies and other chiefs held intraparty democracy to a minimum. They issued directives through the Executive Committee that lower echelons were expected to follow.

To ensure that the DKP would not meet its predecessor's fate, the basic program recognized the Basic Law's democratic principles and the peaceful achievement of socialism. The party did not surmount the 5 percent barrier in any national or Land election, despite assurances of its commitment to democracy and pockets of strength in some cities, which resulted in the election of seventy-four councillors in thirty-five city assemblies.[2] In the 1980s, it still had an estimated forty thousand to fifty-eight thousand members.

The DKP courted workers, especially those organized in trade unions. In 1981, it recruited 40 percent of the thirty-five thousand members in the German Socialist Workers Youth, which it had established as a front organization. The DKP also set up shop floor organizations in three hundred factories. Its effort had only limited success because the bulk of workers were strongly anticommunist. However, numerous DKP members became middle-level functionaries in the metal workers and other progressive unions.

Many intellectuals and students backed the DKP. They predominated in the local units, although older leaders controlled the top policymaking bodies. The party gained support from thousands of university students through its front organization, the Marxist Student League Spartakus. The Spartakus activists had considerable influence in student governments, despite competition from other student groups, including Young Socialists, Greens, and numerous Marxist and New Left splinter groups.[3]

Mikhail Gorbachev's perestroika policy in the Soviet Union had an effect on the DKP. A dissident group, the Renewers, challenged the orthodox pro-Stalinist course that the party leaders had been following faithfully since the DKP's inception. After the January 1989 convention, where the dissidents called in vain for intraparty pluralism, many members resigned. However, the dissidents won their goal at the May 1990 convention. Delegates adopted a new statute to democratize the party and selected a successor to Mies, who declined to be chairman again. But by then, the DKP had become a shadow of its former self, barely surviving the discredited communism in the East, the fall of the Wall, and the end of generous covert yearly subsidies from the SED.

From 1945 to 1990, numerous other smaller radical and independent communist parties, such as the Communist Party of Germany/Marxist-Leninist and the Communist League of West Germany, were active on the left fringe of the political spectrum. In cities and university towns, they competed with the KPD and its successor DKP for members and voters but had only minuscule support.[4]

Right Radical Parties

The Socialist Reich Party

Nationalist right-wing parties have existed in Germany since the Empire era. The horrors of the Nazi regime had no effect on a small minority of citizens in western Germany, who have backed new ultra-right-wing parties or action groups in the decades since 1945. After the war, the Western Allies permitted nationalists but not neofascists to organize. In March 1946, in the British zone of occupation, the German Conservative Party–German Right Party was founded, a result of a merger of several small rightist parties. It attracted former Nazis, especially in Lower Saxony, which had been a pro-Nazi stronghold. In October 1949, the party's nationalist majority expelled the former Nazis, who were becoming too strong.[5]

On the day of expulsion, the neo-Nazis formed the Socialist Reich Party (SRP), which became the magnet for most right radical groups, especially in northern Germany. The party was led, among others, by General Otto Ernst Remer, who had played a central role in crushing the anti-Hitler putsch of June 1944. The SRP, rejecting the democratic system, called for the linkage of a people's community and German "socialism," code words for a new national socialism.

In 1951, the SRP gained 11 percent of the vote in Lower Saxony and nearly 8 percent in Bremen. Many of its supporters were refugees and expellees from East Prussia and other eastern territories formerly inhabited by Germans who after 1945 had started a new and precarious existence in western Germany. Others were ultranationalists who dreamed of a reconstituted powerful Germany. To counter the SRP's strong showing, the federal government requested the Länder governments to limit its activities and to outlaw its paramilitary units, including its strong-arm squads, and its youth division. In 1952, the Constitutional Court, acting on a request of the federal government, declared the party unconstitutional for its failure to support the democratic system, its anti-Semitism, and its authoritarian party structure.

Many SRP supporters thereupon joined the German Reich Party (DRP), which had been formed two years earlier by rightist leader Adolf von Thadden. The party won seats in the Lower Saxony legislature but had only minimal support (1.1 percent or less of the vote) in the Bundestag elections of 1953, 1957, and 1961. Thereupon the DRP looked for allies to strengthen its position in national politics.

The National Democratic Party of Germany

In 1964, the DRP fused with other small rightist regional parties to form the National Democratic Party of Germany (NPD). Friedrich Thielen, leader of the rightist German Party, became chairman. The NPD had less than fourteen thousand members in 1965 and received only 2 percent of the vote in that year's federal election. However, in eleven Länder elections between 1966 and 1969, the party captured seats in seven legislatures. Its supporters were angry that the CDU/CSU, which for many had been their political home, had betrayed their trust and allied itself in Bonn in a grand coalition with the hated SPD.

In the 1969 federal election, the party received 1.4 million votes, or 4.3 percent of the total vote, but not enough to occupy seats in the Bundestag. The protest vote, much publicized abroad as a sign of a resurgent neo-Nazism, resulted primarily from an ailing economy, especially in the coal and steel industries, which had led to serious unemployment. Among NPD voters were disgruntled workers, the self-employed, and farmers, who blamed the establishment parties for not ending the economic crisis, and law-and-order conservatives and neo-Nazis, who were outraged by the 1968 student revolt and its challenge to traditional values. These voters were attracted to the NPD's commitment to ultranationalism and reunification of the two Germanys and its antileft program.[6] However, in the early 1970s the party, led at the time by von Thadden and numerous former Nazis, swiftly lost influence when the economy had recovered. The NPD's membership fell from twenty-eight thousand in 1969 to six thousand in 1982, and its electoral support in the 1980s shrank to less than 1 percent.

The Republicans

In a third cycle of ultraright activities, the Republicans, popularly known as the REPs, emerged on the political stage in 1982. Franz Schönhuber and other former members of the Bavarian CSU founded the new party after having criticized the CSU's lack of internal democracy and the DM 1 billion ($412 million) credit extended by Franz Josef Strauss, then minister-president, to the communist East German government.

Schönhuber had been a Waffen-SS sergeant during the war and thereafter became a newspaper editor in Munich. In 1975, he was appointed host of a popular Bavarian television political talk show but in 1982 was fired from his job because of the publication of his autobiography, in which he boasted of his SS background. He then began his career in the Republicans, becoming its chairman in 1985.

Schönhuber is a skillful and demagogic speaker, comparable to the French rightist National Front leader Jean-Marie Le Pen and the Austrian rightist Freedom Party leader Jörg Haider. Until 1994, Schönhuber survived numerous power struggles and was always cautious to keep right-wing extremist planks out of the Republicans' program, which proclaims the party's support of the state and the democratic order. As a consequence, the government intelligence agency, the Office for the Protection of the Constitution, while putting the party under surveillance, has not listed it in the category of extremist parties, which could be banned by the Constitutional Court.

However, the Republicans' support for a true democracy is suspect. The 1987 program is replete with anti-West, anti-Europe, ultranationalist, racist, and xenophobic sentiments. It characterizes the party as a "community of German patriots" and warns about the flood of immigrants pouring into Germany. The asylum-seekers especially will weaken the social net and endanger the well-being of German citizens. The program urges women to remain at home raising a family and extends no sympathy for the feminist movement, abortion rights, and homosexuals.[7]

The 1990 platform is more comprehensive and moderate than its 1987 predecessor. Not the consequence of an ideological shift, the change was made to ensure the party's legality and attractiveness to a wider net of voters. To gain their backing, Schönhuber's speeches were replete with hatred against minority groups, yet fell within the constitutional protection of freedom of speech. At the 1990 convention, he said, "But we also say to some club-wielding Turks, we have granted you hospitality in this country but we don't grant you the right to beat up our citizens."[8]

On another occasion, referring to German Jews, he said that they had been responsible for anti-Semitism in postwar Germany because they had had the temerity to constantly meddle in national affairs that did not concern them. He labeled the German Central Council of Jews as the "fifth occupying power" (the others were the four Allied powers) on German soil. In 1989 he said that history books had to be rewritten: "We do not allow that our history be permanently reduced to Auschwitz."[9] In speaking about the Nazi past, he admitted that Hitler brought destruction and defeat to Germany but that the war had also produced self-sacrifice, courage, and patriotism. The party's newspaper wrote, "We have been repressed, sullied, stepped upon and blackmailed by absurd imputations of collective guilt and of sole responsibility for the war."[10]

The Republicans built up their organization first in the conservative Bavarian and Baden-Württemberg bastions. By 1989, they had chapters in all Länder and claimed twenty thousand members. In that year, they gained, most unexpectedly, 7.5 percent of the vote in the West Berlin Land election. Five months later, they received 2 million votes, or 7.1 percent of the West German national vote, in the European Parliament election.

The meteoric Republican surge caused consternation among liberal circles in West Germany and other states. Pollsters were kept busy trying to find answers as to who joined or voted for the party and why. They found that it received the greatest support in urban working-class districts from eighteen- to twenty-four-year-old men, many unemployed, who cast twice as many votes for the party as women. The young men had a minimum education, grew up in asocial families, and lived in bleak housing projects with few social and cultural amenities. Seeking new forms of community in right-wing groups, they did not base their views necessarily on the virulent Nazi ideology of the 1930s but rather on an ultraright ideology (a strong leader, a Germanic race, and antipathy toward Jews) that differed from it only in degree.

The party also received support from middle-class salaried employees and civil servants, including police officers, who were worried about their own future or who approved the party's law-and-order and other conservative goals. In previous elections, these groups had voted for the CDU or CSU and, to a lesser extent, the SPD. They shifted to the Republicans as a protest against corrupt establishment politicians and the government's immigration policies, which they saw as a threat to their jobs, housing, and social welfare.[11]

In small towns and rural areas, many shopkeepers and farmers, the latter allured by the party's promise to restrict foreign food imports competing with their own crops, voted Republican. However, most women, whether living in urban or rural areas, were repelled by a party that was patriarchal, aggressive, ready to use force if necessary, and antifeminist—one party plank called on the government to institute a compulsory social year, which would include courses for females "relating to [their] tasks as a woman, mother, and housewife."[12]

The government never saw the Republicans as an immediate threat to the democratic order, especially because of the party's internal and external problems. Internally, the Republicans have been rent by continual feuds, expulsions, defections, and litigations in national headquarters and state organizations. Externally, Chancellor Kohl, during the 1990 campaign, took up the nationalist theme of one united Germany—a theme that the Republicans had used with some effectiveness in previous years. These problems contributed to the party's loss of nearly one-half of its membership and to its steep electoral decline in the postunification years (see Chapters 11 and 12).

The German People's Union

The Republicans also lost strength because a new rightist party competed with them. In 1987, Gerhard Frey, a Munich right-wing publisher, converted the German People's Union (DVU), which he had founded in 1971, from an association into a party (DVU–List D).[13] Although at first it had branches only in Bavaria and Bremen (later in other Länder), it attracted enough support in Bremerhaven, a part of Land Bremen, that its top candidate became a deputy in the state legislature, the first rightist deputy in any Land in nearly twenty years.

Frey has become wealthy as a result of his firms publishing right-wing newspapers and books, making records and video cassettes, casting medals, and owning profitable rental properties. The party's two newspapers, with a combined weekly circulation of one hundred thousand, have been shrilly nationalist and xenophobic. They have called for a "Germanization" of the Germans, warned about the "invasion" of foreigners, defamed democratic institutions, made light of Nazi crimes, and denied German responsibility for World War II. The newspapers' antidemocratic stance made it possible for the Office for the Protection of the Constitution, after a lengthy surveillance, to include the party in its "right-wing extremist" category. Such a step does not mean the party is banned (only the Constitutional Court can do that), but it is a warning that the party's future is in danger unless the DVU moderates its message.

In 1989, the DVU, with twenty-five thousand members, garnered only 1.6 percent in the European Parliament election, but subsequently the party maintained strength in a few regions of western Germany. However, as a result of leftist counterdemonstrations and harassment of DVU campaign rallies, the DVU leaders curtailed the party's public activities and instead recruited new members and voters by mailing out propaganda leaflets.[14] In West Germany's last year before unification in 1990, the DVU and the Republicans were the chief contenders for right-wing voters, but they faced minor competition from the NPD and the League for a German People and Homeland, which had splintered off from the Republicans.

Conclusion

Minor left and right radical parties in West Germany from 1945 to 1990 had a checkered record of emerging and vanishing and of squabbling internally and splintering. Members or voters of leftist parties are often ideological rebels against the status quo who are seeking to shape a better world. They find the Greens or the SPD too supportive of the system and want its complete transformation. Members or voters of rightist parties protest the government's inability to deal with pressing economic and social issues. However, many are also ideological crusaders seeking a fascist revival. They are alienated and dissatisfied with the establishment parties' policies or lack of policies and with an alien cultural milieu and modernization that marginalize or exclude them. However, the minor radical and extremist parties, with a 10–15 percent potential support from the electorate, were never strong enough during this period to pose a threat to the state's existence, even though there were times when the NPD and the Republicans seemed to replicate the early successes of the Nazi Party during the Weimar period. In the end, Bonn never became Weimar.[15]

To sum up our odyssey through the West German party landscape so far: The CDU/CSU, SPD, and FDP, joined by the Greens in the 1980s, occupied the bulk of the political space, giving the system great political stability. The left and right radical parties were vocal opponents, protesting the system but with only a moderate effect on the country's political agenda. The government's toleration of most radical parties gave their supporters a means to express their dissatisfaction but within constitutional boundaries. Such a policy sustains the country's commitment to pluralism and democracy. As we turn to the rival East German state's party system, striking differences, but also some similarities, to the West German system emerge.

Notes

1. Manfred Rowold and Stefan Immerfall, "Im Schatten der Macht: Nicht-etablierte Kleinparteien," in *Parteien in der Bundesrepublik Deutschland,* ed. Alf Mintzel and Heinrich Oberreuter (Opladen: Leske und Budrich, 1992), pp. 405–406.

2. Eva Kolinsky, *Parties, Opposition, and Society in West Germany* (New York: St. Martin's Press, 1984), p. 223; see also pp. 209–220.

3. In 1981, 70 percent of the sixty-one thousand Spartakus members had joined the DKP (ibid., pp. 221–222).

4. Andrei S. Markovits and Philip S. Gorski, *The German Left: Red, Green, and Beyond* (New York: Oxford University Press, 1993), pp. 61–65.

5. All German parties accepted former Nazis as (mostly nominal) members. For details on one rightist party, see Horst W. Schmollinger, "Die Deutsche Konservative Partei—Deutsche Rechtspartei," in *Parteien-Handbuch: Die Parteien der Bundesrepublik Deutschland, 1945–1980,* ed. Richard Stöss (Opladen: Westdeutscher Verlag, 1983), vol. 1, pp. 982–1024.

6. For an early overview of the NPD, see John D. Nagle, *The National Democratic Party: Right Radicalism in the Federal Republic of Germany* (Berkeley and Los Angeles: University of California Press, 1970).

7. See Die Republikaner, *Programm der Republikaner* (Munich: Die Republikaner, n.d.); personal interview with a Bavarian REP official, Munich, December 10, 1990.

8. Hans-Joachim Veen, Norbert Lepszy, and Peter Mnich, *The Republikaner Party in Germany: Right-Wing Menace or Protest Catchall?* (Westport, Conn.: Praeger, 1993), pp. 17–18.

9. Dieter Roth, "Die Republikaner," *Aus Politik und Zeitgeschichte,* supplement to *Das Parlament,* B 37–38/90 (September 14, 1990):45–46.

10. Veen, Lepszy, and Mnich, *The Republikaner Party in Germany,* p. 19.

11. Ibid., pp. 29–40; Franz Urban Pappi, "Die Republikaner im Parteiensystem der Bundesrepublik: Protesterscheinung oder politische Alternative?" *Aus Politik und Zeitgeschichte,"* supplement to *Das Parlament,* B 21/90 (May 18, 1990):37–44.

12. *Frankfurter Rundschau,* June 20, 1989.

13. "D" stands for Deutschland (Germany). The party is hereafter referred to as DVU, its common abbreviation.

14. *DVU: Organisation—Ziele—Perspektiven* (Stuttgart: Landesamt für Verfassungsschutz Baden-Württemberg, 1992); Gerard Braunthal, "The Rise of Right-Wing Extremism in the New Germany," in *The Domestic Politics of German Unification,* ed. Christopher Anderson, Karl Kaltenthaler, and Wolfgang Luthardt (Boulder: Lynne Rienner, 1993), pp. 103–104.

15. See Armin Pfahl-Traughber, *Rechtsextremismus: Eine kritische Bestandsaufnahme nach der Wiedervereinigung* (Bonn: Bouvier, 1993), pp. 228–251.

PART THREE

East German Parties Since World War II

• *9* •

The Socialist Unity Party and the Bloc Parties

A PARTY SYSTEM REFLECTS a state's political system. As noted in Chapter 1, two or more parties compete for power in democratic systems, whereas one party normally rules in dictatorial systems. In turning our attention to West Germany's rival state, the German Democratic Republic, in existence from 1949 to 1990, we find a slight deviation from the dictatorial pattern. In this instance, power lay with one party, but its leaders tolerated, even during the Soviet period of occupation from 1945 to 1949, other noncompeting and satellite parties to provide a democratic facade and to indoctrinate noncommunist members.

To gain an understanding of how the GDR party system evolved and operated, this chapter first deals with the influence of the Soviet military authorities, whose grand design, replicated in all Eastern European countries, was to prevent the rise of a democratic political system. As the initial power holders, the Soviets determined the destiny of the eastern Germans for close to half a century. The chapter then deals with the fusion of the Communist and Social Democratic Parties into the powerful Socialist Unity Party, the role of the four bloc parties, and the history of the SED, its structure, and its control of the country's politics, economics, and social life.

The Soviet Occupation

In 1945, the Allied powers carved up a defeated Germany. The Soviet Union administered the country's eastern zone (except for west Berlin) until 1949, when the zone became a semisovereign state, the GDR. During this time, the Soviets gradually imposed an economic system, which corresponded somewhat to their own, in the eastern zone, while the Western Allies, especially the United States, made sure that neocapitalism emerged in a pluralist system in their zones. The Soviets set about to destroy all vestiges of fascism and militarism and to establish centralized planning and state socialism during the rebuilding of the shattered economy.

They were the first among the occupying powers to allow Germans to form political parties. Initially the Soviets did not want to impose a communist political system on their territory for fear of alienating the Western Allies, on whom they were dependent for war reparations from western Germany for their devastated state. The Soviets also hoped, in vain, that the new party system in their zone would become the model for one in a future all-German state.

The KPD and the SPD

On June 10, 1945, the Soviet military administration permitted "antifascist democratic" parties to organize. On the following day, not surprisingly, the Communist Party of Germany was the first party to be founded. The KPD considered itself heir to the Weimar KPD, and its leaders, many of whom during the Hitler era had been incarcerated in German concentration camps or had lived in Soviet exile, wanted to create a party that would be in the vanguard of the antifascist movement and support Soviet interests. Paradoxically, they initially rejected a plan to introduce the communist system into the Soviet zone and opted instead to establish a parliamentary republic, which would have allowed a mixed economic system to emerge. These objectives did not mean that KPD leaders had given up their long-range goal of achieving a socialist society; rather, their tactical move was meant to decrease the level of potential hostility to the party.

The KPD was headed by Wilhelm Pieck, who had been one of the founders of the Communist Party in 1919, an executive committee member of the Communist International, and, during the Nazi period, the chairman of the KPD in Soviet exile. After returning to Berlin in 1945, he rejected as premature the call from some members for a merger of the KPD and the newly reconstituted eastern German Social Democratic Party as the best means to strengthen the leftist camp. He wanted first to build up the KPD, which most eastern Germans did not back. They remembered only too vividly Soviet soldiers' plunder and rape in eastern Germany at war's end and the continuing massive war reparations of German factories and goods to the Soviet Union. Pieck feared that the KPD's weakness would lead to the SPD's domination of a fused party.

On June 15, 1945, four days after the KPD's creation, the eastern SPD was formed. Otto Grotewohl, heading its Central Committee, called for the creation of a democratic state and a socialist economy. He had been a member of the SPD from 1912 to 1933, a deputy and top regional administrator during Weimar, and a businessman who was frequently arrested during the Nazis' reign of terror. In 1945, he supported the proposal for an SPD-KPD merger because he did not want to witness once again the Weimar feuds between the two parties, which had facilitated the rise of Nazism, and because a fraternal bond had arisen between SPD and KPD resistance members against the hated Nazi regime. He believed that a leftist party would achieve socialism through democratic, rather than revolutionary, means. Not all SPD officials shared his optimism about a merger; they feared that the SPD would be swallowed up by the KPD. At the same time, KPD officials in the Soviet zone abandoned their initial opposition to a swift merger. Now they hoped that KPD cadres, loyal to the Soviet authorities, would dominate the projected united party and not fall prey to a moderate SPD ideology.

In December 1945, sixty leaders of the two parties, including many hesitant SPD officials, met to prepare for unification. Thereafter Soviet authorities, using coercion, did not permit those SPD officials who objected to a merger to speak at meetings and arrested them. In February 1946 in west Berlin (administered by the Western Allies), 82 percent of SPD members voted in a referendum against a merger. Soviet authorities forbade the eastern Berlin SPD to hold a similar referendum on the same day, knowing that the result would be equally negative.

In April 1946, delegates of the KPD and SPD approved a merger of their parties at a unity convention in east Berlin. The KPD chiefs, supported by the Soviet officials, had achieved their goal of forcing the SPD to end its independent existence and fuse into the new party, the Socialist Unity Party of Germany. To reassure SPD members, who automatically became SED members, Pieck and Walter Ulbricht, the communist deputy chairman, emphasized that the SED was not an extension of the KPD, had no intention of forming a one-party dictatorship, and, as a new workers' party, stood ideologically halfway between the KPD and the SPD, incorporating Marxism but not the dictatorial concepts of Leninism into its program. Despite this statement, power shifted within the SED to the former KPD—the result of continuing Soviet pressure—even though the KPD had 600,000 members to the SPD's 680,000.

Before the October 1946 Land parliament elections, SED leaders, knowing that a majority of voters did not support the party, permitted the SED's ancillary mass organizations (e.g., trade unions, youth, women) to run their own candidates. The strategy paid off. The SED gained only a plurality of votes but together with those cast for the ancillary organizations obtained a majority of legislative seats.[1] The SED, on the Soviet model, had created these mass organizations to serve as transmission belts for its directives.

Enrolling millions of members, the organizations mobilized the masses but in the process robbed them of the opportunity to create groups free of state control.

The Bloc Parties

The SED's rivals in the eastern German parliaments were two bourgeois parties, the Christian Democrats and the Liberals, that the Soviet administration had allowed to form in summer 1945. On June 26, the Christian Democratic Union was organized, months ahead of its western German counterpart. In the founding manifesto, the eastern CDU affirmed its commitment to Christian democracy; supported private enterprise, except for the nationalization of natural resources and key industries; and approved central planning during the reconstruction period. Jakob Kaiser, one of its founders and a former Catholic union leader, attempted to create a four-zonal CDU, but Adenauer vetoed the plan. The western German CDU leader feared that it would lead to Soviet influence in the western zones (see Chapter 4). The eastern CDU grew swiftly from 119,000 members in 1946 to 231,000 in 1948.

On July 5, 1945, the Liberal Democratic Party of Germany (LDPD) was organized. Its founders, former leaders of the German Democratic Party in the Weimar years, sought the backing of conservative citizens in their call for the creation of a free enterprise system based on individual initiatives. The party had some success: It registered 113,000 members in 1946 and 197,000 in 1948.[2]

The CDU and LDPD leaders, who had been active antifascists in the Nazi period, believed that in the postwar reconstruction period all parties would have to cooperate with one another rather than engage in fratricidal conflicts. Thus, in July 1945 they joined the United Front of Antifascist Democratic Parties, which the KPD and SPD had established. The front was headed by a committee of five delegates of each of the four parties (KPD, SPD, CDU, LDPD). Decisions had to be taken unanimously, giving any party a veto power. However, the bourgeois parties could not afford to veto KPD decisions because their activities would have been limited further. They realized belatedly that they had become an acclamation machine for the more powerful KPD, later SED, which had full Soviet backing. Thus, they had to make concessions to the Soviet authorities, such as having to dismiss two conservative leaders to preserve the parties' nominal independence.

In 1948, the SED, worried about the popularity of the CDU and LDPD, allowed, with Soviet official blessing, two more parties—the National Democratic Party of Germany (NDPD) and the Democratic Farmers Party of Germany (DBD)—to form in order to dilute the opposition vote. The nationalist NDPD called for an end to discrimination against nominal Nazi members and for support of private shops and small businesses. It was backed primarily by former German army officers (many reeducated to socialism while in Soviet captivity), former Nazi Party members (frozen out of the other parties), and bourgeois middle-class members. About 30 percent of NDPD members were salaried employees, and 22 percent were tradespeople and artisans. The DBD, headed by a former KPD deputy, was supported primarily by conservative farmers. By 1982, it had an enrollment of 103,000 members, of whom 30 percent were women. They were expected to support the SED's agricultural policies, including the campaign to collectivize farms.

To ensure that the NDPD and DBD would remain SED satellites, the new parties' executive officers had to be SED sympathizers. The NDPD and DBD were admitted into the SED-dominated United Front of Antifascist Democratic Parties, renamed in June 1949 the Democratic Bloc of Parties and Mass Organizations (hence, the expression "bloc parties"). The SED permitted the four bloc parties to exist as long as they did not compete with it for political supremacy. Thus, they could not engage in any political activity in large firms, the armed forces, and the universities. The SED instead used the parties as a channel for its propaganda and for feedback of views from their bourgeois or ex-bourgeois adherents. Ironically, the more the SED nationalized small firms and farms, the fewer bourgeois voters there were, and the less justification the SED had to perpetuate the bloc system. One SED official remarked that the multiparty system was justified as long as "the reeducation of the entire population in the spirit of Communism has not been completely carried through."[3]

In sum, during the 1945–1949 occupation period the SED pursued a double strategy. On the one hand, it permitted subservient bloc parties and mass organizations; on the other hand, it deprived the old ruling and propertied classes of their power. The SED thereby set the preconditions for revolutionary transformations in business, agriculture, education, and the judiciary. In this process, it abandoned its 1946 position as the "German road to socialism," which meant at the time pursuing a reformist course toward socialism, and adopted instead in 1950 the slogan "party of a new type," which meant that it was determined to prevent any opposition to the creation of a socialist system.[4]

The German Democratic Republic

The outbreak of the cold war had sealed Germany's division into two states. Once the GDR was created on October 7, 1949, the SED, whose structure, program, and functions were modeled on those of the Soviet Communist Party, assumed full control of the country. The provisional Parliament elected former KPD leader and SED cochairman Pieck as the country's president (titular head of state) and former SPD leader and fellow SED cochairman Grotewohl as prime minister (chairman of the Council of Ministers).[5] The council, comprising ministers of all parties, had the same executive powers as Western-style cabinets but served primarily as a transmission belt for SED policy directives. Thus, the prime minister stood in the shadow of Walter Ulbricht, soon to be the SED general secretary, who also had a seat on the council.

The SED's power meant that its cadres occupied all key positions in the national and Länder ministries and in the economy. From 1950 on, the SED forced the other parties to put up candidates for elections to the People's Chamber (Parliament) on a so-called unity list of the National Front of the GDR, created by it one year earlier.[6] On each list, the SED received 25 percent of the seats; the CDU and LDPD, 15 percent each; the NPD and DBD, 7.5 percent each; and the mass organizations, the remainder. (In 1963, the allocation of seats was changed slightly.) Even though the bloc parties and mass organizations had only a meager plurality in the national legislature—which met rarely, hardly voted on any bills, and when it did passed them unanimously—the SED chiefs knew that both groups would support the party. The voters, lacking alternative lists, gave nearly 100 percent support to the unity lists. They had to approve or reject the lists, a further indication that the purported pluralist system was a fiction.

In justifying this electoral system, the SED chiefs said that voters in the West had few programmatic choices among the major competing parties. Thus, the Western claim to pluralism was a sham. But in the GDR, they said, the electoral process served to mobilize the voters for the socialist state. The leaders knew, however, that a vote for their lists did not guarantee popular approval for their policies.

The Politburo, the SED's top organ, made the key decisions on domestic and foreign policies, which the national, district, and local executive and legislative bodies had to carry out. The SED's control of the government and the armed forces was assured through the establishment of "basic units" (the core group of reliable SED members) in each ministry and military detachment. As in the Soviet Union, political officers in the military were given control responsibilities.

The Ulbricht Era

From 1950 to 1971, Walter Ulbricht, general secretary of the SED, was East Germany's dominant policymaker. He was born in 1893, grew up in a socialist worker's home, trained as a cabinetmaker, and joined the SPD in 1912 but switched to the KPD soon after its founding in late 1918. After serving as deputy in the Reichstag from 1928 to 1933, he fled Nazi Germany and settled in Moscow, where he became a Politburo member of the exiled KPD. In 1945, he returned to Germany with the Soviet troops to reestablish a nationwide KPD. He rose to prominence in the eastern zone's politics and then became GDR deputy prime minister in 1949, SED general secretary in 1950, and Council of State president (titular head of the country) in 1960. (That year, the council, a collective presidency, supplanted the position of the president.) As party head, he was a hard-line communist loyal to the Soviet Union and a skillful but humorless leader who paid attention to the most minute bureaucratic details.

Ulbricht survived national crises, such as the 1953 workers' uprising against the regime in Berlin, which spread to other areas and was forcibly put down by Soviet troops. In its aftermath, Ulbricht made enough concessions to the workers to defuse their anger about economic hardships and the Soviet action. Later he purged rival leaders and their supporters from the SED and appointed instead loyal officials to top posts by making use of the party's entrenched patronage system. From 1958 on, Ulbricht, secure in his post, quickened the economy's collectivization. As in the Soviet Union, the state made central planning a key instrument for ensuring that the nationalized industries and small businesses carried out the government's five-year plans. After agriculture was collectivized between 1959 and 1960, only a few private retail trade and artisan shops remained in private hands.[7]

In response to economic hardships and political repression, masses of dissatisfied people moved to West Germany, which in turn led to Ulbricht's 1961 decision to build the wall to keep the remaining population inside the GDR. (About 4 million citizens moved or fled to the FRG from 1949 to 1961.) From 1961 on, Ulbricht had to make concessions to lessen popular dissatisfaction. He decentralized the GDR economy, modernized its technology, and provided more consumer goods. Yet in 1971 he could not stop a new economic crisis, alienated Soviet and other SED chiefs with his inop-

portune ideological declamations, and opposed the Soviet–West German détente. In May 1971, other senior chiefs removed him as party boss, but he remained titular head of state. He died in August 1973 at age eighty.

The Honecker Era

In 1971, Erich Honecker replaced Ulbricht as SED first secretary. Born in
1912, the son of a coal miner, Honecker joined the KPD youth organization
at age ten, became a party member in 1929, and then accepted a high post in
the party's youth organization. After two years of anti-Nazi underground
work, he was arrested by the Nazis and imprisoned for ten years. In 1945,
following his release, he organized and chaired the KPD-controlled Free
German Youth. In 1958, he became a full member of the SED Politburo,
with responsibility for security.

As the SED first secretary, Honecker reversed Ulbricht's decision to shift
some powers from the SED to government agencies. The SED once again
became the country's sole policymaking body. After Ulbricht's death in
1973, Willi Stoph, who had been prime minister, became State Council
president (titular head of the GDR). But in 1976, Honecker, whose title in
the party was changed from first secretary to general secretary, assumed the
presidency of the State Council as well, relegating Stoph to the post of prime
minister once more. Until Honecker's resignation from his posts in October
1989, he unashamedly continued the Stalinist cult of personality that
Ulbricht had begun. Honecker's photograph adorned placards on thousands
of walls, and his phrases were quoted repeatedly in the government-con-
trolled media.

Honecker also reversed Ulbricht's economic decentralization policy and
reinstated centralized planning. He ordered the conversion of most remaining private businesses into state enterprises; consolidated collective farms
into huge units, on the Soviet model; replaced reformist SED leaders with
loyal ideologues; and changed the state's most recent slogan, "building socialism," to "real, existing socialism," meaning that the state had already
achieved it.

Riots by Polish workers protesting their communist regime's decision to
increase food prices in 1970 was a signal to Honecker that he had to proceed
cautiously. Even though the GDR was one of the most highly industrialized
countries in the world and had the highest living standard of any commu-
nist-ruled state, the people were still dissatisfied with their material conditions, especially in comparison to West German citizens. In response,
Honecker liberalized social welfare support for low-income groups, con-

cluded an informal pact with the Protestant church, and liberalized citizens' rights to visit or emigrate to West Germany.

However, in 1976 he ended a liberal cultural policy and resumed jailing, or expelling from the GDR, those intellectuals, artists, and others who demanded more civil rights for the people. He increased the powers of the Ministry for State Security (Stasi), which kept all citizens under strict surveillance.[8] In foreign affairs, Western countries, including the United States, extended diplomatic recognition to the GDR following its signing in late 1972 of a basic treaty with West Germany, which gave the GDR belated legitimacy as an independent state in the international community. (The four Allied powers still had residual powers in the two Germanys, which in 1973 became U.N. members.)

SED Structure

Following the Soviet model, the SED's statute (1976) assigned the party the task of being "the conscious and organized vanguard of the working class and toiling people of the socialist GDR."[9] The SED's program called the party the "leading force in the creation of the developed socialist society."[10] Thus, based on the Marxist-Leninist assumption that the SED's doctrine was infallible and scientific, and that the working class, constituting the majority of the population, was the most progressive politically, the SED viewed itself as the wave of the socialist future.[11]

From 1946 to 1949, the party admitted anyone as member who supported its principles and was willing to proselytize nonmembers. But thereafter it restricted admission to potential cadres and other able candidates, who, after petitioning for entrance, had to first finish a probationary period. Leaders rewarded the most talented and loyal members with prestigious, well-paying jobs in the party cadre or in other occupations. The SED cadre included many coming from underprivileged families; members were politically screened, trained in party schools, and encouraged to develop technical or administrative skills. The cadre consisted of a veritable army of nearly two hundred thousand full-time paid professional functionaries, who received special privileges unavailable to the average citizen.

The SED was not only a cadre but also a mass party, constituting one of Europe's largest. In 1948, membership stood at nearly 2 million, or 16 percent of the adult population. In the following four years, SED officers purged from the party's rolls an estimated 200,000 former SPD members, whose loyalty was considered suspect. More than 5,000 purged members were incarcerated, of whom hundreds died in prisons or Soviet labor camps. As a result of the mass purges and resignations, membership had dropped to about 1.2 million by 1952 but climbed steadily thereafter, reaching 2.3 million in the mid-1980s. Of these members, 58 percent were workers; 4.9 percent, farmers; 7.4 percent, salaried employees; 22.3 percent, intellectuals; and the rest, students, the self-employed, pensioners, and homemakers. The proportion of workers was high because the SED wanted to maintain the image of being the party of the proletariat. However, the workers' membership total was inflated because it included those who started out as workers but switched to other professions later on. Among members, men predominated two to one over women. Members and functionaries, of whom 40 percent were under forty, were well educated. More than 30 percent of members had finished their study at a university or technical college, and most functionaries had higher education degrees.[12]

The party was built on a hierarchical structure, operating in theory on the principles of democratic centralism. These included (1) the decisions of higher organs being strictly binding on lower ones, (2) all members of decisionmaking bodies being elected and accountable to their organizations, and (3) party members having to maintain strict discipline (if they were in the minority on a disputed issue, they would have to subordinate their interests to the majority). In practice, elections to the top bodies were not democratic because the top officials selected nominees, a practice that is not restricted to the communist world.

The SED was organized on the territorial-production principle. Three or more members were entitled to form a basic or primary unit (*Grundorganisation*) at their workplace and 150 members or more formed a section. The self-employed, homemakers, and others joined the residential units. The local groups' duties included approving the admission and expulsion of members and raising citizens' ideological consciousness and productivity at work.

The SED had executive committees in the GDR's 263 districts (Kreise) and 15 regions (Bezirke). The committees, whose members were elected from one level below, were large bodies. Thus, small secretariats, headed by first secretaries, took care of the daily tasks and maintained a link to central headquarters. In the regions, the secretaries ensured that national policies were implemented in their districts and encouraged talented and loyal SED officials to seek high party office. The regional organs' first secretaries were national Central Committee members.

In theory, the highest party organ was the national congress, convened once every five years. At a typical congress, delegates listened to the top leaders laud the party's achievements and provide details of the coming five-year economic plan. Then the delegates approved the reports and policy recommendations drafted by the Central Committee and other top organs. The congress, handicapped as a policymaking body by its large size and infrequent meetings, delegated powers to the Central Committee, whose more than two hundred members and candidates it selected.

The Central Committee, meeting twice a year, ratified the senior leaders' policies, elected the party's general secretary and members of the Secretariat and the Politburo, and directed the work of the central state organs and mass organizations, in which were party groups to ensure compliance with Central Committee directives and to monitor the views of state employees and the organizations' members. The eleven-member Secretariat implemented party directives, supervised the two thousand staff employees who worked in various departments, selected party cadres, and prepared the Politburo agenda. As noted earlier, the Politburo, the top party organ, headed by the general secretary and the party's senior officers, was the chief political decisionmaking body in the GDR, unlike in Western parliamentary systems, where the cabinets fulfilled that role. The Politburo's size fluctuated during the GDR era between fourteen and twenty-seven members and candidate members. Meeting weekly, the Politburo discussed issues affecting the party, the government, and the economy and approved the decisions, directives, and orders sent to government and party units.[13]

Conclusion

The evolution of eastern Germany's party system illustrates how an occupation power can shape the politics of a defeated state. Without the Soviet occupation, the zone would not have evolved into a communist state. The Soviet authorities knew, based on German history, that the KPD would never receive a majority in a free election. Thus, KPD leaders, subservient to the Soviets, forced the SPD to merge with the KPD. When even the merger did not produce legislative majorities for the newly created SED, the leaders gave the mass organizations, controlled by them, enough seats in parliaments to produce automatic majorities for the SED.

During this time, the leaders permitted the four bloc parties (Christian, liberal, nationalist, and farmers) to organize. They took this action to (1) legitimize, in their view, a democratic state that allowed noncommunist parties; (2) propagandize the parties' noncommunist members; and (3) gauge the members' support for the regime and the nature of their economic and social concerns. However, the leaders made sure to limit the parties' powers by admitting them into the SED-controlled Democratic Bloc and the

National Front. One specialist notes that it was "rather ironic that the GDR, the state whose chief attribute was monolithic unity, had more parties than the pluralistic Federal Republic of Germany."[14]

From 1949 to 1989, the SED was the dominant political organization in the GDR. As was true of communist parties in the Soviet Union and Eastern European states, but not of parties in Western European states, the SED had total control over the government, the economy, the media, and society. Structurally, the SED was pyramid shaped, with a large base of local branches and a narrow band of policymaking organs at the top—typical also of West German parties. In both states, the party elites made key decisions. However, in the GDR the SED demanded that members maintain strict party discipline or else face a purge, justified under the rubric of "democratic centralism," a condition that did not apply as strictly to West German parties. The communist system would have remained entrenched for a long time but for the aging SED leaders' failure to realize that their opposition to any reform movement, such as Gorbachev's glasnost and perestroika, would contribute to the SED's sudden demise in 1989 as the top political force in the GDR. The following chapter deals with the system's swift decline and the rise of a democratic system.

Notes

1. For a detailed analysis, see Henry Krisch, *German Politics Under Soviet Occupation* (New York: Columbia University Press, 1974), pp. 18–25.

2. Dietrich Staritz, "Zur Entstehung des Parteiensystems der DDR," in *Das Parteiensystem der Bundesrepublik,* ed. Dietrich Staritz (Opladen: Leske und Budrich, 1976), pp. 98–100.

3. Cited in Roderich Kulbach and Helmut Weber, *Parteien im Blocksystem der DDR* (Cologne: Wissenschaft und Politik, 1969), p. 34. See also Arnold J. Heidenheimer, *The Governments of Germany,* 3d ed. (New York: Crowell, 1970), p. 272.

4. Hermann Weber, *DDR: Grundriss der Geschichte, 1945–1990* (Hannover: Fackelträger, 1991), pp. 25–30.

5. In 1949, Parliament consisted of the People's Chamber (Volkskammer) and the Chamber of the Länder. In 1952, the five Länder were abolished, and fifteen districts were created instead. Thereupon the People's Chamber became the sole legislative body.

6. The National Front was formed to serve as the link between state and society, to reduce class differences among citizens, and to foster greater "political and moral unity." It had an organizational network throughout the GDR, which included all

parties and organized groups (Hartmut Zimmermann, ed., *DDR Handbuch,* 3d ed. [Cologne: Wissenschaft und Politik, 1985], vol. 2, pp. 928–929).

7. Henry Krisch, *The German Democratic Republic: The Search for Identity* (Boulder: Westview Press, 1985), pp. 15–18; Henry Ashby Turner Jr., *The Two Germanies Since 1945* (New Haven: Yale University Press, 1987), pp. 98–116.

8. Turner, *The Two Germanies Since 1945,* pp. 175–178; Hermann Weber, "The Socialist Unity Party," in *Honecker's Germany,* ed. David Childs (London: Allen and Unwin, 1985), pp. 2–5.

9. *Dokumente zur Geschichte der SED* (Berlin: Dietz, 1986), vol. 3, p. 98.

10. Ibid.

11. This power was underscored in the revised 1974 GDR constitution, which proclaimed that the state was led by the working class and its Marxist-Leninist party.

12. Gert-Joachim Glaessner, "Der politische Prozess in der DDR," in *Deutschland Handbuch: Eine doppelte Bilanz, 1949–1989,* ed. Werner Weidenfeld and Hartmut Zimmermann (Munich: Hanser, 1989), pp. 517–519; Krisch, *The German Democratic Republic,* pp. 30–31; Mike Dennis, *German Democratic Republic: Politics, Economics, and Society* (London: Pinter, 1988), pp. 79–82.

13. Dennis, *German Democratic Republic,* pp. 82–89; Krisch, *The German Democratic Republic,* pp. 31–35; Eckart Förtsch, *Die SED* (Stuttgart: Kohlhammer, 1969), pp. 34–65.

14. David M. Keithly, *The Collapse of East German Communism: The Year the Wall Came Down, 1989* (Westport, Conn.: Praeger, 1992), p. 19.

• 10 •

The Turbulent Transition,
1989–1990

Dictatorial governments can remain in power for decades. Resistance against their rule may be a moral imperative, but it is dangerous for the average citizen. A dictatorship usually ends abruptly when the power holders are thrown out of office as a result of a war (e.g., Adolf Hitler in Germany) or an armed force rebellion (e.g., António Salazar in Portugal). Rare is the case in which the chief of a monolithic party agrees to a country's transformation into a pluralist democracy (e.g., Mikhail Gorbachev in the Soviet Union). Whether a democratic system emerges or survives in the wake of a major upheaval depends on the historic and political factors shaping each state.

In fall 1989 in Czechoslovakia and the GDR, the end of authoritarian rule assumed a different path: The citizens demonstrated en masse for a democratic political system, and the power holders acceded to their demands. Such peaceful revolutions are infrequent and are not necessarily successful. But in these two instances, the leaders knew that their rule was shaky and that the popular yearning for democracy, which both states had experienced decades earlier, was strong. In the GDR's case, the flourishing democratic system of West Germany served as an additional incentive for citizens to oust the communist rulers.

This chapter examines what happens to a party system in the transition from an authoritarian to a democratic state. In looking at the fate of the old and the new East German parties, we span the spectrum from left to right, beginning with the SED. We must ask whether the sprouting of new parties in the post-Honecker transition months of the GDR paralleled those of new parties in the post-Nazi 1945–1949 transition years of western Germany.

The SED

The crumbling of the strongly entrenched Honecker regime in 1989 came as a complete surprise to nearly all observers. They knew about small opposition groups that, under the aegis of the Protestant churches, had formed to support the international peace movement, improve human rights, and strengthen environmental safeguards. But these 150 groups, with about twenty-five hundred members, were under tight surveillance by the Ministry for State Security. The observers did not know that in 1987 Hans Modrow, then SED chief in Dresden but not a member of the inner circle, canvassed senior leaders to find out whether they would be willing to collectively oust Honecker after his rejection of domestic reforms. Most leaders rebuffed Modrow, fearing that reforms would destabilize the regime and lead to serious economic and social consequences.

Honecker obstinately maintained his hard-line course, even when from late 1988 to late 1989 thousands of members resigned from the party and when, according to one late 1988 poll, 90 percent of the SED's youth members supported Gorbachev's reforms.[1] Popular protests increased during the campaign for the May 1989 local elections. On the announcement that the National Front unity lists had captured nearly 99 percent of the vote, members of civil rights groups who had monitored the election claimed the results a fraud. Many citizens also demanded that in the future several candidates run for each elective post and criticized the shortage of consumer goods, poor medical services, and mounting pollution.[2]

The unraveling of the regime came a few months later. When the Hungarian reform communist government opened its frontiers to Austria on September 11, 1989, thousands of GDR citizens headed for West Germany via Hungary and Austria.[3] In the GDR, new civil rights groups and the SPD organized to force the system's democratization, especially after Gorbachev told SED chiefs on October 7, on the occasion of the fortieth anniversary celebration of the GDR, that they would have to pay a high price if they did not learn the lessons of history and make reforms.

In Leipzig and other cities, thousands of dissatisfied citizens demonstrated spontaneously every week against the Honecker regime. Police and Stasi agents often beat up and arrested some of them, but with little effect on the growing opposition. Honecker apparently ordered combat groups to dissolve a huge demonstration in Leipzig on October 9, but as a result of pressures from the city's SED and church officials, and from Kurt Masur, famous Leipzig conductor, the government backed off. This led throughout the GDR to an even greater escalation of protest demonstrations in which citizens demanded free elections and unrestricted travel abroad.

The Beginning of the End

On October 18, nervous Politburo members forced Honecker to resign as SED general secretary and on October 24 as titular head of state. Politburo member Egon Krenz, who had little support among the rank and file, succeeded Honecker. Krenz, viewed by many members as an opportunist who turned with the wind, now forced the resignation of a few other orthodox party leaders, opened talks with the citizens' group New Forum, removed some restrictions on the media, amnestied arrested demonstrators and citizens who had tried to leave the GDR illegally, and promised free elections in 1990. The swift change in the SED did not appease the restless masses. On November 4, hundreds of thousands of demonstrators in East Berlin called for an end to the oppressive system. Their dislike of the SED chiefs was intensified by media revelations about the numerous special privileges (villas, automobiles, hunting grounds) that the chiefs had enjoyed and the widespread corruption among them. In one instance, the chiefs had siphoned off church funds, under the pretext of "church building," for the construction of their private villas.

Several days after the mass demonstrations, all Council of Ministers and Politburo members resigned. Modrow, honest and less compromised by his past than Krenz, was elected, in an unprecedented secret vote, new chairman (prime minister) of the Council of Ministers. Krenz, however, remained general secretary of a smaller Politburo and titular head of state. On November 9, the GDR borders to West Berlin and West Germany were opened, and millions of citizens poured across the breached Wall for a look at the FRG that most had not been allowed to visit since 1961.

In the following weeks, the SED Central Committee issued an action program, which specified that future elections in the GDR would be free and secret. The People's Chamber (the unicameral legislature) struck out of the GDR constitution the clause heralding "the leading role of the working class and its Marxist-Leninist SED." The legislature also established a special commission to investigate cases of corruption by former SED leaders, which led to the SED Central Committee expelling Honecker, Willi Stoph (former head of the Council of Ministers), and ten other top leaders. Two of them (Günter Mittag and Harry Tisch), along with others, were taken into custody and charged with abuse of office, corruption, and gross negligence.[4]

On December 3, in the wake of charges against high SED functionaries, the second group of Central Committee and Politburo members tendered their resignation. Krenz gave up his posts as general secretary and chief of state, and in January he was expelled from the SED. Later he admitted meekly that during the Honecker era he had been less courageous than others in not questioning the party's undemocratic practices.

From the SED to the PDS

On December 9 and 10, a special SED conference was called to decide whether the decimated party should be disbanded or reconstituted. A majority of delegates chose to maintain the party, but with drastic structural and ideological changes. They decided to abandon democratic centralism and abolish the Politburo and the Central Committee. They elected as chairman Gregor Gysi, an SED lawyer who had had contacts with opposition groups during the communist period, had defended dissidents, and was not too closely identified with the discredited regime. The charismatic and charming speaker apologized to the delegates for the past "failures and mistakes" of SED officials and announced that a new party statute would be drafted after consultations with the party's political base.

One week later, the party conference resumed its deliberations. In a brief speech, Honecker admitted to personal responsibility for the country's crisis but denied any wrongdoing. In a major address, Gysi said that the party had to choose democratic socialism as the alternative to Stalinism and capitalism. It should uphold pluralism, tolerance, and civil liberties but oppose capitalist monopolies and transnational corporations. He urged the party to support the positive aspects of communism and social democracy (the utopia of the classless society) and pacifism. As a symbol of the new beginning, the delegates renamed the party SED-PDS.

In February 1990, party officials dropped the name SED. But the change in name could not staunch the rapid loss of members. In December 1989, the party still had 1,780,000 members; by February 1990 more than 1 million had resigned. Nevertheless, the PDS managed to capture 16.4 percent of the vote in the first free election of the People's Chamber on March 18, 1990 (see Table 10.1). The party mustered the support of the old cadres, public servants who feared a loss of jobs, and intellectuals who still dreamed of socialism. Thereafter, with unification approaching, PDS leaders warned about the economic costs to the FRG if the GDR was annexed and about the capitalist state's exploitation of workers.[5]

The New (and Old) Party Landscape

Alliance 90

Before late 1989, the numerous small GDR peace, human rights, and ecology groups, which had formed in the mid-1980s under the Protestant churches' protection, could not coalesce into a united opposition for fear of

TABLE 10.1 East German People's Chamber Election Results, 1990

Party	Percent	Seats
Alliance for Germany		
CDU	40.8	163
DSU	6.3	25
Democratic Awakening	0.9	4
SPD	21.9	88
PDS	16.4	66
League of Free Democrats	5.3	21
Alliance 90	2.9	12
Democratic Farmers Party	2.2	9
Greens and Independent Women's Association	2.0	8
National Democratic Party	0.4	2
Democratic Women's League	0.3	1
United Left	0.2	1
Other	0.4	–
Total	100	400

SOURCE: Statistisches Amt der DDR, *Statistisches Jahrbuch der DDR '90* (Berlin: Rudolf Haufe Verlag, 1990), p. 449 (final figures).

being crushed by the still-powerful SED regime. But they all demanded that the GDR transform itself from rigid "real" socialism to democratic socialism.

In addition, new leftist groups and parties emerged once the SED's popularity plummeted. Whether new or old, they were the ones that sparked the peaceful revolution in October and November 1989. Thereafter they participated in roundtable discussions with government representatives. If they registered as political parties, rather than remain grassroots organizations, they could take part in the new electoral politics. Many formed alliances to strengthen their position before the March 1990 legislative election. Alliance 90, the strongest, linked three groups: New Forum, Democracy Now, and Initiative for Peace and Human Rights.

New Forum was led by, among others, painter Bärbel Bohley; dissident Robert Havemann's widow, Katja Havemann; defense lawyer Rolf Henrich (who, after writing a critical book on the SED, had been expelled from the party); and molecular biologist Jens Reich. In October, New Forum issued an appeal, which was signed swiftly by at least one hundred thousand citizens, calling on sympathizers to join the organization and begin a democratic dialogue on key societal issues. New Forum viewed itself as a countercultural and grassroots citizens' movement rather than a political movement, which turned out to be its weakness. Nevertheless, in late January 1990 it also organized as a party to participate in the coming election. Factionalism rent the party: A Berlin minority group, demanding the GDR's preservation as a democratic socialist system, was pitted against a primarily southern group, demanding a united neocapitalist Germany. The two factions arrived at a compromise by calling for a slower pace toward unification and for the preservation of the GDR's social system.

The second Alliance 90 group, Democracy Now, was also led by intellectuals, such as Ulrike Poppe, cofounder of the group Women for Peace, and church historian Wolfgang Ullmann. Their views did not differ from those of New Forum founders, but personal conflicts between the two groups prevented an early merger. The third Alliance 90 group, Initiative for Peace and Human Rights, had already been founded in 1985. Members of the initiative, which served as a watchdog organization of human rights violations during the SED era, had been harassed, arrested, and sent into exile. In fall 1989, the members, organized into small policy-oriented groups, demanded the system's democratization. The three Alliance 90 groups mustered a total of only 2.9 percent in the March election and received twelve seats in the People's Chamber. (The 5 percent minimum to gain seats did not apply.)

Another leftist alliance, concluded in February 1990, linked the newly formed Green Party and the Independent Women's Association (UFV). The Green Party, which had emerged out of the environmental movement, called in its electoral program for pollution safeguards, expanded women's rights, the SED regime's elimination, and a German confederation. The UFV, founded on December 3, 1989, opened its ranks to women of all parties who supported women's rights and quotas for women in politics. Soon after the March election, in which the alliance received 2 percent of the votes, the UFV left the alliance, charging that the Greens had not honored their pledge to grant one-third of the alliance seats to its candidates.

Other small parties and temporary alliances formed: a Trotskyist party, the Communist Party of Germany, the Alternative Youth List, the Democratic Women's League, and the Action Alliance United Left/Carnations. Among them, the most prominent was the United Left, which was founded on October 2, 1989, and consisted of anarchists, autonomists, and small factory and student groups championing a radical, grassroots, democratic socialist system.[6]

The Social Democratic Party

On October 7, 1989, after preliminary meetings and consultations, forty-three dissidents, including many pastors, academics, and students, met covertly to organize the Social Democratic Party of the GDR. They deliberately adopted the initials SDP in order not to be identified too closely with the West German SPD but in January 1990 changed SDP to SPD (GDR). A lack of workers and salaried employees in the organizing group indicated a weakness in coming free elections. As was true of other party activists, the SDP organizers were overworked and lacked sufficient office space, telephones, mimeograph machines, access to the media, and funds. In the course of time, the SPD in Bonn came to the rescue, which in turn led to worry among SDP officials that their new party was losing its freedom of action.

The SDP recruited about fifteen thousand members by December 1989. Membership rose swiftly thereafter but then settled at about twenty-five thousand in summer 1990. At a conference in January 1990, the party discussed its organizational structure and agreed on a programmatic plank urging slow unification of the two Germanys. One month later, party convention delegates elected Ibrahim Böhme, a former teacher, as chairman. (In April, he resigned when the newsmagazine *Der Spiegel* alleged that he had once been an informant for Stasi.) The convention delegates also accepted a new party statute and basic program, which did not contain the term "socialism" in the party's goals. After the bitter experience of the GDR's command economy, which had discredited the concept of socialism, the SPD (GDR) officials did not want to publicly identify themselves with the term.

The officials were reluctant to enter into an electoral alliance with the citizens' initiative groups (earlier efforts had failed). Thus, the party fought its own campaign, which became bitter when the East German CDU accused the SPD's predecessor of having voluntarily merged with the SED in 1946 and thereby having been largely responsible for the SED regime. The SPD (GDR) vehemently denied this charge. Taking the counteroffensive, it denounced the East German CDU for having been a lackey of the SED throughout the GDR era. In the March 1990 election for the People's Chamber, the SPD had hoped to capture a plurality of the vote, partly because eastern Germany had historically been its stronghold. It fared poorly, however, mustering only 21.9 percent, primarily from well-educated, middle-class, urban citizens but not from the majority of workers, who, voting CDU, wanted a speedy unification.

On Böhme's resignation, Markus Meckel, a Protestant pastor, took over as acting chairman. In June, party delegates chose Wolfgang Thierse as the new chairman. He had been on the staff of two GDR government agencies and had taught at Humboldt University. In the new FRG, he has risen swiftly in the party, becoming one of the deputy chairpersons in the united SPD. The historic joining together of SPD (GDR) and SPD (FRG) occurred in late September 1990, a few days before the two states merged.[7]

The Liberal Bloc

The Liberal Democratic Party of Germany, one of the major bloc parties, had more of a problem than the East German CDU (another major bloc party) in shedding its past. The middle-class LDPD, with about 110,000 members, gave up its support for the SED only in December 1989 and did not meet until February 1990 to reorganize. At a special convention, delegates shortened the party's name to the Liberal Democratic Party (LDP). Chairman Manfred Gerlach, who had been a loyal ally of the SED until a year before the upheaval, did not stand for reelection. Rainer Ortleb, a mathematics professor and Rostock LDPD member since 1968 and district head since 1987, succeeded Gerlach. One specialist aptly commented: "Like so many others inside and outside the party, he had apparently found ritual ways of accommodating himself within the old socialist system. Compared to Gerlach, he seemed like a fresh voice without close and disqualifying ties to the old powerholders."[8] (Yet in 1993, when Ortleb was minister of education in Bonn, *Der Spiegel* revealed that he had once been a staunch supporter of the SED regime. He denied the charge but was eventually replaced as minister.[9])

In late January 1990, dissident LDPD members and other liberals formed two new rival parties; the German Forum Party and the East German Free Democratic Party (FDP). The Forum Party was founded by Jürgen Schmieder of Chemnitz, a patent engineer who had been active in New Forum. When he could not forge unity among the diverse Forum Party factions, which had emerged primarily in Saxony and East Berlin, he resigned in May and was replaced by a liberal leader from East Berlin. The East German CDU and the LDP both courted the new party before the March election; it opted for the liberal bloc.

East German liberal leaders organized the FDP (GDR) in December 1989. The West German FDP threw its support behind the new organization rather than the LDPD, which was still clinging to its past as a bloc party. The East German FDP, formally incorporated as a party in early February 1990, viewed itself as the programmatic counterpart of the West German FDP, but its late entry into politics accounted for its low two thousand to three thousand membership.

The three rival liberal parties—LDP, German Forum Party, and East German FDP—formed an alliance, the League of Free Democrats, to enhance their electoral support. The alliance received full backing from the West German FDP, which sent its most prominent politicians, campaign workers, technical equipment, and advertising posters and other promotional materials to help in the March campaign. The alliance gained only 5.3 percent of the vote and did not survive the election.

Thereupon a new alliance was created between the two former bloc parties, the LDP and NDPD. The NDPD, which at its peak in 1953 had 233,000 middle-class conservative members, sought to shore up its weakened organization after a disastrous showing of 0.4 percent in the March election. The strategy paid off: The new alliance received 6.6 percent in the May local elections.

In preparation for a unified Germany and the first all-German election in October, the West German FDP and the rival East German liberal parties merged at a special convention in Hannover on August 11 and 12, 1990. The merger brought 136,000 East German and 66,000 West German members into the new FDP. However, the West German FDP held the most important leadership positions. East German leaders, aware that their lack of experience did not entitle them to full representation in the top FDP organs, nevertheless resented being swallowed up by the more powerful and wealthy Bonn party.[10] Leaders of other East German parties had similar experiences.

The Christian Democratic Union

The East German CDU, founded in 1945, was one of the four bloc parties that blindly followed SED dictates during the GDR era. Few CDU members dared protest the collaborationist role of their party before 1989. But in early September of that year, a reform group urged a greater independent role for the party. In November, the group forced longtime CDU chairman Gerald Götting out of office.

Lothar de Maizière, a member of the CDU since age sixteen, replaced Götting. De Maizière had started his career as a professional viola player but then became a lawyer, who defended a few political dissidents accused of violating GDR laws. He had also been vice president of the Synod of the Association of Protestant Churches and a member of the CDU Committee on Church Affairs. Because he had supported efforts at political reform and had not been a tool of the SED (or so it was assumed at the time until his connections to Stasi were revealed), he was confirmed as party chairman at a special convention in December. His earlier appointment as deputy chairman of the Council of Ministers also increased his political visibility.

The reformed party viewed itself in late 1989 as a conservative people's party with a Christian profile, although it briefly supported democratic socialism. It also proposed that in the spirit of federalism the former GDR Länder be reestablished. In November, the CDU called for a confederation of the two German states, but when the demonstrators in the cities changed their slogans from "We are the people" to "We are one people," the CDU—and the Kohl government in Bonn—joined the bandwagon for speedy unification.[11] The radical switch in position resulted from the East German citizens' worry that a postcommunist GDR would be too weak economically. They preferred to share quickly in the prosperity of their fellow West Germans.

Initially, Kohl hesitated to back the East German CDU because of its previous status as an SED satellite and because several of its top leaders still lauded the SED's socialist achievements of full employment and public housing. But faced by the possibility that the newly formed SPD might win the People's Chamber election, Kohl put the resources of the West German CDU at the disposal of de Maizière's party. Kohl was gratified by the results: The East German CDU won a plurality of 40.9 percent, including a slim majority of votes of blue-collar workers.[12] The East German CDU merged with its West German counterpart at a unification conference on October 1 and 2, 1990, on the eve of the GDR accession to the FRG.

Democratic Awakening

The East German CDU was the major conservative party in the rapidly evolving party system. One smaller party, which changed ideology, emerged on its periphery. East German theologians, who had called on the SED regime to liberalize its policies since 1988, issued a call in June 1989, when Honecker was still in full control, for those sympathetic to their position to organize a new party, Democratic Awakening (DA). In late October at a national founding conference, delegates from various church groups, representing about six thousand members, agreed on a program to support democratic socialism, economic reforms, and environmentalism. They elected as chairman Wolfgang Schnur, a Protestant church lawyer from Rostock who had defended conscientious objectors and other dissidents. Schnur's commitment to democratic socialism was short-lived. Supported by pastor Rainer Eppelmann, Schnur led a conservative pro–free enterprise faction that sought close contacts with the West German CDU. The left wing, in the minority, called for an independent democratic and socialist GDR.

In mid-December, the majority of delegates at the first DA convention, attended by prominent West German CDU chiefs, approved a liberal-conservative program that emphasized a social free market economy in a united Germany. Thereupon the left-wing founders and about twenty thousand members (one-third of the total) resigned, most of them joining the East German SPD. DA suffered another blow when Schnur quit as chairman before the March 1990 election after he had been unmasked as a Stasi informant.[13] He was replaced by Eppelmann, by then a minister in the Modrow cabinet. To survive in the competitive party system, Democratic Awakening joined the CDU-dominated Alliance for Germany before the March election. In August 1990, with ranks depleted, DA merged with the CDU.

The Democratic Farmers Party and the German Social Union

Since 1948, the SED had received loyal support from the Democratic Farmers Party (DBD). The bloc party, which had 115,000 members in 1987, severed its links to the SED only at the end of 1989 and early 1990. In a new incarnation, the DBD attempted to recruit conservative farmers by pledging to sustain a pluralist system, a free economy, and unification. But its electoral support shrank steadily during the GDR elections of 1990 as most farmers voted for the CDU. On June 26, the DBD merged with the CDU, enriching it by about thirty thousand members.[14]

The German Social Union (DSU), founded in January 1990, amalgamated about a dozen small conservative and Christian parties and groups. Headed by Hans-Wilhelm Ebeling, a church rector in Leipzig, it hoped to rally not only conservative farmers but also blue-collar workers, soldiers, and others. Ebeling, politically moderate, favored an alliance with the West German CDU and CSU, but right-wing populist Hansjoachim Walther, later chairman, favored an alliance solely with the CSU. When Walther's faction, with strength in southern Saxony and Thuringia, won out, the West German CDU did not support the new party, except to let it enter into an electoral alliance in the March election. Instead, the Bavarian CSU, eager to court the ultraconservative citizens in the GDR, generously aided the DSU. The East German party, with thirty-five thousand to fifty thousand members, received 6.3 percent in the March election. But when its vote dipped to 3.4 percent in the May local elections, its prospects in a united Germany looked grim, especially as the Republicans, newly established in the GDR, became the competitor for right-wing votes. (The People's Chamber forbade the Republicans, because of their right-wing ideology, to run candidates in the March election, but the party, after winning a court appeal, was free to resume its electoral activities a few months thereafter.[15])

The Alliance for Germany

East German CDU leaders looked for electoral allies to shore up the conservative parties' prospects in the March election. On February 5, 1990, they formed the Alliance for Germany with Democratic Awakening and the DSU. The DSU joined because it had a late start as a party, and DA joined because it was dependent on CDU funds. To preserve each party's profile and ideological differences, alliance leaders let each one have its own electoral slate rather than a joint list, only too reminiscent of SED bloc parties' practice. The alliance scored an unexpected victory (48.1 percent) in the March election, showing the voters' preference for quick unification. Yet soon thereafter, the alliance broke apart when the DSU bowed out after shifting toward the extremist right.[16]

The Democratization of the Government

December 1989 marked the government's transition to democracy, paralleling earlier changes in the party system. The government organs assumed executive powers once held by the SED. Prime Minister Hans Modrow presided over a caretaker government, the twenty-eight-member Council of Ministers, which consisted of nineteen members of the SED and nine of the bloc parties but none as yet of the newly founded democratic parties. Many members were still of the old guard but realized that the SED regime's collapse meant that they had to support free elections and a competitive party system.

At the insistence of seven new opposition parties and groups, which wanted a dialogue with, and some control over, the five government parties (the SED-PDS and the four bloc parties), the Council of Ministers on December 7 convened the first of many roundtables. (Similar roundtables were established in towns and cities, districts, and regions.) The government, on one side, and the opposition parties and groups, on the other side, had equal representation, with church delegates chairing and mediating the meetings. The representatives, who had been appointed by their respective parties or groups, discussed urgent matters, such as the need for a new security service to replace Stasi, the draft of a new constitution, and the date for the next free election of the People's Chamber. The representatives had no legislative powers, which were reserved to the People's Chamber, but they were in effect able to veto government decisions.

The roundtable lost most of its functions on February 5, 1990, when Modrow, forced to make concessions to the new noncommunist parties, formed a "government of national responsibility," which included most of their representatives. The roundtable members nevertheless continued to meet, using their forum as a policy-advising instrument; indeed, as a parallel government. Thus, eager to maintain a modicum of independence for East Germany, they criticized the West German parties' massive aid to their East German counterparts, voted against letting West Germans speak at East German campaign rallies, called for the preservation of the social achievements of the GDR, approved a new constitution for the GDR, and opted for a slow path to reunification.[17]

After the March election, de Maizière (CDU) formed a new government. He set up a grand coalition of the CDU, the SPD, the League of Free Democrats, the DSU, and DA to spread responsibility widely and to have a two-thirds majority to amend the constitution (e.g., to reorganize the fifteen districts into five Länder). The PDS and small leftist parties went into parliamentary opposition. In summer, the League of Free Democrats and the SPD, after policy disputes with the CDU, quit the government. De Maizière remained head of a minority government until unification day on October 3, when all East German institutions ended their independent existence.

Conclusion

A peaceful revolution of the people led to the fall of the authoritarian SED regime and its replacement by a democratic system. During the transition period from late 1989 to unification day, ideologically diverse groups and parties mushroomed, each seeking space in a crowded political landscape. They had been preceded by the emergence of small, leftist citizens' groups in the mid-1980s, at a time when the SED and Stasi were still powerful. The leaders of the new and old citizens' groups and new parties sparked the mass demonstrations against the regime—a testimony to how a few courageous individuals can shape history. Their democratic ideas, bottled up for such a long time in a one-party dominant state, caught the imagination of others.

In late 1989 and early 1990, many of the groups organized into parties to participate in the emerging democratic parliamentary system. The parties in the CDU/CSU-dominated Alliance for Germany and in the FDP-dominated League of Free Democrats gained the support of a majority of GDR voters in the 1990 elections. These voters opted for the free enterprise system because they had been frustrated by the discredited SED command economy and were beguiled by Kohl's promises of an economic miracle in a unified state. The SPD, PDS, Alliance 90, Greens, and UVF gained the support of a minority of voters, who in most instances favored democratic socialism, which they viewed as a viable alternative to the GDR's real socialism and the FRG's neocapitalism. Paradoxically, the citizens' groups, such as New Forum, which had sparked the democratic revolution, were the losers in the tough political struggles. As movements, rather than as parties, they had wanted to preserve a democratic GDR. History passed them by.

A parallel existed between the post-Hitler 1945–1949 transition years of western Germany and the post-Honecker transition months of 1989–1990. During the two periods, numerous new parties, ranging from left to right, emerged. However, the weaker ones were not represented, or hardly, in the new parliaments and disappeared or maintained a marginal existence. In the post-Hitler period, it took years before the party system in the FRG assumed its present configuration; in the post-Honecker period, the pace of events was so swift that the party system had only months to develop before it was engulfed by the West German juggernaut.

Notes

1. Leipzig Institute for Youth Research poll; cited in Henry Krisch, "From SED to PDS: The Struggle to Revive a Left Party," in *The New Germany Votes: Unification and the Creation of the New German Party System,* ed. Russell J. Dalton (Providence, R.I.: Berg, 1993), p. 167.

2. Dieter Grosser, "The Dynamics of German Reunification," in *German Unification: The Unexpected Challenge,* ed. Dieter Grosser (Oxford: Berg, 1992), pp. 12–13. See also Michael G. Huelshoff and Arthur M. Hanhardt Jr., "Steps Toward Union: The Collapse of the GDR and the Unification of Germany," in *German Unification: Process and Outcomes,* ed. M. Donald Hancock and Helga A. Welsh (Boulder: Westview Press, 1994), pp. 73–91.

3. For a chronology of events, see Hermann Weber, *DDR: Grundriss der Geschichte, 1945–1990* (Hannover: Fackelträger, 1991), pp. 343–353.

4. In March 1991, Honecker fled to the Soviet Union. In November 1992, he was charged with manslaughter for ordering, as party general secretary, the shootings of East Germans trying to flee over the Wall. He returned to Berlin to face trial, but the court halted the proceedings in January 1993 when Honecker became too sick to stand further trial. In May 1994, he died of cancer in Chile (*New York Times,* May 30, 31, 1994).

5. David M. Keithly, *The Collapse of East German Communism: The Year the Wall Came Down, 1989* (Westport, Conn.: Praeger, 1992), pp. 214–216; Thomas Ammer, "Die Parteien in der DDR und in den neuen Bundesländern," in *Parteien in der Bundesrepublik Deutschland,* ed. Alf Mintzel and Heinrich Oberreuter (Opladen: Leske und Budrich, 1992), pp. 432–460.

6. Michaela W. Richter, "Exiting the GDR: Political Movements and Parties Between Democratization and Westernization," in *German Unification,* ed. Hancock and Welsh, pp. 105–106; Gerard Braunthal, "An Analysis of the German Elections of 1990," *Politics and Society in Germany, Austria and Switzerland* 5 (1993): 33.

7. For details of the SPD (GDR), see Gerard Braunthal, *The German Social Democrats Since 1969: A Party in Power and Opposition,* 2d ed. (Boulder: Westview Press, 1994), pp. 27–44; Gero Neugebauer, "Die SDP/SPD in der DDR: Zur Geschichte und Entwicklung einer unvollendeten Partei," in *Parteien und Wähler im Umbruch: Parteiensystem und Wählerverhalten in der ehemaligen DDR und den neuen Bundesländern,* ed. Oskar Niedermayer and Richard Stöss (Opladen: Westdeutscher Verlag, 1994), pp. 75–104.

8. Christian Søe, "Unity and Victory for the German Liberals: Little Party, What Now?" in *The New Germany Votes,* ed. Dalton, p. 110.

9. *Der Spiegel,* August 23, 1993, pp. 44–47.

10. Søe, "Unity and Victory for the German Liberals," pp. 110–118; Thomas Pfau, "Aspekte der Entwicklung liberaler Kräfte in der DDR vom Herbst 1989 bis zum Herbst 1990," in *Parteien und Wähler im Umbruch,* ed. Niedermayer and Stöss, pp. 105–112.

11. Ute Schmidt, "Transformation einer Volkspartei—Die CDU im Prozess der deutschen Vereinigung," in *Parteien und Wähler im Umbruch,* ed. Niedermayer and Stöss, pp. 37–74.

12. David P. Conradt, "The Christian Democrats in 1990: Saved by Unification?" in *The New Germany Votes,* ed. Dalton, p. 65.

13. Richter, "Exiting the GDR," pp. 106–107.

14. Ammer, "Die Parteien in der DDR und in den neuen Bundesländern," pp. 470–471.

15. Gert-Joachim Glaessner, "Parties and the Problems of Governance During Unification," in *German Unification,* ed. Hancock and Welsh, pp. 146–147, 150–151.

16. Richter, "Exiting the GDR," pp. 121–122; Glaessner, "Parties and the Problems of Governance During Unification," p. 147.

17. Uwe Thaysen, "The GDR on Its Way to Democracy," in *German Unification,* ed. Grosser, pp. 73–86.

PART FOUR

Parties in the Unified Germany

• 11 •

The First Three Years

T HE ACCESSION OF THE German Democratic Republic to the Federal Republic on October 3, 1990, marked a milestone in German history and led to the transformation of the party system. The eastern and western parties, with the exception of the Greens and the PDS, had already merged before unification. The Greens in the FRG and GDR had agreed not to merge until after the first all-German election of the Bundestag on December 2, 1990, to let the eastern Greens freely develop at their own pace without western Green influence. The PDS had no West German counterpart; thus the question of a merger or of western dominance—evident among the CDU, SPD, and FDP—was moot.

This chapter deals with the new party system, which quickly took on the coloration of the West German system, from October 1990 to the end of 1993. The period was highlighted by the first all-German election of 1990, the resultant increase in the number of parties that won representation in the Bundestag, and the parties' confrontation with internal changes and the state's postunification problems.

In surveying party developments from 1990 to 1993, we must ask whether one democratic state (in this instance, western Germany) was able to successfully transplant its multiparty system to a postcommunist state (eastern Germany) that had once had a monolithic party system (but with a multiparty facade). If the answer is positive, then we may assume that the new system will be a mirror of the old FRG system; if negative, we must ask what the impediments were to transplantation.

The 1990 Election Campaign

No doubt, the eastern Germans had difficulty coping psychologically with the rapid political changes, already evident during the transition era before unification. Many resented the blatant intrusion of most western German parties, which, as noted in Chapter 10, provided massive speaker, organizational, and financial assistance to their eastern counterparts. Eastern Germans, obviously with exceptions, viewed the western blitz as too intrusive. Not having enjoyed democratic freedoms since 1933, they would have preferred changing their own institutions and political culture at their own pace and with less interference from the western Germans.

However, in the months before unification conservative and liberal party leaders in the FRG and GDR favored a swift unification under Article 23 of the Basic Law. This article stipulates that new Länder (created in eastern Germany in October 1990) had the right to accede to the FRG. The leaders said that accession would be the quickest way to achieve German unification and lead to stability in a period of swift change. In response, leaders of the SPD, Greens, PDS, and small leftist parties argued that Article 23 in effect would lead to an FRG annexation of the GDR. Calling for a different route to unification, they preferred a later merger of the two states under Article 146 of the Basic Law, which provides for a popular referendum on replacing the Basic Law with a new constitution. Such a procedure would allow time for discussion in a constituent assembly as to which GDR institutions, such as its comprehensive social welfare network, could be preserved. The leftist leaders called in vain for a referendum in the FRG and GDR on the question of whether Article 23 or 146 should prevail.

The parties thereupon quarreled over the dates of unification and the all-German election and over the politically sensitive question of whether the West German electoral law should apply unchanged to the national election. On the latter issue, the small East German parties, knowing that they would not obtain the minimum 5 percent of the vote in western Germany, opposed the law's applicability. One West German political scientist, supporting their views, wrote that the dispute showed the West German parties' quest for dominance by setting an "unconditional surrender mood" in their relations with East German parties.[1]

To defuse the East German parties' opposition, Minister of the Interior for the FRG Wolfgang Schäuble (CDU), chairman of a newly appointed commission, proposed to make one exception to the existing law. Small parties could form joint lists with bigger parties to surmount the electoral barrier. The proposal would have meant, for instance, that the DSU in East Germany could "piggyback" with the Bavarian CSU. The PDS, aware that it could not form a joint list with any major party, opposed Schäuble's proposal. The West German Greens, sympathetic to the PDS position, requested the West German Constitutional Court in Karlsruhe to rule on the CDU proposal's constitutionality.

On September 29, the court, supporting the PDS and Greens position, said that the proposed law would discriminate against small parties that were unable to find a major party as electoral partner. Therefore, the law violated the principles of an equal vote for all citizens and an equal opportunity for all parties. The court urged the Bundestag to enact a law stipulating that East German parties needed to obtain the minimum 5 percent of the votes only in the new Länder (the former GDR)—and to include a similar provision for West German parties in the old Länder (FRG)—to be represented in the new all-German Bundestag. The West German Parliament complied but added a provision that the law was applicable only to the 1990 election and not thereafter. The new law helped the PDS and Alliance 90/Greens gain Bundestag seats, but not the DSU and the western Greens, whose vote did not reach 5 percent.

The interparty disputes before the December election made campaign planning uncertain. In early summer, the East German party managers had to prepare first for the legislative elections in the newly created Länder, scheduled for October 14, less than two weeks after unification day. On election day, the eastern German CDU, repeating its March triumph in the People's Chamber election, won a majority vote in Saxony and pluralities in Mecklenburg-Pomerania, Saxony-Anhalt, and Thuringia. As a consequence, the CDU formed governments in the four Länder. De Maizière, the eastern CDU chief, hailed the results as a vindication of his party's call for swift unification and as a "final farewell to the centralism of the Communist regime."[2] The SPD's sole victory was in Brandenburg, where it formed the government.

The CDU/CSU and FDP on the Offensive

Once the national election campaign moved into high gear after the October Länder elections in the former GDR, party managers had to tailor their efforts to each part of Germany.[3] The CDU campaign centered on Chancellor Kohl's support of swift unification and his pledge that the government would fully support efforts at economic recovery in the new Länder. Imitating U.S. president George Bush, Kohl made a "read my lips" promise that the government would not increase taxes to help finance the recovery. Rather, he said, the government would make greater outlays through temporary budget deficits, to be offset by selective tax cuts in fields not related to economic recovery. He also expected private western companies to invest in former GDR state enterprises.

In the usual campaign ritual, CDU officials assailed the SPD for not shedding its socialist goals and for making a pre-1989 rapprochement with Eastern European communist governments rather than with their freedom movements. Cleverly, the CDU equated the SPD's democratic socialism with the GDR's real socialism. Such statements hardly differed from CDU claims made in earlier West German campaigns, but in 1990 the CDU managers played up to the eastern German voters' disillusionment with the socialism they had experienced while trying to arouse their nascent nationalist feelings ("Germany is our fatherland; Europe is our future").

The CDU and the CSU wooed the same conservative constituency in eastern Germany, unlike in western Germany, where they had a long-standing accord that the CDU campaigned in all Länder except Bavaria and the CSU only in Bavaria. In Bonn, tensions developed between Kohl and Theo Waigel, CSU chairman and federal finance minister, who attempted to shore up the faltering, ultraconservative DSU and thereby take potential votes away from the CDU.

The FDP, eager to form another governing coalition with the CDU/CSU in Bonn, hoped to attract the large liberal vote in eastern Germany. There the popular FRG foreign minister Hans-Dietrich Genscher (FDP) capitalized on his being a native citizen. In Halle, where he was born, French, British, and Soviet foreign ministers, whom he had invited for politically convenient sightseeing tours of the city, accompanied him on separate visits.[4] Count Otto von Lambsdorff, FDP chairman since 1988, emphasized in his campaign speeches the FDP's competence in foreign policies, its opposition to any tax increases, and its proposal, at variance with the CDU/CSU's, to give East Germans tax easements during the transition period.

The SPD on the Defensive

Oskar Lafontaine, the SPD candidate for the chancellor post, spearheaded the party's campaign but did not give the voters a positive vision of a unified Germany. He ran a negative campaign in which he predicted that Kohl would break his promise to minimize the population's financial burdens to assist eastern Germany. Lafontaine's prediction proved to be true in 1991, when Kohl announced that higher taxes would be imposed. But the SPD leader did not realize that in late 1990 the voters, euphoric over unification, wanted an upbeat message rather than a reminder of upcoming financial and economic hardships.

Lafontaine and other top SPD officials raised other issues—a liberalized abortion law, an eventual end to nuclear energy, child-care reforms, and structural changes in the economy to minimize unemployment—that normally would have aroused discussion during a campaign. But in 1990 the focus was almost exclusively on unification, and the SPD could hardly take credit for that when it had opposed the government's decision to take the speedy Article 23 route.

The costly campaign ran into difficulties in eastern Germany, where the SPD had only a rudimentary organization. Many former GDR citizens, convinced by the CDU propaganda, identified the SPD with socialism, even with the discredited SED-inspired ideology. Therefore, some of the SPD campaign activists were harassed, such as a Hesse shop councillor who, having volunteered to put up placards in Thuringia, kept being called a "red pig."[5]

Left and Right Parties

The western Greens also tried to convince voters, and even the majority of their own members who favored unification, that the party's opposition to a speedy unification was motivated by a genuine concern for the eastern Germans' inability to shape their own destiny. The Greens accused the Kohl government of turning the former GDR into a "banana" or "deutsche mark" republic, a mere appendage of the Federal Republic. They prophesied that a unified Germany would increase its economic might on the continent and would witness a mounting nationalism and racism within its borders.

The Greens faced electoral handicaps. The long-smoldering internal rift between the pragmatic Realos and the radical Fundis continued (see Chapter 7). In Hamburg, the radical Greens defected to the PDS before the election. The Greens' best-known leaders, such as Petra Kelly and Antje Vollmer, could not become candidates again because the party, in an effort to prevent encrustation in office, prohibited its deputies from running for reelection.

In most of the new Länder, the Alliance 90 and the Greens had campaigned separately in the March 1990 People's Chamber election. For the all-German election, they formed a new electoral organization, Alliance 90/Greens, to increase their chance of getting a 5 percent minimum vote. The alliance leaders, echoing western Green leaders, criticized the hasty *Anschluss* (annexation) of the GDR to the FRG. They warned about pending economic hardships, which would prevent the restructuring of an ecologically sound economy. They favored greater democracy in society, a minimum income for all residents, affordable rents, sufficient child-care facilities, gender equality, civil rights safeguards, integration of minorities, dissolution of secret police units, and Germany's demilitarization.

The PDS had its own ticket in eastern Germany but in western Germany allied itself with communist and other leftist groups and individuals under the rubric "Left List." The PDS faced its own set of handicaps. Unable to shake off its SED past, the PDS was vulnerable to media reports about the many members who had been Stasi agents and about the PDS treasurer smuggling SED funds out of the country to prevent their seizure by the government. In response to the latter report, the PDS Executive Committee announced that an independent commission would check the party's finances and that a public trustee would be given all PDS assets, except those needed to meet the party's liabilities and to fund its political activities.

Despite, or perhaps because of, the party's numerous difficulties, its chief, Gysi, became a media star. In his speeches, laced with humor and brilliance, he once again, as in the March 1990 campaign, told his listeners that the PDS provided the third way between capitalism and the GDR's state socialism. He denounced the CDU/CSU, FDP, and SPD for their defamatory statements that the PDS was but a disguised SED. He said that in 1989 the West German CDU/CSU and FDP had made the collaborationist East German CDU and LDPD respectable, but only when they had chosen the capitalist system.[6]

In 1990, the right-wing Republicans faced numerous problems, which reduced their electoral threat. Franz Schönhuber, party chief, was expelled briefly from the faction-ridden organization but then was reelected chairman. Once the ban against the party had been lifted in the GDR, the party officials attempted to strengthen their weak eastern organization, having only twenty-eight hundred members (in West Germany, membership was stagnating at twenty-three thousand). The officials also continued their national campaign against foreigners and against Soviet and U.S. troops stationed on German soil. Taking a nationalist stance, Schönhuber warned that eastern Germany must not become a "Coca-Cola republic." The party put up posters captioned "The boat is full," picturing foreigners packed into one small German rowboat. The poster's implication was clear: Foreigners were filling up the limited German *Lebensraum* (living space).

The Election Results

In the first free all-German election since 1932, the CDU/CSU and the FDP gained 54.8 percent of the votes (CDU/CSU, 43.8 percent; FDP, 11 percent); the SPD, 33.5 percent (35.7 percent in western Germany; 24.3 percent in eastern Germany); the PDS/Left List, 2.4 percent nationwide but 11.1 percent in eastern Germany; and the Alliance 90/Greens, 6.1 percent in eastern Germany. Thus, these five parties were represented in the Bundestag, but the PDS and the Alliance 90/Greens only because they had topped the 5 percent minimum in eastern Germany. The election's major surprise was the western Greens' low vote of 4.8 percent, which shut them out of the Bundestag. As predicted, the Republicans obtained only a fraction (2.1 percent) of the vote. Nearly one-half came from dissatisfied voters who had previously supported one of the major parties (330,000 CDU and 110,000 SPD voters).

Although the CDU/CSU gained a plurality, its failure to top its 1987 vote in West Germany alone indicated that if the unification issue had not arisen, which Kohl handled with aplomb, the party might not have exceeded the SPD vote. Before the 1989 peaceful revolution, the West German CDU had done poorly in the FRG Länder elections because it was being blamed for the sluggish economy. The FDP, however, did well in the December 1990 election, primarily owing to Genscher's popularity in eastern Germany.

The SPD was shocked by the magnitude of its defeat. Its percentage of the vote was the lowest in thirty-three years. Before the campaign, SPD managers saw Lafontaine's candidacy as an asset because of his youth, dynamic personality, and fine track record as Saar minister-president, but his wavering position on unification proved a liability during the campaign.

As polls predicted, the PDS and the Alliance 90/Greens shared the opposition benches with the SPD in the Bundestag. The presence of the three parties did not threaten the governing parties' comfortable 398 to 264 majority of seats. Therefore, the Kohl government gained approval for most of its legislation, much of which dealt with postunification problems, in the four-year parliamentary session.

The West German Greens' defeat was caused by their negative position on unification and their factional feuds. They had announced months earlier that they did not want to merge with their East German counterpart until the day after the election in order to underline their opposition to the Kohl government's "colonialization" of eastern Germany. If they had merged earlier, they would have been in the Bundestag again. It took time for them to recover from the shock of defeat, although they continued to do well in 1991 and 1992 Länder elections.

Government and Opposition, 1990–1993

The CDU

Kohl's new CDU/CSU-FDP coalition government seemed off to a good start in late 1990, but it knew obstacles loomed ahead. For instance, the CDU—and the other parties—had difficulty integrating their eastern and western organizations. The eastern CDU members, many of them churchgoers, had joined their bloc party during the GDR era as a career move or as a refuge from the SED's official atheism. Many had collaborated with the regime, others had remained passive, some had resisted. From late 1989 on, new young East German CDU members in the local chapters demanded that those older members who had collaborated with the regime and were then holding a party or political office step down. At the 1991 convention, Kohl, trying to defuse the internal controversy, backed a resolution, which was then adopted, urging all eastern members to reflect privately on their past and then make a personal decision whether to continue in politics.[7] The controversy contributed to the CDU's difficulty in gaining new members in the former GDR.

De Maizière was among those CDU politicians who, once in office, had been accused of collaborating with the SED. Before unification, he had been GDR prime minister and East German CDU chairman. After the East and West CDU merged, he was elected CDU deputy leader, and after the national election Kohl appointed de Maizière minister without portfolio in the new cabinet. In late 1990, the press made damaging allegations that during the GDR era he had informed Stasi about dissidents whom he had defended as a lawyer. Even though he denied the allegations, he promptly resigned from the cabinet, but he kept his top party posts until September 1991, when the pressure on him to retire from politics became too great.

De Maizière's resignation from political office did not stop the internal controversy. Many eastern CDU members resented their western colleagues' self-righteous posturing. They believed that the western Germans were applying a higher standard to them than had been the case when western German officials, after the collapse of Hitler's Germany, measured the citizens' collaboration with the Nazis and allowed most collaborators to continue in politics. The eastern CDU members also resented the worsening economic and social problems in their Länder. Although Kohl met their Bundestag deputies on a regular basis to discuss their concerns, the deputies formed their own caucus to promote eastern interests within the party and the government.[8]

The East and West CDU merger meant that power within the party shifted away from the southern tier of states and toward the northern and eastern Protestant states, with their less homogeneous and more secular population. This shift had policy implications in making assistance to the east one of the top CDU priorities from 1990 to the present. But the policy—imposition of a temporary 7.5 "solidarity" surtax on incomes and an increase in oil and gasoline taxes in 1991—meant that Kohl could not keep his 1990 election promise that the Germans would be spared additional burdens to finance unification.[9]

The result was a political fallout in western Germany, which was also fueled by popular resentment against the continuing influx of foreigners, ethnic Germans, and eastern Germans. Voters in numerous western Länder elections in 1991 and 1992 turned against the CDU. In April 1991 in Rhineland-Palatinate, Kohl's home state, the CDU lost to the SPD for the first time in forty-three years. In April 1992 in Baden-Württemberg, another CDU bastion, the party lost nearly 10 percent of the vote (when compared to the previous election) and had to form an unprecedented grand coalition with the SPD. In the same election, the Republicans made striking gains, indicating strong voter dissatisfaction with the CDU and other establishment parties.

Polls showed that western voters were dissatisfied with the CDU's inability in the Länder it governed to cope with environment, housing, and transportation crises and were dissatisfied with its lackluster or corrupt leaders. Lothar Späth, the technocratic minister-president of Baden-Württemberg, had to resign his post in early 1991 when accused of having accepted free vacation trips from business firms in his state. In the new Länder, polls in July 1991 showed a drop in CDU support among those who voted for it in 1990 because they blamed the CDU/CSU-led government in Bonn for closed factories and mounting unemployment.[10] Eastern voters' suspicion that many of their own politicians were crooked was confirmed when Bonn minister of transportation Günther Krause (CDU) resigned from Kohl's government over accusations that in 1991 he had used DM 6,600 ($4,000) of public funds to pay his family's private moving expenses from eastern Berlin to his hometown near Rostock (in the former GDR).

CDU leaders were also worried about the party's problems in western Germany—the lethargy; the inactivity of local branches, which they had neglected for years; and the stagnating and aging membership of less than 700,000, with a corresponding decline of young members from 260,000 in 1983 to 196,000 in 1991. According to critics, the western CDU would have been in better shape if Kohl had not surrounded himself with leaders who were in his debt and lacked their own power base and if the leaders had allowed more intraparty democracy, more discussions about policies, and more tolerance of dissidents.

The CDU's problems were compounded by the continuing strained relations between Kohl and CSU chief Waigel. Kohl could not afford to alienate Waigel, who as minister of finance occupied a key Bonn cabinet position. Waigel, in turn, continued to have policy discords with the Bavarian minister-president, Edmund Stoiber, which hurt the CSU image.[11]

The FDP

The FDP shared some of the same concerns as the CDU. In western Germany, FDP membership remained stable at about 66,000, but in eastern Germany it plummeted from 202,000 in July 1990 to 124,000 in June 1992 because of rising political apathy and disillusionment with Bonn policies. However, the remaining eastern members still formed a majority in the party; their leftist-liberal views could not be disregarded by the more conservative Bonn leaders.[12]

The FDP has had its share of leadership problems. During the post-1990 election negotiations between the CDU/CSU and FDP to form a new cabinet, the usual jostling for favorite posts took place among the leaders of both parties. The ambitious Jürgen Möllemann (FDP) of North Rhine–Westphalia became minister of economics, despite his lack of economic expertise. He announced, with Lambsdorff's blessing but not those of other FDP chiefs, that he would become a candidate for the post of party chairperson in 1993, when Lambsdorff planned to retire.

In April 1992, Genscher's sudden resignation as foreign minister, after a record eighteen years in office, led to an internal party crisis. The FDP leaders announced unilaterally that Irmgard Schwaetzer, then minister of housing, would assume his post. However, FDP Bundestag deputies, who would have the final say in such a selection (as agreed on earlier by the coalition partners), rebelled against Schwaetzer's selection because they deemed her too weak for the position and feared that Chancellor Kohl would then also become de facto foreign minister. They chose instead Klaus Kinkel, then minister of justice, as foreign minister. Kinkel, a former associate of Genscher in the Foreign Office and later head of the West German secret service, had impressed many deputies with his imaginative policies and administrative skills. The FDP leaders, without success, had wanted him to remain minister of justice because of pending debates on important constitutional amendments. According to critics in the FDP, the crisis, damaging to the party, would never have occurred had proper procedures been followed.[13]

In June 1993, the fifty-six-year-old Kinkel, who had not even joined the FDP until January 1991, succeeded Lambsdorff as party chairman. His rival Möllemann, who had resigned as minister of economics months earlier because of a scandal over letters he wrote on behalf of a relative's business, did not contest Kinkel's nomination. But Möllemann remained the powerful party boss in North Rhine–Westphalia. Kinkel's rapid rise to the top in the party and in German politics did not end the fratricidal leadership feuds as the party prepared for the 1994 elections.

The SPD

The SPD has not been spared a turnover in leaders since 1987, when Willy Brandt resigned as chairman. Hans-Jochen Vogel led the party until 1991 and then made way for the younger Björn Engholm, minister-president of Schleswig-Holstein. In May 1993, Engholm resigned his posts after admitting that he had lied to an investigative commission established in 1987 to probe a CDU election scandal. Johannes Rau briefly became acting chairman until Rudolf Scharping, the forty-five-year-old minister-president of Rhineland-Palatinate since 1991, won the coveted position. He had gained a plurality among SPD members in an unprecedented referendum, designed to enhance internal democracy, of candidates for the chairmanship. He triumphed over two rival candidates, Gerhard Schröder, minister-president of Lower Saxony and former Juso chairman, and Heidi Wieczorek-Zeul, Bundestag deputy and former Juso chairwoman. In June 1993, a party convention formally elected Scharping chairman.

Scharping had been one of the young protégés of Brandt, despite his sympathies for the party's centrist-right wing. Although not an eloquent speaker, he has been honest and reliable. He rose swiftly in the SPD, becoming Land chairman in 1985. But his meteoric rise to the top faltered when he failed in his bid to become chancellor in 1994 and when Lafontaine replaced him as party chairman in 1995 (see Chapter 12 and Conclusion). Scharping remains head of the SPD Bundestag Fraktion.

The SPD, mirroring other parties, has lost members since the 1980s, partly because of popular dismay about scandals and the party's inability to solve economic problems in the Länder it governs. In 1993 alone, SPD membership dropped by 21,000 to less than 865,000. For the SPD, which had more than 1 million members in 1976, the trend was disturbing, especially because only 4 percent of members were under twenty-five and less than 30 percent of all members were women.[14]

After unification, the party hoped to build an effective organization and increase its membership in eastern Germany, especially in Saxony and Thuringia, its strongholds before 1933. The SPD did not succeed; indeed, it has been lucky to hold onto most of its twenty-five thousand members in eastern Germany. Bonn SPD officials have given eastern leaders representation on all the top party organs, including one of the posts of deputy chairperson, held since 1990 by Bundestag deputy Wolfgang Thierse. But in the five new Länder, few top leaders, other than Manfred Stolpe, the Brandenburg minister-president, have become well known. Intraparty disputes and media accusations that some leaders, Stolpe included, worked for

The Wall between East and West Germany came down in 1989. But the lack of a psychological rapprochement between western and eastern Germans created negative stereotyping that led to their imagining a new wall was going up. In this cartoon, the western German thinks the eastern Germans (colloquially known as "Ossis") "are lazy, naive, and feel sorry for themselves"; conversely, the eastern German thinks the western Germans ("Wessis") "are arrogant, egotistical, and inconsiderate." *Source:* Walther Keim and Hans Dollinger, eds., *Schöne Aussichten: Karikaturisten sehen die wahre Lage der Nation* (Munich: List, 1994), p. 36. Reprinted by permission.

Stasi have also weakened the party. As a consequence, discouragement and lethargy have become widespread among leaders and the rank and file. To add to the gloom, the shortage of members, especially youths, who are apolitical or gravitate toward the PDS, prevents the party from running candidates in some districts.

In Bonn headquarters, SPD officials decided to assist the party in the new Länder by imposing a special tax on all SPD members. Many "Wessi" (slang for West German) members, feeling no solidarity with their "Ossi" (East German) colleagues, quit the party in protest. Eastern members in turn were displeased when some western leaders tried to run their organization or took policy positions prejudicial to their interests. To illustrate: In 1993 Lafontaine, Saar minister-president, proposed that to hold down national budget deficits, wages and pensions in the new Länder should only be raised gradually to western levels. Stolpe, taking issue with Lafontaine, warned Bonn SPD chiefs that such a position would harm the party in the 1994 elections.

In the new Länder, the SPD's problems—a small membership, structural weaknesses, leadership struggles, lethargy, and discouragement—result partly from the party's operating within a transforming political culture apathetic toward parties and partly from the growing pains that most new organizations suffer. The western SPD has given much help, but in the long run the efforts to build an effective party must be indigenous.[15]

Alternative 90/The Greens

The western and eastern Greens, as planned, merged their organizations on the day after the December 1990 national election. (Saxony held out for a while, not wanting to jeopardize its cooperation with Alliance 90.) The western Greens had little time to reflect on their election loss because important Länder elections were in the offing in 1991 and 1992. Led by Realo chief Joschka Fischer, the party portrayed itself as a moderate and responsible organization willing to enter coalition cabinets. Party managers pitched their message to new and young voters who sympathized with the party's platform. The Greens secured more than the 5 percent minimum in five Länder elections but missed by a fraction in Schleswig-Holstein. The future looked promising. They participated in a so-called traffic light coalition with the SPD (red) and the FDP (yellow) in Bremen and in Brandenburg and in a coalition with the SPD in two other Länder. They also had seats in thirteen of sixteen Länder legislatures and in thousands of local councils.

The party's emphasis on electoral work was complemented by discussions about its organization and policy. In April 1991, national conference delegates voted to increase the role of elected state party leaders and deputies in national decisionmaking, to have two chairpersons (one from the West and one from the East), and to eliminate the requirement that deputies rotate in office. The party was concerned about the problems encountered by the eastern Greens. Although the latter had two deputies in the Bundestag (grouped with six Alliance 90 deputies), their organization in the new Länder was spotty, their finances weak, and the number of members (1,250 in 1992) small. They had to compete with the major parties receiving substantial assistance from western Germany.[16]

After the 1991 convention, a group of radical fundamentalists, led by Jutta Ditfurth, split off from the party because it had become too pragmatic. As a result, fewer intraparty feuds rent the Greens. In June 1992, the Greens began merger talks with the eastern Alliance 90 leaders. Both parties realized that they could become major players in German politics only if they agreed to a merger. The talks were often marred by personality conflicts and ideological differences. The centrist Alliance 90, with less than three thousand members, also feared being engulfed by the leftist thirty-six-thousand-member Greens. Thus, Alliance 90 demanded that its name symbolically precede that of the Greens (as was already true of the eastern group of deputies in the Bundestag). After difficult negotiations on many topics, the two organizations merged at the May 1993 Leipzig convention and named themselves Alliance 90/the Greens (informally, the Greens). According to the consensus document, the new party stands for human rights, ecology, democracy, social justice, gender equality, and a society free of force. The Greens abandoned their advocacy of participatory grassroots democracy and accepted a representative state but remained ambivalent toward the market economy, championed by Alliance 90. Many Greens decried the turn toward the political center; some defected.[17]

The PDS

After success in the 1990 national election, the PDS tried to establish a new identity and legitimate itself as a democratic party within the pluralist system. The party's task was difficult because the public was hostile, several Länder Offices for the Protection of the Constitution had it under surveillance, its isolated Bundestag deputies could not engage in official party-to-party contacts, its old SED cadres and young radicals had few fraternal links, the unaccounted-for SED funds remained an object of media attention, its small but vocal orthodox communist caucus (Kommunistische Plattform) led to intraparty frictions, its membership had dropped from 284,000 in December 1990 to 150,000 in 1993, and it had a minuscule staff of 150 for all of Germany (of whom half were part-timers on contract).[18]

Despite the difficulties, the PDS remained strong in eastern Germany, especially in east Berlin, where it received over 30 percent of the vote in the May 1992 local election. About 150 small municipalities had PDS mayors, and nearly all city councils had PDS representatives. The party's strength was caused by continuing dissatisfaction with cutbacks in jobs and social welfare programs and by worsening intra-German relations (see Table 11.1)

In June 1993, the party adopted a new basic program to replace the outdated 1990 program, which had been premised on the continued existence of the GDR. The 1993 program's ideology has similarities with and differences from those of the SPD and the Greens. Reflecting an eclectic mix of

TABLE 11.1 Eastern German Perceptions of Unification Consequences, 1994 (in percentages)

Perception	CDU	SPD	FDP	Alliance 90/ Greens	PDS	Total
My personal situation today is:						
Better than in GDR	80	51	50	54	17	56
Worse than in GDR	6	17	17	8	43	18
Not different	14	33	25	37	37	26
Economic situation:						
Better than in GDR	75	47	72	46	24	53
Worse than in GDR	8	20	24	5	38	20
Not different	17	33	4	48	36	27
Social welfare:						
Better than in GDR	33	14	36	15	6	20
Worse than in GDR	39	70	52	64	80	60
Not different	27	15	12	19	13	19
Personal freedom:						
Better than in GDR	86	68	77	76	44	71
Worse than in GDR	3	6	8	3	14	6
Not different	11	26	15	17	42	22
Relations to fellow citizens:						
Better than in GDR	11	2	3	1	5	6
Worse than in GDR	47	65	57	51	69	56
Not different	42	33	40	46	26	37

Note: Percentages do not necessarily add up to 100 because of varying response rates and rounding off.
SOURCE: *Politbarometer, Sept. 1994* (Mannheim: Forschungsgruppe Wahlen, 1994).

communist, green, social democratic, feminist, and radical democratic elements, it calls for a fundamental transformation of society and democratization of the economy, which would eventually lead to a democratic socialism. The program rejects dictatorship and the use of force and does not claim, as the SED did, that the party is the sole representative of the Left but rather the fulcrum of different leftist streams.

Thus, the party, especially in western Germany, sees itself as a mixture of party and movement, which would be open to the Greens, left-wing SPD members, and independents. In western Germany, the strategy did not work, partly because former German Communist Party members dominated many meetings and thereby alienated potential members. To make a new start, PDS organizers founded a separate West German regional organization and held a convention in May 1993 to open links to the PDS Executive (Vorstand) and parliamentary group and to prepare for the 1994 election.[19]

To improve the party's image and decentralize power, the PDS made internal reforms. It instituted term limits for officeholders; increased the number of elected, rather than appointed, top officials; dissolved the Presidium; and transferred its policymaking function to a smaller executive committee. Gysi, tired of factional disputes, resigned as chairman in 1993 but continued to head the PDS group in the Bundestag. Lothar Bisky, a longtime SED member and former head of the GDR University for Film and Television, replaced Gysi. Bisky, who had supported dissident professors and students during the GDR era, viewed himself in 1993 as a hybrid left-wing social democrat and reform communist.[20]

Right-Wing Parties

The Republicans and other rightist parties, despite their poor showing in the December 1990 election, did not give up hope. Their optimism paid off when they received nearly 11 percent of the vote in the Baden-Württemberg 1992 election, thereby becoming the third strongest party in that Land. (In 1988, they had mustered only 1 percent of the vote.) The German People's Union also did well in the Bremen 1991 and the Schleswig-Holstein 1992 elections.

The rightist parties gained support because of their criticism of the Basic Law's Article 16, which specifies that persons persecuted on political grounds in their home countries shall enjoy the right of asylum in Germany. Few asylum seekers qualified for permanent residence on that basis; most of the 430,000 in 1992 came for economic reasons. The Republicans in their propaganda stirred up racist and xenophobic sentiments among the Germans, who were becoming increasingly concerned about the continuing influx of foreigners. In response, the major parties—the SPD most reluctantly—agreed in late 1992 to amend Article 16 by tightening the asylum provisions. The parties thereby robbed the Republicans of a key propaganda weapon, but the result was that Germany lost the distinction of having had one of the most liberal asylum policies in the world.

Conclusion

From 1990 on, the party system assumed new dimensions. The number of parties in the new Bundestag had jumped from four to five when the PDS deputies took their seats. The merger of the western and eastern branches of the CDU/CSU, FDP, SPD, and, later, Greens meant that the eastern branches had to be strengthened, major organizational changes had to be made, and eastern leaders had to be given positions in the enlarged policy-making units of each party. The changes produced uneasiness and tensions, causing people to question whether the former West German state could successfully transplant its multiparty system to the former East German state. Normally, the answer would be negative, considering differences in political, economic, and social factors between sovereign—or in the case of Germany, near-sovereign—states. But the two Germanys had a common history, political culture, and societal pattern from 1871 to 1945. Thus, the answer should be positive, but in this instance only with qualifications. True, the eastern Germans supported a genuine multiparty system and democratic values, but they resisted becoming a dependent colony of the FRG. In the transplantation process from west to east, the western trappings of the 1990 election campaign and the competition of parties did not alleviate the belief among resentful eastern Germans that their welfare was being negatively affected by Bonn policymaking.

Notes

1. Klaus von Beyme; cited in H. G. Peter Wallach and Ronald A. Francisco, *United Germany: The Past, Politics, Prospects* (Westport, Conn.: Greenwood Press, 1992), p. 85.

2. *The New York Times*, October 15, 1990.

3. For details, see David P. Conradt, *Unified Germany at the Polls: Political Parties and the 1990 Federal Election*, German Issues No. 9 (Washington, D.C.: American Institute for Contemporary German Studies, 1990); Gerard Braunthal, "An Analysis of the German Elections of 1990," *Politics and Society in Germany, Austria and Switzerland* 5 (Summer 1993):29–53.

4. *Die Zeit*, November 16, 1990; *Frankfurter Rundschau*, November 20, 1990.

5. *Tageszeitung*, November 30, 1990.

6. PDS, *Links wählen—Wahlzeitung zur Bundestagswahl 1990* (Berlin: PDS, n.d.).

7. *New York Times*, December 19, 1991.

8. Clay Clemens, "Disquiet on the Eastern Front: The Christian Democratic Union in Germany's New Länder," *German Politics* 2, no. 2 (August 1993): 205–208.

9. Ibid., pp. 209–219.

10. Polls cited in David P. Conradt, "The Christian Democrats in 1990: Saved by Unification?" in *The New Germany Votes: Unification and the Creation of a New German Party System,* ed. Russell J. Dalton (Providence, R.I.: Berg, 1993), p. 72. See also William M. Chandler, "The Christian Democrats and the Challenge of Unity," in *Parties and Party Systems in the New Germany,* ed. Stephen Padgett (Aldershot, England: Dartmouth, 1993), pp. 138–140.

11. Werner A. Perger, "Die CDU," *Aus Politik und Zeitgeschichte,* supplement to *Das Parlament,* B 5/92 (January 24, 1992):4–5; Peter Fehrenholz, "Die CSU vor einem schwierigen Spagat," *Aus Politik und Zeitgeschichte,* supplement to *Das Parlament,* B 1/94 (January 7, 1994):17–20.

12. Christian Søe, "Unity and Victory for the German Liberals: Little Party, What Now?" in *The New Germany Votes,* ed. Dalton, pp. 118, 128–131.

13. The deputies agreed on Sabine Leutheusser-Schnarrenberger to replace Kinkel as minister of justice (Geoffrey K. Roberts, "The Free Democratic Party and the New Germany," in *Parties and Party Systems in the New Germany,* ed. Padgett, pp. 165–166).

14. *Der Spiegel,* May 17, 1993, p. 29.

15. For an overview, see Gero Neugebauer, "Die SDP/SPD in der DDR: Zur Geschichte und Entwicklung einer unvollendeten Partei," in *Parteien und Wähler im Umbruch: Parteiensystem und Wählerverhalten in der ehemaligen DDR und den neuen Bundesländern,* ed. Oskar Niedermayer and Richard Stöss (Opladen: Westdeutscher Verlag, 1994), pp. 93–104.

16. Donald Schoonmaker and E. Gene Frankland, "Disunited Greens in a United Germany: The All-German Election of December 1990 and Its Aftermath," in *The New Germany Votes,* ed. Dalton, pp. 152–160; Gerd Langguth, "Bündnis 90/Die Grünen nach ihrer zweiten Parteigründung: Vier Thesen," *Politische Studien* 45, no. 334 (March–April 1994):37–38.

17. Thomas Poguntke and Rüdiger Schmitt-Beck, "Still the Same with a New Name? Bündnis 90/Die Grünen After the Fusion," *German Politics* 3, no. 1 (April 1994):91–110; Jürgen Hoffmann, *Bündnis 90/Die Grünen: Ein schwieriges Bündnis in der Bewährungsprobe,* Interne Studien No. 86/1994 (Sankt Augustin: Konrad-Adenauer-Stiftung, September 1994), pp. 9–16.

18. Eric Canepa, "Germany's Party of Democratic Socialism," in *Socialist Register 1994,* ed. Ralph Miliband and Leo Panitch (London: Merlin Press, 1994), p. 324; Patrick Moreau, *PDS: Anatomie einer postkommunistischen Partei* (Bonn: Bouvier, 1992), pp. 332–337.

19. Ann L. Phillips, "Socialism with a New Face? The PDS in Search of Reform," *East European Politics and Societies* 8, no. 3 (Fall 1994):521–525; Gero Neugebauer, "PDS—What's Left?" (Berlin: Free University, September 26, 1994), pp. 5–8, unpublished ms.

20. *New York Times,* June 29, 1994.

• 12 •

"Super" Election Year 1994

Politics in advanced industrialized states has become increasingly unstable and unpredictable. The incumbent party or parties cannot necessarily expect to win the next electoral contest and determine again the direction of government policies. In recent years, U.S., British, French, Italian, and other voters have often been dissatisfied with the performance of their governments, regardless of whether left, center, or right parties have held the reins of power. The voters have been angry about the numerous corruption scandals that seem endemic in any system and about the policymakers' failure to solve the most urgent national problems, be they high unemployment, crime, immigration, or increased taxation. In protest, many voters have switched their support to newly founded or existing opposition parties. Others, wary of the programmatic similarities between the major parties or too disgusted with politics, have not bothered to vote. Civic fatigue and resignation have set in, which can be dangerous for a democratic polity.

This chapter asks whether the German national election of October 16, 1994, one of twenty local, state, and European Parliament contests in the "super" election year 1994, was the prototype for one in which voters were dissatisfied with the status quo. To gain some answers, the chapter examines the parties' internal problems, planning for the campaigns, positions on public issues, social group targets, views about coalitions, and electoral performance.

The Christian Democrats: From Defense to Offense

In a democratic polity, there is always some dissatisfaction with the government in power because voters range themselves widely along the political spectrum from left to right and cannot concur on basic policies. Thus, in Germany it is perhaps not too surprising that in a 1994 poll showing the electorate's ideological self-estimate, a high percentage of respondents put

The nonvoter is wooed by all the parties, as this cartoon, entitled "Plea for a small vote," shows. *Source: Der Spiegel,* March 15, 1993, p. 4. Reprinted by permission.

themselves on the left, an indication not only of their traditional values but also of their opposition to the conservative government's policies (see Figure 12.1). The reasons were clear: In 1994 the euphoria over unification had dissipated. In the former GDR, Kohl's promise of a speedy economic takeoff had not materialized. In western Germany, citizens grumbled over the prospect of new taxes to assist eastern Germany. Nationally, the public debt and unemployment (over 4 million) had mounted to unprecedented levels. Thus, from late 1993 until May 1994 opinion polls indicated that the CDU/CSU would lose and the SPD would win the national election. Respondents said that the CDU/CSU and its coalition ally, the FDP, were less competent to deal with unemployment and social problems than the SPD and that as chancellor they preferred Scharping (SPD candidate) to Kohl (see Figure 12.2).

To improve the CDU's chance of electoral victory, Kohl, Secretary-General Peter Hintze, and other officials devised a vote-maximization strategy,

FIGURE 12.1 Ideological Self-Estimate of the Electorate, 1994

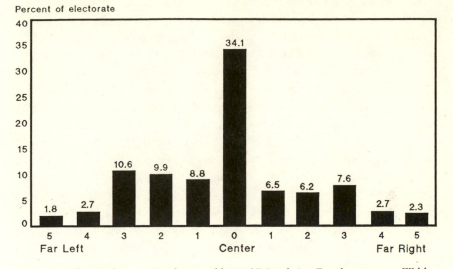

SOURCE: *Blitz-Umfrage zur Bundestagswahl, 1994* (Mannheim: Forschungsgruppe Wahlen, 1994).

FIGURE 12.2 Chancellor Preferences of the Electorate, 1994

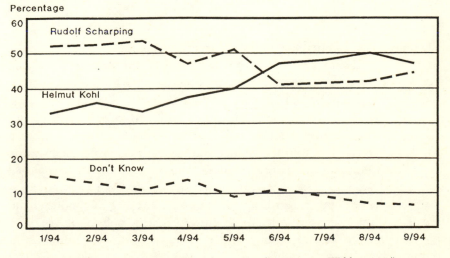

SOURCE: *Politbarometer (G003.3)* (Mannheim: Forschungsgruppe Wahlen, 1994).

which they urged delegates at the September 1993 party convention to endorse. It included a tough government law-and-order policy, adopted partly to woo voters supporting rightist parties.

Kohl's nomination in 1993 of Steffen Heitmann, Saxony's minister of justice, to be the CDU candidate for the federal presidency in 1994 tarnished the party's image. Kohl chose the politically unknown, conservative east German leader as a symbol of national integration. But progressive CDU politicians, such as former secretary-general Heiner Geissler and Bundestag president Rita Süssmuth, objected to his statements urging further limits on immigration of foreigners to protect the Germans' right of identity and recommending that more women be at home caring for children. Despite the criticisms (the feminist magazine *Emma* cited him as the year's "enemy of women") and the objections of conservative CSU leaders that they had not been consulted sufficiently before the nomination, Heitmann remained the party's nominee until November 1993, when Kohl finally realized that Heitmann could not win against Johannes Rau, North Rhine–Westphalia SPD minister-president.

Thereupon Kohl chose Roman Herzog, Federal Constitutional Court president, to be the new nominee. In May 1994, in a special federal convention Herzog won the presidency in the third round of balloting, when only a plurality, rather than a majority, was needed. Most FDP delegates, who had backed their own candidate in the first two rounds, supported Herzog rather than Rau, a clear signal that the FDP would remain a coalition partner of the CDU/CSU should the two parties gain a majority in the October election.[1]

Herzog's victory symbolized a turnaround for the CDU/CSU. However, the public was less interested in that contest (indeed, Rau was more popular than Herzog) than in the improving economy. As a consequence, polls from early summer 1994 on showed that the government parties would win in October. Yet, the CDU and CSU campaign managers took no chance on the steadfastness of the voters' views. Making heavy use of television, the managers sought to win over potential switch voters or nonvoters. They featured Kohl as the chancellor who had unified the two Germanys in 1990, was responsible for eastern Germany's economic recovery, and was a recognized European statesman. The strategists knew that the sixty-four-year-old chancellor was more popular than his party because of his successful policies and his personality. Therefore, they put up posters showing only his image, with the caption "Chancellor of unity." Many citizens empathized with a down-home leader who spoke with a rustic Rhineland-Palatinate accent, who had difficulty keeping his weight (three hundred pounds) down, who invited visiting politicians to his family home near Ludwigshafen for a sauna and a helping of a spicy dish of sow's belly, and who, while on a visit to

Washington in early 1994, was told by President Clinton that he had dreamed that Kohl was a sumo wrestler.

At the CDU convention in February 1994, delegates adopted a new party program that affirmed the CDU's backing for an "ecological" social market economy and for the European Union (formerly, the European Community). In April, CDU and CSU leaders agreed to wage a joint electoral campaign under the bland slogans "Security," "Stability," and "Future." They appealed to their traditional clientele—entrepreneurs, the middle class, farmers, and Catholic blue-collar workers—and to other groups for support. They said that all Germans had the duty to safeguard existing jobs and create new jobs in a highly competitive world. They claimed that eastern German economic growth was strong and living standards were improving. The CDU triumph in the Saxony election in September 1994, the result of Minister-President Kurt Biedenkopf's popularity, buoyed the party's hopes for an October national victory.

CSU leaders were also confident of success in the October election because they captured in September, once again, an absolute majority of votes in the Bavarian Land election. Polls had shown that CSU voters saw the party as the most competent to deal with the economy and crime. In the Land election, the CSU even received the votes of nearly one-half of the unorganized workers, although the SPD did better among organized workers.

The Free Democrats: On the Brink of Disaster

The FDP had to overcome a series of setbacks in 1994 that nearly spelled its oblivion. It failed to get 5 percent in all 1994 Länder elections and in the European Parliament election, an indication that its voter support was rapidly eroding. The lack of a new generation of popular leaders to replace the well-known older ones was only one of the party's many problems. Its new chairman, Kinkel, Germany's foreign minister since 1992, was overworked and too bureaucratic and did not have the strength and popularity of Genscher. Kinkel was unable to narrow the gap between the party and its parliamentary group or between the dominant conservative free-enterprise wing and the weakened pro–civil rights left-liberal wing. (He resigned as FDP chairman in 1995 after further losses that year in Länder elections. Wolfgang Gerhardt, the deputy national chairman and party leader in Hesse, succeeded him, but Gerhardt's selection was far from unanimous and lacked enthusiasm. Guido Westerwelle, the popular thirty-three-year-old general secretary, is expected eventually to become the next FDP chairman.)

The catalog of other FDP problems included a search for identity in a society polarized between Christian and social democracy, which left little room for liberalism. The FDP appealed primarily to the business community and to the middle class, many of them the "well-to-do," as one FDP leader foolishly said early in the campaign. The party was too beholden to the CDU/CSU because early in the campaign it had pledged to remain in a Kohl cabinet and lacked the force to make its own imprint on government policy. In eastern Germany, the FDP was riddled with strife among contending leaders, lacked an organization in many towns, was unable to attract new members, and lost most of its older members, who in the GDR decades had belonged to the liberal and nationalist bloc parties.[2]

To counter the FDP's image problem, delegates at the June 1994 convention adopted an election program that favored continued cuts in government spending and taxes, more privatized state properties, and fewer government bureaucrats. As a sop to the party's liberal minority, the program demanded more protection of individual rights and laws to let foreigners acquire German or dual citizenship. The program also opposed the CDU/CSU law-and-order proposal to use electronic surveillance in apartments to gather evidence on organized crime.

Kinkel attempted thereby to regain the confidence of the left-liberal secular, well-educated professional, and other middle-class voters who had switched parties when the FDP took a conservative path. Yet he missed an opportunity to resuscitate the party's liberal past and to improve its image as a party not beholden solely to business interests. He should have urged the FDP members in the parliamentary constitutional commission revising the Basic Law to be in the forefront of discussions on more participatory rights for citizens and more protection for minorities and foreigners.

The Social Democrats: From Offense to Defense

From late 1993 until May 1994, the SPD leaders were optimistic about winning the October 1994 election; polls showed that if the election had been held then, the SPD would have garnered 41 percent of the vote (up from 38 percent); the CDU/CSU, 37 percent (up from 32); the Greens, 9 percent; the FDP, 6 percent; and the PDS, at least three direct seats in the districts. The SPD's euphoric mood was confirmed in March 1994 when the party gained an unprecedented majority of seats in the Lower Saxony legislature, permitting Minister-President Schröder not to govern any longer with the Greens. The SPD leaders were also optimistic because the party was a member of eleven out of sixteen Länder coalition governments and held the minister-presidency in nine of them. Thus, in 1994 the SPD continued to have a sizable majority in the Bundesrat, giving it an opportunity to block government bills.

In early 1994, Scharping, in consultation with top officials, appointed an unoffical kitchen cabinet of specialists who were to give advice on the party's electoral program and to mobilize SPD members and voters. To achieve these goals, the specialists urged that employment, housing, and taxation be major campaign themes. They targeted the blue-collar workers, who no longer cast their ballots automatically for the party, and the large group of undecided voters. The voters were told that only an SPD-led government would turn the country around and improve their standard of living. The specialists also planned the various phases of the campaign, including the "hot" one in the weeks before the election when Scharping was to travel throughout Germany in a special train and deliver about 120 speeches.

To achieve an election victory, Scharping knew that intraparty feuds had to be minimized. Left and right factions, often at odds in the past on key domestic and foreign issues, fell in line and, with few exceptions, supported his policy recommendations. They knew that the SPD had a chance to beat a weakened Kohl government if their differences were buried, at least until after the election. Scharping insisted that the party adopt centrist positions on issues (shades of President Clinton in his first two years in office) to have a chance to win. Thus, he retreated on liberal political asylum and civil liberties issues, over the protest of the party's leftist faction, which with some justification claimed that the party was becoming a CDU/CSU clone.

In keynote speeches, Scharping and Lafontaine, the party's spokesman on economic and financial questions, dealt primarily with ways in which an SPD-led government would improve employment, the economy, finances, and the social welfare system—problems of greatest concern to voters, as shown by opinion polls. The SPD proposals included tax increases on the wealthy (a 10 percent tax surcharge on incomes of over DM 52,000 [$35,000]); cuts in national expenditures, including welfare programs; and a meshing of the national budget with improvements in the economy, which in turn would be linked to productivity increases. Only then, so ran the argument, would the economy become internationally more competitive and unemployment be reduced.

Scharping's statements on foreign policy hardly differed from those of Kohl. Thus, after years of intraparty discussion the SPD chairman said that German troops should be allowed to participate in U.N. peacekeeping operations, provided that they would not be involved in combat and that Parliament give prior approval in each case.

The SPD domestic and foreign policy proposals were incorporated into an "SPD government program," which was unveiled in March 1994 and was affirmed on June 22 at a special election convention in Halle. Delegates nominated Scharping as the party's candidate for chancellor. The program shows that the party's differences with the CDU/CSU had narrowed considerably.[3] As if to underline the SPD trend toward conservatism, Scharping told business leaders that the party wanted to conclude a solidarity pact with them. If the SPD won the election, it would be willing to limit wage increases of public employees in 1995, lower the costs of fringe benefits, and promote investments. Such a position did not endear him to the trade union officials, most of them stalwart SPD members. They were aware, however, that the SPD still stood to the left of the CDU/CSU in its commitment to social justice and in its support of the growing underclass in western and eastern Germany.

Prospects for an SPD victory did not last. The economy began to improve, redounding to the benefit of the Kohl government. Scharping committed a series of faux pas, which did not help the lackluster campaign. When he unveiled the new SPD election program, he confused gross with net income in stating which citizens would have to pay higher taxes. In response, critics questioned his competence in economic affairs. Moreover, Scharping was unable to avoid internal party disputes over a speed limit on the Autobahnen (superhighways) and liberalized abortion laws. He showed he was a poor loser by overreacting to the election of Herzog to the federal presidency. These image problems contributed to the CDU/CSU receiving 39 percent to the SPD's 32.2 percent of the vote in the European Parliament election in June. (The SPD had 5 percent less than in 1989.)

To recoup some of the loss, the SPD planners portrayed the party as being friendly to the citizens by using such slogans as "More money for children" and "Affordable apartments." In the U.S. style, placards and media advertisements pictured Scharping as a family man who excelled at bicycling and other sports. But the lack of emotion and charisma in his campaign speeches was a serious liability.

Belatedly, at the end of August, Scharping announced the names of his shadow cabinet members, including his two main rivals, Lafontaine (to become minister of finance) and Schröder (to become minister of economics, transportation, and energy), and numerous women leaders. If the selection of potential cabinet members had been announced earlier, Scharping would not have been solely responsible for the several campaign mishaps that had plagued the party. It promptly printed 150,000 copies of a placard showing the three minister-presidents as the confident troika that could achieve an SPD victory. Some female SPD members in the shadow cabinet were displeased that not one of them had been selected as being worthy of troika status on the photo.[4]

On September 4, the beginning of the hot phase of the campaign, the SPD unveiled at a mass rally its first 100-day government program, to be introduced in the Bundestag should the party regain political power in Bonn. Soon thereafter, a solid majority of voters in a Brandenburg Land election cast their ballots for the SPD ticket headed by Minister-President Stolpe, a reaffirmation of his popularity. Thus, the SPD's hopes for October rose, even though the CDU triumphed solidly in Saxony on the same day.

The Greens: Hoping for a Comeback

At the February 1994 Greens' convention in Mannheim, delegates adopted an electoral program designed to drum up more support for the party. The program envisaged a German society based on environmentalism and social solidarity rather than on high technology. It favored greater investments in mass transit, decentralization of the energy system, and creation of environmentally friendly new products. The Greens claimed that these proposals, if adopted, would help end the recession and create new jobs. To preserve existing jobs, working hours would have to be reduced drastically.

The program also demanded dual citizenship for those foreigners seeking it, voting rights for all foreigners who had resided at length in Germany, liberalization of the existing immigration system, and renewed guarantees of a legal hearing for political asylum applicants. A majority of delegates reaffirmed the Greens' commitment to pacifism, opposition to obligatory military service, and call for eventual dissolution of the Bundeswehr.[5]

Thus, at the beginning of 1994 the party, having shed some of its radical image, was on its way to becoming the FDP of the 1990s. The Realos, aware that pending elections would not be decided to the left of the more conservative SPD, pushed the Greens to the left-center. However, in Saxony Green leaders said before the 1994 Land election, to the consternation of the Realos in Bonn, that they were not averse to joining, if necessary, a black-green coalition with the CDU. The CDU's absolute majority made any coalition unnecessary.

In June 1994, at the Greens' Länder council meeting in Magdeburg, officials presented ten reform projects designed to appeal to centrist voters. The projects, which received final approval at a September conference, were to be presented to a SPD-Green government, if formed, for enactment during the four-year legislative session.

During the campaign, the Greens' central headquarters approved newspaper advertisements and television spots, commissioned an artist to design posters, and drafted a series of slogans (e.g., "Secure peace without weapons," "Women in front," and "Equal rights for all"). Headquarters also authorized the Länder and district organizations to initiate their own campaign propaganda, featuring their top candidates.[6]

In eastern Germany, especially after the party's disastrous showing in the September 1994 Saxony and Brandenburg elections, Green leaders, over some local opposition, waged a strong anti-PDS campaign to win over leftist voters. These leaders also criticized their western colleagues for emphasizing ecological problems, which were of less immediate concern to eastern Germans than economic and social problems. The eastern Greens, shut out of all their parliaments, except for Saxony-Anhalt, were pessimistic about their appeal in the October election.

The PDS: Optimism Prevails

Most observers predicted from 1990 on that the PDS, unable to gain 5 percent of the national vote or a plurality in at least three districts in 1994, would fade into obscurity. They did not accurately gauge the PDS's continuing strength in eastern Germany, as seen in numerous 1994 local and state elections, in which the party gained one-third more votes than in 1990.

PDS leaders Gysi, Bisky, and André Brie, the chairman of the party's 1994 electoral campaign, pursued a double strategy to gain maximum backing for the party in the October election by targeting both leftist citizens and those dissatisfied with the status quo. In western Germany, these included communist youth and radical Greens who were seeking a new political home. In eastern Germany, these included voters, not necessarily leftists, who criticized the western parties as being too indifferent to their economic and social plight and who therefore identified with the PDS as their regional party. According to polls, PDS supporters included not only former SED functionaries but also academics, salaried employees, and pensioners, all of whom had lost status and privileges and were worried about the future. They did not include many workers, artisans, and farmers.[7]

In March 1994, delegates at a PDS convention in Berlin adopted, for the European Parliament election in June, a platform that committed the party to a peaceful, socially just, democratic, and environmentalist Europe. They endorsed Hans Modrow, the party's honorary chairman, as the top candidate for the European Parliament. For the October election, they also adopted a program that criticized the government's failure to deal adequately with mass unemployment, the housing shortage, environmental destruction, and right-wing radicalism. The program characterized the PDS as a community providing hearth and solidarity in a hostile world.

The antiestablishment mood in eastern Germany redounded to the PDS's benefit. It received enough support in 1994 local contests to elect 160 mayors and to gain administrative posts in 100 cities, where PDS officials were working well with colleagues from other parties. For the October election, the PDS also secured the endorsement of prominent nonparty members, some of whom ran as independent candidates on the PDS ticket. Among them was Stefan Heym, a well-known GDR author, who became a candidate in a central Berlin district—and won.[8]

New Minor Parties

In 1993, two centrist "antiparty" parties were formed, which seemed to presage a realignment of parties. In Hamburg, Markus Wegner, a disgruntled CDU member, founded the Instead Party to protest the corruption and greed of politicians and the major parties' failure to deal effectively with national problems. The party received more than 5 percent of the vote in the 1993 Hamburg election, enough to become the junior partner in the government led by the SPD, which claimed that it could not find a more suitable partner. However, the Instead Party, despite the publicity it received, did not achieve a similar victory in the 1994 national election because the voters, even though disgruntled with the establishment parties, thought twice about "wasting" their vote on a splinter party. In this case, potential Instead Party supporters cast their ballots for the CDU or SPD, where their vote would count in a tight election.

The nationalist Free Citizens' Federation, the second centrist party, was founded in January 1994 by Manfred Brunner, formerly of the FDP, to capitalize on the public's worry that a European currency would eventually replace the German currency in a united Europe. Not getting the hoped-for backing from dissatisfied CDU and FDP members, the party did poorly in the European Parliament election and did not run candidates for the 1994 election. Thus, the prediction that new parties would be serious competitors to the establishment parties in the 1994 contests proved false.

The Coalition Debates

During the national election campaign, the parties shied away from a discussion of issues, focusing instead on possible governing coalitions after the election. The CDU/CSU leaders asked the SPD repeatedly about its choice of coalition partner if it received a plurality of votes. They wanted Scharping to commit himself to a coalition with the Greens (red-green) because they were confident that such a coalition would be anathema to the many centrist voters whose support the SPD was seeking. Scharping, knowing that any prior commitment was bound to lose party votes among those who would disapprove of whatever coalition might emerge, did not fall into the trap. He said that the party would not decide on a coalition partner until after the election. He also doubted that a red-green government could span differences on several major policy issues, such as the Greens' demand that NATO be disbanded and the Bundeswehr be phased out. But most leftist or centrist SPD leaders, knowing that the Greens were making maximum demands for bargaining purposes, expected such a coalition to settle its differences. Scharping may have reluctantly agreed with them because, according to one press report, he told colleagues that he was willing to form a coalition with the Greens but without announcing his position publicly before the election.[9]

Most Green leaders favored a red-green coalition because it gave their party a chance to participate in national policymaking. But they mistrusted Scharping, who as Rhineland-Palatinate minister-president had asked the FDP, not the Greens, to join him in a coalition government and who in 1994 was making the SPD "a carbon copy" of the CDU. In frustration, Joschka Fischer, Hesse's minister of environment, denounced Scharping's position as a "fatal signal" for a possible red-green coalition. Another Green official warned SPD chiefs that his party would not enter a coalition with them if they supported a policy of austerity and relegated environmental issues to second place. A few Green leaders, opposed on principle to a coalition with the SPD, said that such a government would betray the original Greens' intent to be a populist movement rather than a party machine intent on winning elections. The coalition opponents also worried about losing the party's leftist adherents should the Greens move to the center.[10]

The media speculated not only about a possible red-green coalition but also about a less likely CDU/CSU-SPD grand coalition, similar to the one that had governed West Germany from 1966 to 1969. On the record, SPD leaders were opposed to it ideologically and feared that it would create an ineffective parliamentary opposition of only minor parties. But a grand coalition could not be ruled out should the FDP fall under the 5 percent barrier. In that case, the CDU/CSU, if it had a plurality but not a majority, most likely would turn to the SPD. A traffic light (red, yellow, green) coalition of SPD, FDP, and Greens was also a possibility, but observers predicted that it would be politically too unstable and would not last the four-year legislative term.

Few citizens could have foreseen that another coalition debate would erupt after the Saxony-Anhalt election in June 1994. In this former GDR territory, the SPD and Greens formed a coalition, as they had done previously in a few other Länder. However, the two parties' failure to get a majority of seats in the Land parliament meant that their minority government needed the legislative support or tolerance of another party; in this instance, the PDS.

The CDU knew immediately that it had the perfect election issue to assail the leftist parties. Reviving the dormant anticommunist views held by most citizens, the CDU stepped up its anti–"red sock" (the symbol of the PDS) campaign. It denounced the "unholy" alliance and "left front" of the three parties, implying that the SPD and the Greens were sympathetic to the PDS and had sold out to it. The CDU demanded that the SPD distance itself completely from the PDS. Kohl said that if this "treasonous act" was replicated in Bonn, a "change of system in our Republic" would result.[11] In response, the SPD distributed posters showing a photo of Kohl meeting GDR chief Honecker, with the caption that 63 percent of CDU deputies from the former GDR had been members of the communist National Front before unification. Scharping said repeatedly that the SPD had no intention of ever forming a political alliance with the PDS.

Eastern German CDU leaders did not want the national CDU to put up anti-PDS placards ("Into the future, but not in red socks," and "Future instead of left front") in the new Länder. They argued that the placards' message and Kohl's statement that the PDS supporters were "red-lacquered fascists" would play into the hands of the PDS, which could (and did) mobilize its potential voters more easily once the CDU pursued an anti-PDS campaign. Similarly, many eastern German SPD officials, supported by Minister-President Schröder, disagreed with Scharping's denunciation of the PDS as an antidemocratic party. They wanted the PDS to be integrated into the democratic system rather than demonized. According to them, such a conciliatory position would make the SPD a more attractive alternative for eastern German voters.[12]

The National Election

Election night showed that the CDU had gained more votes in western and eastern Germany than its nearest rival, the SPD. Exit polls indicated that in the former GDR those voters who were better off than in 1990 and who were optimistic about the future (they were known as the unification winners) had cast their ballots for the CDU, but those who were not yet better off (the unification losers) had switched to other parties. Because there were many losers, the CDU/CSU's 41.5 percent of the vote in both parts of Germany was its lowest since the 1949 West German election.

In the end, the low CDU/CSU vote did not matter because the party's coalition ally, the FDP, received 6.9 percent (a considerable drop from its 11 percent in 1990), for a combined total of 48.4 percent (see Table 12.1). This enabled both parties to hold a majority of 341 to 331 in the 672-member Bundestag (see Figure 12.3). A slim 10-seat lead over the opposition parties can spell danger for the government's longevity.

As expected, many CDU and CSU voters had split their tickets, giving the first vote to their own local candidates but the second vote to FDP candidates on the Länder lists. By doing so, these voters, wanting the governing coalition to continue in office, made sure that the FDP was not frozen out of the Bundestag. From summer 1994 on, Kohl's popularity and an improved economy contributed greatly to the coalition's victory.[13]

The left-center and left opposition parties (SPD, Greens, and PDS) received considerably more votes than they had in 1990, mustering 48.1 percent. Despite Scharping's colorless personality and gaffes during the campaign, the SPD received 36.4 percent of the vote, a gain of 2.9 percent over 1990, stemming partly from a switch of 700,000 former CDU voters and 600,000 former FDP voters (out of a total of 17 million votes for the SPD and 19.5 million for the CDU/CSU). The voters who had switched to the SPD, many living in eastern Germany, had been dissatisfied with the record of the governing parties, which they had supported four years earlier. However, as further proof of the citizens' eroding partisan loyalties, the SPD lost two hundred thousand votes cast for it in 1990 to the PDS in 1994 and more to the other parties.[14]

The Greens became the third strongest party nationwide, trailing the CDU/CSU and SPD but ahead of the FDP. Having been shut out of the Bundestag for four years, the western Greens had cause to celebrate their return to the legislature. They were able to fully mobilize their sympathizers in western Germany, especially the younger voters, and to attract disaffected SPD voters in former SPD strongholds, such as Hamburg and Frankfurt.

TABLE 12.1 Bundestag Election Results, 1994 (1990 results in parentheses)

Party	Percentage of Second Votes		Number of Seats	
	1994	(1990)	1994	(1990)
CDU/CSU	41.5	(43.8)	294	(319)
SPD	36.4	(33.5)	252	(239)
FDP	6.9	(11.0)	47	(79)
Alliance 90/Greens	7.3	(5.0)	49	(8)
PDS	4.4	(2.4)	30	(17)
Republicans	1.9	(2.1)	–	–
Other	1.5	(2.0)	–	–
Total	100.0	(100.0)	672	(662)

Note: Percent totals have been rounded off to the nearest whole number.
SOURCE: *Bundestagswahl 1994* (Mannheim: Forschungsgruppe Wahlen, 1994)
(preliminary figures).

FIGURE 12.3 Distribution of Seats in the Bundestag, 1994

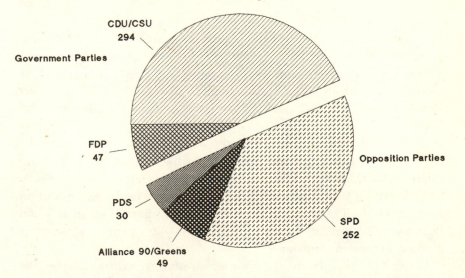

SOURCE: *Bundestagswahl 1994* (Mannheim: Forschungsgruppe Wahlen, 1994).

The CDU/CSU victory in 1994 produced this cartoon, in which one worker hanging up a picture of Kohl says to the other, "Scharping for the time being into storage." *Source:* Walther Keim and Hans Dollinger, eds., *Schöne Aussichten: Karikaturisten sehen die wahre Lage der Nation* (Munich: List, 1994), p. 96. Reprinted by permission.

However, in eastern Germany the Greens fared worse than in 1990, losing about one hundred thousand votes to the PDS and failing to attract older voters. The poor results were caused by infighting among leaders, lack of a clear profile, and intraparty schism concerning possible coalition partners. Partly because of the Greens' difficulties, the PDS outpolled them and pushed them into fourth place in eastern Germany.[15]

The PDS, despite the bitter attacks by its opponents, achieved its goal on election day. It won four seats outright in central and east Berlin districts (a minimum of three was necessary to gain Bundestag representation). But because it had gained 4.4 percent of the nationwide vote, on the basis of proportionality the PDS received thirty seats. The party's strength in eastern Germany (17.6 percent of the vote) was offset by its disastrous showing (0.9 percent) in western Germany.

In the 1994 election, many minor leftist, centrist, rightist, religious, and other parties were on the ballot, but none of them received enough votes to gain Bundestag seats. The radical right Republicans, the party that had achieved such prominence in 1989 local and state elections in West Germany, could gain only 1.9 percent of the vote. Their support had crumbled as a result of internal leadership squabbles, such as the ouster a few weeks before the election of Schönhuber from his chairmanship for having met with the ultranationalist Gerhard Frey, chairman of the German People's Union. A Berlin court reinstated Schönhuber three days before the election because of procedural errors in his ouster.[16] The Republicans also fared poorly because of the already cited decision of the major parties in 1993 to call for a limit to political asylum. The decision robbed the Republicans of their virulent anti-immigration campaign but showed that they, and other small rightist parties, had successfully moved the political agenda to the right.

The election results indicated that much of the CDU/CSU's clientele remained in Catholic areas, whose population was engaged in agriculture and small trades. The SPD did well in most of its traditional Protestant urban bastions in western Germany, gaining 50 percent of the workers' votes and 60 percent of those organized in trade unions but trailing the Christian Democrats in the other occupational categories. The FDP was backed by well-educated professionals and salaried employees, especially in Baden-Württemberg and Hesse. The Greens scored high in urban areas with a tertiary (service) labor force and in university cities, continuing to attract young voters, especially women. In eastern Germany, men over forty-five, many of whom had lost their jobs, and women under thirty-five, who were embittered about cuts in child care and the tougher law on abortion, voted for the PDS. Among voters between the ages of twenty-five and thirty-four, the SPD gained the most votes (39 percent), ahead of the CDU/CSU (32 percent) and the Greens (13 percent); conversely the CDU/CSU did best among older voters.[17]

After the election, the governing parties negotiated on the composition of the cabinet, agreeing finally that the CDU would hold ten posts; the CSU, four; and the FDP, three. They also discussed the projected policies for the 1994–1998 legislative period, agreeing to create jobs, reduce bureaucracy, consolidate the federal budget, fight crime, aid families with children, move government agencies to Berlin, and integrate Europe. They could not agree on electronic surveillance of suspected criminal hideouts (a CDU/CSU demand), naturalization of children of foreign residents, and a time limit on the 7.5 percent solidarity tax for eastern Germany (FDP demands). These issues were therefore dropped from the legislative package. On November 15, Kohl was reelected chancellor, but by a margin of only one vote more than the minimum necessary for election. Whether the government, with its slim legislative majority, can survive the Bundestag term until 1998 remains to be seen.

Conclusion

The 1994 national election was not a prototype of voter expression of deep dissatisfaction with the status quo, although earlier Länder elections, in which national policies were not at stake, had given such an indication. Thus, Germany was an exception among countries whose incumbent national government had been ousted in recent years by the opposition (e.g., France, Italy, Poland, South Africa) or whose left or right radical parties had made significant electoral gains (e.g., Russia, Austria). The SPD, Greens, and PDS were unable to end the protracted reign of Chancellor Kohl, indicating that enough people were satisfied with him and, to a lesser extent, with the governing parties. The voters who supported the opposition parties disagreed with Kohl's policies, but most of them did not advocate a radical transformation of the system. The expectation that minor fringe parties would take away votes from the major parties in the 1994 election failed to materialize.

In an era in which conservatism seems the driving ideology, the German parties on the left received more votes in the 1994 election than they had four years earlier. Conversely, the conservative governing parties lost votes, but not in sufficient numbers to be relegated to the opposition benches in the Bundestag. The election also indicated that the two distinct political cultures of western and eastern Germany were still far apart. In eastern Germany, many citizens abstained from voting or voted for the PDS, which showed their dissatisfaction with Bonn. Yet on balance, the 1994 election results epitomized a remarkable stability in the democratic party system of the fledgling united Germany.

Notes

1. The FDP's candidate was Hildegard Hamm-Brücher, a former minister of state in the Foreign Office. The fourth candidate, an independent, was Jens Reich, a former East German citizens' movement leader (GIC, *The Week in Germany*, September 17, 1993; May 20, 1994).

2. *Der Spiegel*, April 25, 1994, pp. 32–34, 43, 45.

3. SPD, "Das Regierungsprogramm '94," in *Politik* (Bonn: SPD, June 1994); Gerard Braunthal, "The Perspective from the Left," *German Politics and Society* 13, no. 1 (Spring 1995):36–40.

4. *New York Times*, August 30, 1994; *Der Spiegel*, September 5, 1994, pp. 18–26.

5. GIC, *The Week in Germany*, March 4, 1994.

6. Jürgen Hoffmann, "Bündnis 90/Die Grünen: Ein schwieriges Bündnis in der Bewährungsprobe," Interne Studien No. 86/1994 (Sankt Augustin: Konrad-Adenauer-Stiftung, September 1994), pp. 18–20.

7. *Berliner Morgenpost,* July 2, 1994. See also Laurence H. McFalls, "Political Culture, Partisan Strategies, and the PDS: Prospects for an East German Party," *German Politics and Society* 13, no. 1 (Spring 1995):50–61.

8. PDS, *Pressedienst,* no. 11/12, March 25, 1994.

9. *Die Zeit,* June 17, 1994.

10. *Der Spiegel,* February 7, 1994, pp. 40–41, 44.

11. *Boston Globe,* August 29, 1994.

12. *Die Zeit,* July 29, 1994; *Der Spiegel,* July 25, 1994, pp. 25–28; August 15, 1994, pp. 20–22.

13. For election analyses, see the special issue "Bundestagswahl 1994: The Culmination of the Superwahljahr," ed. Russell J. Dalton and Andrei S. Markovits, *German Politics and Society* 13, no. 1 (Spring 1995); David P. Conradt, Gerald A. Kleinfeld, George K. Romoser, and Christian Søe, eds., *Germany's New Politics* (Providence, R.I.: Berghahn, 1995); Russell J. Dalton, ed., *Germans Divided* (Oxford: Berg, forthcoming).

14. *Frankfurter Rundschau,* October 18, 1994.

15. Infas, "Report für die Presse," October 21, 1994, pp. 3, 4.

16. Timothy G. Ash, "Kohl's Germany: The Beginning of the End?" *New York Review of Books,* December 1, 1994, p. 21.

17. *Die Zeit,* October 21, 1994; *Bundestagswahl 1994: Eine Analyse der Wahl zum 13. Deutschen Bundestag am 16. Oktober 1994* (Mannheim: Forschungsgruppe Wahlen, 1994), pp. 9–29.

Conclusion

THE CURRENT GERMAN party system is merely the latest in a series of discontinuous ones since the Empire era. From 1871 to 1918, parties played only a limited role in the nondemocratic political system; instead power was wielded by the kaiser, the chancellor, and the traditional elites—the bureaucracy, the military, the nobility, and the large landowners. During the brief Weimar era (1918–1933), the multiparty system, in which major democratic parties competed with numerous extremist, regional, and special interest parties, mirrored the deep fissures within the state. Unstable coalition cabinets had a short life span, contributing to the economic and social problems that peaked in the Great Depression. During the Hitler era (1933–1945), the monolithic Nazi Party crushed all opposition. After World War II, new and restructured parties emerged in the western and eastern zones. Thereafter a dominant two-party system in the Federal Republic confronted a dominant one-party system in the German Democratic Republic. When the GDR collapsed, its accession to the FRG led to popular acceptance of the western party configuration.

True, many other European states also lacked continuity in their party systems, but Germany's failure to develop a democratic one at crucial times in its history had disastrous consequences, including its launching of aggressive wars in 1914 and 1939.

The Central Role of Parties

One of the two themes underlying this book is the centrality of German parties in the post-1945 political systems. In the GDR, the ruling Socialist Unity Party, created out of a merger of the KPD and SPD under Soviet pressure, was at the core of the system, marginalizing the bloc parties, the unions, and other social organizations. Thus, during the four decades of the GDR's existence, its authoritarian SED leaders, who shaped party and government policies, were more powerful than their CDU/CSU or SPD counterparts in Bonn.

In West Germany and currently in the united Germany, CDU/CSU or SPD chancellors and ministers have determined, with their coalition partner or partners, the country's domestic and foreign policies. The parties' central role is derived from the Basic Law. They are to help form the political will of the people but can be declared unconstitutional if the Constitutional Court rules that they intend to do away with the democratic basic order. Legislation grants parties substantial public funds. Their central role extends beyond the policymaking level to their attempted domination of the bureaucracy, the judiciary, and public television and radio.

Parties have much power, but, as in most parliamentary systems, they face constraints. Whether in Bonn or the Länder, a multitude of interest groups—business, agriculture, labor, and others—seek to influence bills affecting them. Group specialists bypass parties and lobby the bureaucrats, or provide assistance to them, as they draft legislation. Interest group functionaries are chosen as candidates on party tickets to ensure that the groups are represented directly in the Bundestag or Länder legislatures.

In the 1970s and 1980s, environmental, peace, antinuclear, and women's movements mushroomed as parallel political organizations to the parties. Frustrated by the parties' failure to address their concerns, these movements organized single-issue citizens' groups, which subsequently became national organizations. They staged mass demonstrations or took other direct political actions to pressure the government decisionmakers, who also happened to be party leaders. By the time the parties realized that the groups constituted a groundswell of protest, the environmental movement had transformed itself into a political party—the Greens.[1]

Political Stability

The second thesis of this book is that the parties have provided the political stability underpinning the FRG since 1949 (close to half a century) and the GDR from 1949 to the fall of the Wall in 1989. In the GDR, the SED and its ancillary state security agency imposed on the country a stability, inherent in all dictatorial systems but not necessarily in all democratic systems, that few citizens dared to challenge until 1989. At that time, the Soviet Union and several Eastern European governments had allowed more freedoms to their citizens, which in turn led to the successful peaceful revolution of East Germans against their regime. The subsequent accession of the GDR to the FRG in 1990 showed that East German citizens preferred the stability of the FRG to that of the GDR.

In the FRG, the limited multiparty system, in which two dominant people's parties are flanked by a few minor parties, facilitated the formation of stable CDU/CSU-led or SPD-led coalitions. The CDU/CSU governed from 1949 to 1969 and from 1982 to the present. The FDP has been its perennial coalition partner, except from 1949 to 1961, when the CDU/CSU allied itself with two or three minor parties (including the FDP for some of these years) and from 1966 to 1969, when the CDU/CSU formed a grand coalition with the SPD. The SPD also allied itself with the FDP, in its more liberal incarnation, from 1969 to 1982.[2] Thus, the small FDP has served as a national kingmaker in the country's politics for an unusually long time—a role that the FDP may finally lose to the Greens in the 1998 election as a result of its catastrophic showing in the 1994 and 1995 Länder elections.

The coalition governments have usually remained in office for the full four-year Bundestag sessions, with only a few exceptions, such as in 1982, when the SPD-FDP coalition toppled two years early over serious policy differences. Normally stability prevails because of the lack of fundamental cleavages between the increasingly centrist governing parties, which have little difficulty concurring on most domestic and foreign policies whenever they form a government. If they do not reach an accord on a policy, say health reform, the cabinet will leave it off the government agenda unless consensus is eventually achieved. Since the 1960s, the narrowing of differences between the CDU/CSU and the SPD on domestic and foreign policies has led to a remarkable continuity in policies, regardless of which one is the major political actor.

Stability has also been enhanced because the party topography did not change appreciably in the FRG. For decades, only three parties (CDU/CSU, SPD, and FDP) had seats in the Bundestag; in 1983 the Greens and in 1990 the PDS joined the privileged ranks. Despite the change from a three- to a five-party system, stability was not threatened because the political system adapted to the changes and because the Greens and the PDS channeled much of the anger of disaffected groups into the parliamentary arena. Antisystem leftist and rightist parties have been too weak politically to surmount the 5 percent barrier in the Bundestag, although they have had seats in Länder and city legislatures.

Political stability does not mean that cleavages between and within the center-right CDU/CSU and the center-left SPD have disappeared entirely. There are programmatic differences (e.g., on nuclear energy policy), but ideology has played a secondary position to pragmatism. In the 1990s, a two-bloc party system has emerged in which the conservative CDU/CSU and conservative-liberal FDP bloc is pitted against the center-left SPD, leftist Greens, and socialist PDS bloc. The 1994 election results indicate that each bloc has about equal strength, although the PDS is currently not seen by the SPD and Greens as a potential coalition partner. All parties have their squabbling factions and elite rivalries, which are inevitable in catchall organizations that bundle diverse social groups and which allow a modicum of intra-party democracy. But these differences and disputes, if kept to manageable proportions, can only strengthen, rather than weaken, the democratic fiber of a state.

A Crisis of Parties?

In spite, or perhaps because of, the centrality of parties and the political stability they have provided, their role in politics has increasingly come under fire. Critics have voiced justifiable complaints about the parties' failure to deal with or to resolve important issues and about the parties' involvement in graft, corruption, and patronage. What are the roots of this criticism, epitomized in the frequently used expression *Parteienverdrossenheit?* Until the 1970s, the West German parties, quiescent and supportive of the status quo, mirrored the country's social peace and affluence. But then, as in other advanced industrial states, social and cultural changes produced a new assertive middle class of young, well-educated civil servants, salaried employees, and professionals. They demanded that the established parties deal with hitherto neglected postmaterialist issues, such as the environment. However, party leaders could not easily accede to these demands because their core constituencies wanted them to deal with equally important materialist demands, such as jobs. The party leaders still have not been able to resolve this dilemma. In the 1990s, these leaders, on the defensive, have claimed that they should not be blamed for their inability as government policymakers to solve many domestic and foreign policy issues because they have little control over the globalization of the economy, transnational migrations, the autonomy of the Bundesbank (Federal Bank), and the enhanced power of the European Union—all of which limit their capacity to make independent decisions.

Internal Challenges

The transformation of West Germany's social structure has affected the parties' internal life. From the 1960s until the 1980s, party functionaries successfully recruited new members, but since then the pattern has been a steady decline in membership. Many young people have resigned from parties or do not join one in the first place. They are wary of a regimented life and big organizations and critical of the parties' lack of intraparty democracy, which limits younger members' access to leadership positions. The parties' future as membership organizations becomes endangered if youth's élan and imagination are missing. This decline in members is paralleled by political apathy among most remaining members, which is not a new phenomenon.

Cartoonists accurately gauge the growing distance, and consequent dissatisfaction, between "the citizen" (looking up) and "the parties" perched high in a cloud. *Source: Frankfurter Rundschau,* May 12, 1993. Reprinted by permission.

A 1991 poll indicated that only 26 percent of respondents had ever attended an election or party rally, a figure that hardly differed from similar polls taken in earlier decades.[3] Party officials find little consolation in the similarity between their problems and those experienced by parties in other countries.[4]

The German parties also face the problem of integrating their decentralized organizations. The officials' attempt to center more power in their Bonn headquarters has never been too successful because the Länder chiefs jealously maintain a modicum of power. One writer aptly characterizes the CDU/CSU and SPD as being a "loosely coupled anarchy."[5] Since 1990, the gap between the western and eastern Länder organizations has compounded the parties' difficulties.

External Challenges

In the 1990s, the voters charge party leaders, whose promises to create a better society are no longer believed, with acting first to protect their own interests and only secondarily those of the public. The voters' critique is reinforced by the media, which are not reluctant to publicize the leaders' personal enrichment and involvement in financial corruption scandals (the leaders' "self-service store" mentality has become a favorite expression). In a poll taken in fall 1993, politicians were close to the bottom (9 percent) in the prestige of their profession. Doctors, clergy, and lawyers topped the list, while booksellers and trade union leaders, ranking below politicians, made up the bottom.[6] Such had not always been the case. In 1978, only 25 percent of those queried in another poll claimed that they were disillusioned by the CDU/CSU, SPD, and FDP, but by December 1993 the total had risen to 66 percent (in eastern Germany, 61 percent).[7]

When most social groups, except for the wealthy, experience hardships, disillusionment increases. For instance, a new peripheral labor market has developed in which the number of dead-end jobs has grown exponentially. Workers holding such jobs belong to the underclass, which also includes the long-term unemployed, the homeless, and alcohol and drug users. Marginalized in a consumer-oriented society, they decry the parties' lack of concern about their plight. Many drop out of society and see voting as useless.[8]

A shift in class, religious, and other social patterns means that the traditional constituencies on which CDU/CSU and SPD leaders could rely for voter support are fading. There are fewer devout Catholics and farmers voting for the CDU/CSU and fewer organized workers voting for the SPD. The new middle class lacks the religious and class identification of an earlier generation.[9] This in turn affects the programmatic direction of the CDU/CSU and the SPD. As noted, if the two parties appeal primarily to their shrinking traditional constituencies, they will be unable to attract many of the new middle-class voters, whose partisan attachments are weak or who have become strong Green adherents. In short, the major parties are losing their capacity to integrate diverse constituencies, which is made even more difficult by the different groups supporting them in eastern and in western Germany. For instance, the CDU/CSU, unlike the SPD, receives few votes from organized workers in western Germany but many from those in eastern Germany.

The number of voters who switch their party allegiance from one election to another has risen sharply. Survey data indicate that in 1972 55 percent of respondents still showed either very strong or strong party affiliations but that by 1993 the number had declined to 24 percent in western and 21 percent in eastern Germany.[10] Because of this declining level of partisan identification, the CDU/CSU and SPD together have seen their voting support drop from over 90 percent in 1969 and 1972 to 78 percent in 1994. The 1995 North Rhine–Westphalia Land election illustrates the shift in partisan voting: For the first time in fifteen years the SPD lost its absolute majority, the FDP plummeted below 5 percent, and the Greens doubled their vote to 10 percent.

This volatility in voting causes the party system to become more fragmented. In a realignment of parties, dissatisfied voters have increasingly supported new parties on the left, right, and center. The changed political topography meant that in the 1990s the Greens and the PDS on the left, the Republicans and the German People's Union on the right, and the Instead Party in the center, as well as others, challenged the established parties. Among these parties, only the Greens and the PDS have gained Bundestag seats, but the others, small in size, have occasionally won seats in Land legislatures and, in the case of the Republicans, the European Parliament.

In addition, as in other Western European countries, the percentage of Germans who have voted in elections has declined in recent decades. In West Germany in the 1970s, more than 90 percent of citizens, bound by a tradition of civic duty to vote, went to the polls, but by 1994 their number in the old and new Länder had dropped to 79 percent. (By U.S. standards, that is still a high turnout when compared to, say, the 39 percent in the 1994 congressional election.) In the united Germany, the "Party of Nonvoters" has grown steadily, especially in Land and European Parliament elections and among youths and eastern Germans who are convinced that their votes would make little difference in Bonn's policies. This nonvoting trend has worried party leaders, although some trenchant observers, seeing it as a healthy sign for democracy, point out that frustrated voters are expressing their disenchantment with parties by staying at home in protest against a system unresponsive to their needs.[11]

The lower level of partisan identification and voting has been offset by a relatively high interest in politics. A poll in 1991 showed that in western Germany 73 percent of respondents discussed politics (22 percent frequently and 51 percent occasionally), while 27 percent never did. In eastern Germany, the corresponding figures show 85 percent discussing politics (36 percent frequently and 49 percent occasionally) and only 15 percent never doing so.[12] Discussion of politics, however, does not indicate satisfaction with the crisis-laden political system. A 1993 Emnid poll revealed that the level of satisfaction had plummeted from 74 percent in 1987 to 28 percent in 1993.[13]

Many dissatisfied citizens and groups have proposed that more direct democracy be infused into the political system. However, in 1994 the CDU/CSU blocked a proposal by the leftist parties in the constitutional commission (set up by Parliament after unification) that would have provided for national initiatives and referenda in a revised Basic Law. A CDU le-

"His majesty, the voter." Voters increasingly question their importance in the political system. The cartoonist portrays the royal gown being held up by two party officials, with one saying to the other, "Thank God, it happens only once every four years." *Source: Schwäbisches Tagblatt Tübingen,* October 4, 1980. Reprinted by permission.

gal scholar critical of the proposal said that it would atomize the electorate, to which one SPD leader retorted, "Why is it you distrust the people so much?"[14]

Despite the CDU/CSU's negative position, pressure continues within its ranks, as within the SPD, to let the rank and file participate more directly in their organizations, such as allowing them to nominate and vote for their party's candidates for public office. Progress has been slow, except for the SPD's innovative polling of its members in 1993 on their choice of party chairperson.

A crisis of legitimacy can be avoided if the parties become more democratic and responsive to people's needs, especially in the east, where economic and social conditions can be expected to improve only slowly in coming years. Eastern party leaders and members, except for the PDS, feel disadvantaged by being in a permanent minority within the all-German parties. Their difficulties are compounded by a clash of values with their western colleagues. One wry joke tells it all: In 1990 demonstrators in Leipzig chanted, "We are one people;" in 1995 when Germans meet each other, the easterner says, "We are one people," to which the westerner replies, "Us too."[15]

Confronting the Future

Speculations and predictions about future party developments are fraught with danger. Unlike in the United States, where a presidential election is certain to be held every four years, in parliamentary systems there is no guarantee that a government, especially if it is a coalition, will last the normal parliamentary cycle (Italy is a prime example). In Germany, Kohl's conservative government has had such a slim Bundestag majority since 1994 that the defection of a few government deputies in a crucial vote, or an irreconcilable cleavage between the CDU/CSU and FDP, would end his reign prematurely. Even if the coalition remains in office until 1998, the next regularly scheduled election, the prospect of another victory for CDU/CSU and FDP is uncertain. In 1994, Kohl announced that he would not become a candidate for chancellor in 1998. Since the announcement, reports indicate that he may change his mind and run again, adding to the uncertainty. Within the CDU, there are few viable candidates in line for the posts of chairperson and national chancellor. Wolfgang Schäuble, the ultraconservative leader of the CDU/CSU Fraktion, remains the most likely candidate.

The CDU/CSU officials realize that if the FDP should fall by the wayside in 1998, their coalition options are extremely limited. The end of the FDP as a national party is a distinct possibility if, without representation in most Länder legislatures, it cannot muster more than 5 percent of the vote in 1998 without the assistance of CDU/CSU voters. If the Christian Democrats gain a plurality of votes in 1998 and the FDP does not surmount the 5 percent barrier, the most likely scenario would then be a CDU/CSU grand coalition with the SPD. There has been some speculation that the CDU/CSU might even ask the Greens in 1998 to join it in a cabinet, but that possibility, given the parties' ideological differences, is remote.

In 1995, the SPD was beset by a fratricidal leadership struggle between Scharping and Schröder. As a consequence, the party's ranking in polls plummeted to a dangerous low. Delegates at the November convention, partly blaming Scharping for the disaster, did not support his renewed candidacy as chairman and voted for the left leaning Lafontaine to succeed him. If eventually the moderate Schröder becomes the chancellor candidate in 1998, a possibility, the SPD's electoral prospects may improve significantly. By then, the CDU/CSU and FDP will have been in power for sixteen years, and many of their voters may decide to switch. The voters' choice will also depend on the SPD's 1994–1998 parliamentary record, especially its position on legislation being considered by the Bundesrat, in which it has a majority. Finally, the voters' choice will depend on their perception of the SPD's competence on crucial economic issues and on their assessment of the SPD's policy alternatives to the Kohl government.

The Greens have lost the image of being the bugaboo of German politics. According to one 1994 poll, about one-half of the respondents give the party positive values on a political sympathy scale.[16] Their future as an established party, at least in western Germany, where they have become the third strongest party, is no longer in doubt, yet the danger of a schism between the western and eastern Greens or the withdrawal of Alliance 90 from the party cannot be ruled out.

The prospects for the PDS in 1998 are unpredictable. It has a core of loyal followers whose antipathy toward western Germany and backing of eastern German interests are bound to remain strong, but its fringe adherents may switch to other parties as economic and social conditions improve. Conversely, the party may muster more strength in western Germany from disgruntled SPD and Green voters who believe that their parties have become too conservative. If the PDS succeeds at least in holding onto its 1994 voters, it has a chance of remaining in the Bundestag in 1998.

Red-green coalitions are now commonly accepted in the Länder, and a national red-green coalition is becoming one of the possibilities after the 1998 election. The formation of such a coalition in Bonn, which would be without precedent in any national government worldwide, presupposes a willingness on the part of the SPD and Greens to compromise on important policy differences. SPD chairman Lafontaine can be expected to support a red-green coalition, especially because he will steer the SPD toward the left in coming years and away from the center, unlike his predecessor Scharping. But a coalition between the SPD, Greens, and PDS is not in sight, given historical, ideological, and political cleavages.

Since 1990, the rightist parties have become a negligible force in German politics, unlike their Italian, French, Austrian, and other European counterparts. The Republicans would have maintained their appeal to some voters if two of their objectives, German unification and a toughening of the asylum laws, had not been achieved, although fulfillment of the first was not of the Republicans' making and realization of the second occurred only because the powerful CDU/CSU had the same objective and the SPD caved in to the CDU/CSU's goal to limit immigration. Yet the Republicans and the German People's Union have succeeded in moving the nation's political agenda, especially on immigration and the status of foreigners within Germany, to the right. If in the future a major economic and social crisis erupted, the rightist parties would probably regain their previous strength. Polls have shown that they could reach 10–15 percent of the vote from citizens with a racist, anti-Semitic, and authoritarian frame of mind.[17]

The neo-Nazi–inspired group violence against foreigners and other minorities, which continues on a reduced scale, is of more immediate concern to most Germans, who are worried about their international image or outraged about a resurgence of neo-Nazism. Democratic parties and groups, to counter such rightist views and actions, have supported political education in schools, pleaded for a more tolerant civic culture, and staged massive prodemocracy demonstrations in which hundreds of thousands of citizens have participated.

In sum, the future of several German parties, especially the FDP and PDS, is uncertain. Therefore, predictions about election and coalition outcomes will become increasingly difficult to make. The CDU/CSU and SPD will remain the chief political actors, even though party membership is declining, partisan attachments are weakening, and fewer citizens are voting. But these trends reflect societal and cultural changes visible in other countries too and are not necessarily damaging to the democratic system. Thus, parties are not in an inexorable state of crisis and decline from which they can no longer extricate themselves.[18]

Yet German party leaders are worried about the many citizens with antiparty views. To create a more favorable climate for parties, the leaders would need to reduce the cleavage between the western and eastern electorates and incorporate eastern German goals into the party programs; inject more democracy and less technocratic management into their organizations; and stop planning electoral campaigns in which issues are less important than their own personalities. Party leaders would also need to provide voters with different policy choices concerning major economic and social problems, which then need to be addressed; and end their own personal enrichment and involvement in corruption scandals. It is up to the leaders whether they can regain the confidence of the citizens, especially youths, by making these necessary changes. If they respond positively, a party system attuned to the volatility of democratic politics on the eve of the twenty-first century could flourish.

Notes

1. See Stephen Padgett, "Introduction: Party Democracy in the New Germany," in *Parties and Party Systems in the New Germany,* ed. Stephen Padgett (Aldershot, England: Dartmouth, 1993), pp. 5, 10; Peter H. Merkl, "The Challengers and the Party Systems," in *When Parties Fail: Emerging Alternative Organizations,* ed. Kay

Lawson and Peter H. Merkl (Princeton: Princeton University Press, 1988), pp. 561–565.

2. In 1949, ten parties gained seats in the Bundestag; by 1961 the number was down to three (CDU/CSU, SPD, and FDP). For a list of chancellors and cabinets (including the number of seats held by the coalition parties) from 1949 to 1994, see Wichard Woyke, *Stichwort: Wahlen; Wähler—Parteien—Wahlverfahren,* 8th ed. (Bonn: Bundeszentrale für politische Bildung, 1994), pp. 24–25.

3. Elisabeth Noelle-Neumann, "Wandlungen der deutschen Demokratie, 1953–1991," in *Civitas: Widmungen für Bernhard Vogel zum 60. Geburtstag,* ed. Peter Haungs, Karl-Martin Grass, Hans Maier, and Hans-Joachim Veen (Paderborn: Ferdinand Schöningh, 1992), p. 437.

4. Alf Mintzel and Heinrich Oberreuter, "Zukunftsperspektiven des Parteiensystems," in *Parteien in der Bundesrepublik Deutschland,* ed. Alf Mintzel and Heinrich Oberreuter (Opladen: Leske und Budrich, 1992), pp. 490–501. For membership in parties from 1946 to 1990, see M. Donald Hancock, "The SPD Seeks a New Identity: Party Modernization and Prospects in the 1990s," in *The New Germany Votes: Unification and the Creation of a New German Party System,* ed. Russell J. Dalton (Providence, R.I.: Berg, 1993), p. 91.

5. Peter Lösche, "Zur Metamorphose der politischen Parteien in Deutschland," *Gewerkschaftliche Monatshefte* 43 (September 1992):531–537.

6. Deutscher Akademischer Austauschdienst, *Letter,* no. 4/93 (1993):9.

7. Elisabeth Noelle-Neumann, "Die Demokratie geht rückwärts: Eine Dokumentation des Beitrags in der FAZ vom 19. Januar 1994" (Allensbach: Institut für Demoskopie, 1994), p. 4, hectographed. For still another poll, with somewhat different results, see *Der Spiegel,* December 27, 1993, p. 32.

8. Hans-Georg Betz, "Krise oder Wandel? Zur Zukunft der Politik in der postindustriellen Moderne," *Aus Politik und Zeitgeschichte,* B 11/93 (March 12, 1993):3–6, 12.

9. Hans-Joachim Veen and Peter Gluchowski, "Die Anhängerschaft der Parteien vor und nach der Einheit—eine Langfristbetrachtung von 1953 bis 1993," *Zeitschrift für Parlamentsfragen* 2 (1994):165–186.

10. Russell J. Dalton, "Two German Electorates?" in *Developments in German Politics,* ed. Gordon Smith, William Paterson, Peter H. Merkl, and Stephen Padgett (Basingstoke, England: Macmillan, 1992), p. 71; Birgit Hoffmann-Jaberg and Dieter Roth, "Die Nichtwähler: Politische Normalität oder wachsende Distanz zu den Parteien?" in *Das Super Wahljahr: Deutschland vor unkalkulierbaren Regierungsmehrheiten?* ed. Wilhelm Bürklin and Dieter Roth (Cologne: Bund, 1994), p. 135.

11. In a poll taken in February and March 1994, 49 percent of respondents believed that it made no sense at times to go to the polls, 42 percent disagreed, and 9 percent were undecided (Elisabeth Noelle-Neumann, "Wählen und Familientradition: Eine Dokumentation des Beitrags in der FAZ, Nr. 63 vom 16. März 1994" [Allensbach: Institut für Demoskopie, 1994], Table A8, hectographed). See

also Ursula Feist, *Die Macht der Nichtwähler: Wie die Wähler den Volksparteien davonlaufen* (Munich: Knaur, 1994).

12. Noelle-Neumann, "Wandlungen der deutschen Demokratie, 1953–1991," p. 436.

13. *Der Spiegel,* December 27, 1993, p. 29.

14. GIC, *The Week in Germany,* July 8, 1994.

15. *New York Times,* January 24, 1995.

16. Forschungsgruppe Wahlen, September 1994; cited in "Die Bundestagswahl vom 16. Oktober 1994—eine erste Analyse" (Sankt Augustin: Konrad-Adenauer-Stiftung, 1994), pp. B13–14.

17. Klaus Leggewie, *Die Republikaner: Phantombild der neuen Rechten,* 2d ed. (Berlin: Rotbuch, 1989), p. 54. See also Brigitte Young, "The German Political Party System and the Contagion from the Right," *German Politics and Society* 13, no. 1 (Spring 1995):62–78.

18. See Steven B. Wolinetz, "Party System Change: Past, Present, and Future," in *Parties and Party Systems in Liberal Democracies,* ed. Steven B. Wolinetz (London: Routledge, 1988), pp. 296–316; Wolfgang Luthardt, "'Krise' der Volksparteien—oder 'Differenzierung' und 'Verfestigung' im bundesdeutschen Parteiensystem?" *Journal für Sozialforschung* 31, no. 2 (1991):140.

Appendix: Self-Portraits
of the Bundestag Parties, 1994

TㅎHIS APPENDIX contains the statements submitted by parties to the German government agency Inter Nationes before the 1994 national election. The statements are reprinted in Inter Nationes, *Special Election Report: Procedures, Programmes, Profiles*, Special Topic, SO 10–1994.

The Christian Democratic Union of Germany

Following their experience with the splinter parties which existed during the Weimar Republic (1919–1933) and having been shocked by the 12 years of nazi totalitarianism, the founders of the CDU resolved in 1945 to create a non-denominational people's party based on Christian principles. Then, as now, the CDU regarded Christian values and concepts as the best foundation for a truly humane, free, democratic and social state. The new post-war German state, the Federal Republic of Germany, bears the strong imprint of the CDU: the federal structure, the separation of powers and the emphasis on individual civil rights, and above all adherence to the goal of German unity, to the free part of Germany's integration into the western community, to the pursuit of European Union, and to the social market economy.

During the time Germany was divided the CDU's candidates served as chancellor in the Federal Republic from 1949 to 1969 (Konrad Adenauer, Ludwig Erhard and Kurt-Georg Kiesinger) and from 1982 (Helmut Kohl). Many significant achievements in the Federal Republic's history have largely been due to the influence of the CDU. In the field of foreign and security policy they include the systematic progress towards European integration leading to the European Union, as well as Germany's strong position in the western defence alliance, NATO.

An economically and politically strong Germany in Europe and the world, pursuing a clear and reliable course, then paved the way for the ultimate political goal of national unity. The peaceful revolution in eastern Germany, which also involved many people who are now members of the CDU, coupled with the speedy and resolute action of the Federal Government under Helmut Kohl which created the internal and external conditions for reunification, made it possible for the eastern part of the nation to accede to the Federal Republic of Germany on 3 October 1990.

The last four years in united Germany have mainly been taken up with joint efforts to give substance to the formal act of unification. Good progress has been made towards harmonizing conditions in east and west, and the CDU aims to complete the process as quickly as possible. Despite the considerable achievements, however, it will be some time before conditions are the same in every respect.

Thus the task of completing German unity internally is the nucleus of the CDU's policy document adopted in Hamburg in February 1994. In it the Christian Democrats renew their commitment to a free and responsible society and their intention to develop the social market economy into an ecological and social market economy. They aim to redefine and strengthen Germany's role alongside the free nations of the world. In order to maintain the welfare state's efficiency and ensure that it can be funded, the necessary restructuring process will also entail qualitative improvements.

The focal point of CDU policy remains the citizen, who as both an individual and a social animal needs society as a whole in order to be able to exercise his freedom in responsibility.

The Christian Social Union

The Christian Social Union (CSU) is a party which, from an organizational point of view, is confined to Bavaria but is involved in policy-making at national level. Ever since the founding of the Federal Republic of Germany it has been a party to major decisions taken by CDU/CSU-led federal governments. Together with its "sister party," the CDU, it forms one parliamentary group in the German Bundestag. The CSU is made up of people from all social strata. Its members are conscious of their responsibility for their fellow-citizens, society as a whole and the country's democratic system.

The CSU bases its political activity on the Christian image of man. It is thus aware of its commitment to history and to the intellectual and cultural heritage of the whole nation. The party faces present-day responsibilities in the light of past experience. This enables it to work out solutions for the problems of tomorrow.

By dint of its responsibility towards the individual, the state and its citizens, the CSU defends the rights and interests of the individual and the different groups in society. It advocates a fair distribution of benefits and burdens among them. The CSU is a people's party. As an independent political force it carries out its responsibilities in and for Bavaria, for Germany, and for Europe. It is committed to world peace.

The CSU is a conservative party because it subscribes to a permanent system of values. It is a liberal party because it stands up for the individual's fundamental rights and freedoms. It is a social party because it supports all citizens, especially the weakest members of society. It stands for an equitable social order.

The CSU's manifesto for the elections for the European Parliament on 12 June 1994 summarizes the basic tenets of its policy as follows: "The CSU's policy is founded in our native Bavaria, the main source of our responsibility. From its Bavarian base the CSU influences German policy, leaving its own strong, unmistakable imprint and showing a sense of national responsibility. Our policy has not only a Bavarian and German but also a European dimension. The continent's future lies in the European Union."

The Social Democratic Party of Germany

The SPD is ready to assume the responsibility of government. We stand on the threshold of a new epoque. The post-war era has ended and Germany is no longer divided. Two parts that belonged together are now one. The task is now to improve the lot of the people. The SPD responds to the question as to the interplay of freedom and justice and describes how society should be shaped as well as the individual's rights and responsibilities towards society and vice-versa. Its objectives, as set out below, would find concrete expression in the programme of an SPD administration.

Workers' freedom means: more codetermination and more humane working conditions. Freedom for young people means: better opportunities for education and training. Social Democratic policy means: safeguarding and developing personal freedom in a society based on solidarity. For instance, the introduction of the flexible retirement age has given millions of employees the freedom to decide themselves when they wish to retire.

The crucial issues today are the safeguarding of peace, the modernization of the economy in the light of ecological requirements, the combating of unemployment, and the solution of problems associated with German unity. The SPD will seek to harmonize conditions in united Germany and pursue a policy of social and ecological reconstruction. It will complete Germany's internal unification and bring the people closer together, step by step.

The Free Democratic Party

The guarantee of inviolable basic rights, the free development of personality, the protection of minorities, the separation and control of public authority, and a body politic based on freedom and the rule of law are the fundamental precepts of Liberalism which, after many attempts and setbacks, have been established step by step. The murderous lunacy of National Socialism sought to destroy these historic achievements of German Liberalism, but they survived. These fundamental liberal values were trampled underfoot during the 40 years of Communist dictatorship in East Germany, but they did not perish.

Since the inception of the Federal Republic of Germany the FDP has been involved in determining the fate of the country, both as a coalition partner in the Federal Government and as an opposition party. The Liberals played a major part in drafting the Basic Law for the free western part of Germany as the foundation for a democratic society. They have ensured that Germany has been governed not from the extremes but from the centre of the political spectrum. The FDP has always been and will continue to be the axis of democracy in Germany.

The Liberals in the eastern part of the country were for a very long time unable to live in freedom as they had wished. The removal of the wall dividing Germany was for them, too, the day of liberation. The people from the former GDR brought about a peaceful revolution, but a major contributory factor was the consistent foreign policy and commitment to civil rights and the social market economy of the Liberals. Since 1990 Liberals throughout the country have been united in the Free Democratic Party. They now together pursue their liberal objectives.

To Liberals the notion of freedom is comprehensive. It must be the common asset of all social strata. There is an indissoluble link between social and economic freedom. Freedom is the opportunity of the future and must be used accordingly: by enhancing the free market economy so as to provide jobs and training opportunities for the young generation; by promoting technological advancement with a view to improving the environment; by encouraging individual initiative and codetermination and thus less government involvement; and by securing more civil rights and thus making for a more virile democracy. Government controls can nowhere do justice to the diversity of the people's wishes or effectively ward off dangers, but they can make it difficult for people to use their opportunities. An open society of free citizens acting with courage and confidence can best master the tasks of the future.

We Liberals intend to continue the successful coalition with the CDU and the CSU after the general election on 16 October 1994. We say to the electorate: Anyone wishing to prevent the election of an SPD and Alliance 90/Greens government or a grand coalition of CDU/CSU and SPD must vote FDP.

Alliance 90/the Greens

In the 1994 general election the Greens, due to the political changes resulting from Germany's reunification, will join forces with Alliance 90, which is the umbrella for the east German civil rights movements which played a crucial role in removing the Communist regime in the former German Democratic Republic. In contrast to the Christian Democrats and Liberals, who joined forces with the old block parties in the GDR, cooperation between the Greens and Alliance 90 is a grassroots movement which was sealed by a general ballot of all members in the autumn of 1993. As a result, this new political force Alliance 90/Greens has lost most of its dogmatists and acquired a better image through its commitment to human and civil rights throughout the world. Alliance 90/Greens wants a socio-ecological and equitable market economy which does not give human rights lowest priority at any (human rights) price, as in China, for instance.

The Party of Democratic Socialism

The PDS is a socialist party and adopts radical-democratic and anti-capitalist positions. Human survival, a social, ecological and cultural perspective, require far-reaching changes in society. Such changes will remain impossible so long as profiteering and capital exploitation dominate society. That is why the party's route is that of democratic socialism.

The PDS is particularly powerful in the new states of eastern Germany, where in the final days of the GDR it emerged in response to the wishes of tens of thousands of members of the former Socialist Unity Party of Germany (SED). Since 1990 it has been active in the whole country. It is represented in the Bundestag and six of the state parliaments, and it has gained members in the old German states and West Berlin.

Dangerous trends have emerged in Germany in recent years. Big-power aspirations, nationalism and right-wing extremism are on the increase. The long overdue radical change in the country's economic policy, which is necessary for human survival, leading to a world economy based on mutual solidarity and ecological change, has not taken place. The global ecological, social, cultural and security crisis has intensified.

The gains in terms of political rights, travel and consumerism which national unity has brought the people in the GDR are unmistakable. But instead of the two German states being united on equal terms, the GDR was merely attached to the old Federal Republic. An unprecedented destruction of industry, agriculture, and culture has taken place in eastern Germany. One third of the people capable of work have been denied it. It has become increasingly apparent that the Federal Government and the employers' associations regard eastern Germany as a place to experiment with measures aimed at reducing welfare and democracy which will be applied increasingly throughout the country. But democracy must stand the test precisely in times of domestic crisis. The PDS, as a left-wing, socialist opposition, demands exclusively democratic solutions.

Selected Bibliography

THE FOLLOWING IS a list of books and articles, primarily in the English language, on German political parties. Several important survey books in the German language are also included. For additional sources, see the notes at the end of each chapter.

Binder, David. *The Other German: Willy Brandt's Life and Times.* Washington, D.C.: New Republic Book Company, 1975.

Braunthal, Gerard. "An Analysis of the German Elections of 1990," *Politics and Society in Germany, Austria and Switzerland* 5 (Summer 1993):29–53.

————. *The German Social Democrats Since 1969: A Party in Power and Opposition.* 2d ed. Boulder: Westview Press, 1994.

————. The 1989 Basic Program of the German Social Democratic Party." *Polity* 25, no. 3 (Spring 1993):375–400.

————. "The Perspective from the Left." *German Politics and Society* 13, no. 1 (Spring 1995):36–49.

————. "The Rise of Right-Wing Extremism in the New Germany." In *The Domestic Politics of German Unification,* ed. Christopher Anderson, Karl Kaltenthaler, and Wolfgang Luthardt. Boulder: Lynne Rienner, 1993.

————. "Social Democratic–Green Coalitions in West Germany: Prospects for a New Alliance." *German Studies Review* 9, no. 3 (October 1986):571–597.

————. "The Social Democratic Party." In *West German Politics in the Mid-Eighties: Crisis and Continuity,* ed. H. G. Peter Wallach and George K. Romoser. New York: Praeger, 1985.

Burkett, Tony. *Parties and Elections in West Germany: The Search for Stability.* New York: St. Martin's Press, 1975.

Canepa, Eric. "Germany's Party of Democratic Socialism." In *Socialist Register 1994,* ed. Ralph Miliband and Leo Panitch. London: Merlin Press, 1994.

Chalmers, Douglas A. *The Social Democratic Party of Germany.* New Haven: Yale University Press, 1964.

Chandler, William M. "The Christian Democrats." In *The Federal Republic of Germany at Forty,* ed. Peter H. Merkl. New York: New York University Press, 1989.

Childs, David. *From Schumacher to Brandt: The Story of German Socialism, 1945–1965.* Oxford: Pergamon Press, 1966.

Clemens, Clay. "Disquiet on the Eastern Front: The Christian Democratic Union in Germany's New Länder." *German Politics* 2, no. 2 (August 1993):200–223.

Conradt, David P. *The German Polity.* 5th ed. New York: Longman, 1993.

————. *Unified Germany at the Polls: Political Parties and the 1990 Federal Election.* German Issues No. 9. Washington, D.C.: American Institute for Contemporary German Studies, 1990.

Conradt, David P., Gerald A. Kleinfeld, George K. Romoser, Christian Søe, eds. *Germany's New Politics.* Providence, R.I.: Berghahn, 1995.

Dalton, Russell J. *Politics in Germany.* 2d ed. New York: HarperCollins, 1993.

———, ed. *Germans Divided: The 1994 Bundestagswahl and the Evolution of the German Party System.* Herndon, Va.: forthcoming.

———. *The New Germany Votes: Unification and the Creation of a New German Party System.* Providence, R.I.: Berg, 1993.

Dalton, Russell J., and Andrei S. Markovits, eds. "Bundestagswahl 1994: The Culmination of the Superwahljahr." *German Politics and Society* (special issue) 13, no. 1 (Spring 1995).

Dennis, Mike. *German Democratic Republic: Politics, Economics, and Society.* London: Pinter, 1988.

Documents on Democracy in the Federal Republic of Germany. 2d ed. Bonn: Press and Information Office, 1994.

Döring, Herbert, and Gordon Smith, eds. *Party Government and Political Culture in Western Germany.* London: Macmillan, 1982.

Duverger, Maurice. *Political Parties: Their Organization and Activity in the Modern State.* Trans. Barbara North and Robert North. 2d English ed. London: Methuen, 1959.

Dyson, Kenneth. "Party Government and Party State." In *Party Government and Political Culture in Western Germany,* ed. Herbert Döring and Gordon Smith. London: Macmillan, 1982.

Edinger, Lewis J. *Kurt Schumacher: A Study in Personality and Political Behavior.* Stanford: Stanford University Press, 1965.

Frankland, E. Gene, and Donald Schoonmaker. *Between Protest and Power: The Green Party in Germany.* Boulder: Westview Press, 1992.

Grosser, Dieter, ed. *German Unification: The Unexpected Challenge.* Oxford: Berg, 1992.

Hancock, M. Donald, and Helga A. Welsh, eds. *German Unification: Process and Outcomes.* Boulder: Westview Press, 1994.

Heidenheimer, Arnold. *Adenauer and the CDU: The Rise of the Leader and the Integration of the Party.* The Hague: Martinus Nijhoff, 1960.

Hülsberg, Werner. *The German Greens: A Social and Political Profile.* London: Verso, 1988.

Keithly, David M. *The Collapse of East German Communism: The Year the Wall Came Down, 1989.* Westport, Conn.: Praeger, 1992.

Kirchheimer, Otto. "Germany: The Vanishing Opposition." In *Political Oppositions in Western Democracies,* ed. Robert A. Dahl. New Haven: Yale University Press, 1966.

———. "The Transformation of the Western European Party Systems." In *Political Parties and Political Development,* ed. Joseph La Palombara and Seymour Weiner. Princeton: Princeton University Press, 1966.

Kolinsky, Eva. *Parties, Opposition, and Society in West Germany.* New York: St. Martin's Press, 1984.

Krisch, Henry. "From SED to PDS: The Struggle to Revive a Left Party." In *The New Germany Votes: Unification and the Creation of a New German Party System,* ed. Russell J. Dalton. Providence, R.I.: Berg, 1993.

———. *The German Democratic Republic: The Search for Identity.* Boulder: Westview Press, 1985.

———. *German Politics Under Soviet Occupation.* New York: Columbia University Press, 1974.

Lawson, Kay. *The Comparative Study of Political Parties.* New York: St. Martin's Press, 1976.

———, ed. *Political Parties and Linkage: A Comparative Perspective.* New Haven: Yale University Press, 1980.

Markovits, Andrei S., and Philip S. Gorski. *The German Left: Red, Green, and Beyond.* New York: Oxford University Press, 1993.

202 / Selected Bibliography

McFalls, Laurence H. "Political Culture, Partisan Strategies, and the PDS: Prospects for an East German Party." *German Politics and Society* 13, no. 1 (Spring 1995):50–61.

Merkl, Peter H. "The Challengers and the Party System." In *When Parties Fail: Emerging Alternative Organizations,* ed. Kay Lawson and Peter H. Merkl. Princeton: Princeton University Press, 1988.

————, ed. *The Federal Republic of Germany at Forty.* New York: New York University Press, 1989.

————. *The Federal Republic of Germany at Forty-Five.* New York: New York University Press, 1995.

Michels, Robert. *Political Parties: A Sociological Study of the Oligarchical Tendencies of Modern Democracy.* Trans. Eden Paul and Cedar Paul. New York: Dover, 1959; reprint of 1911 ed.

Miller, Susanne, and Heinrich Potthoff. *A History of German Social Democracy: From 1848 to the Present.* Leamington Spa, England: Berg, 1986.

Mintzel, Alf, and Heinrich Oberreuter, eds. *Parteien in der Bundesrepublik Deutschland.* Opladen: Leske und Budrich, 1992.

Nagle, John D. *The National Democratic Party: Right Radicalism in the Federal Republic of Germany.* Berkeley and Los Angeles: University of California Press, 1970.

Neumann, Sigmund, ed. *Modern Political Parties: Approaches to Comparative Politics.* Chicago: University of Chicago Press, 1957.

Nicholls, A. J. *Weimar and the Rise of Hitler.* London: Macmillan, 1968.

Niedermayer, Oskar, and Richard Stöss, eds. *Parteien und Wähler im Umbruch: Parteiensystem und Wählerverhalten in der ehemaligen DDR und den neuen Bundesländern.* Opladen: Westdeutscher Verlag, 1994.

Orlow, Dietrich. *The History of the Nazi Party, 1919–1933.* 2 vols. Pittsburgh: University of Pittsburgh Press, 1969, 1973.

Ostrogorski, Mosei. *Democracy and the Origin of Parties.* Garden City, N.Y.: Doubleday, 1964; reprint of 2 vols., 1902 ed.

Padgett, Stephen, ed. *Parties and Party Systems in the New Germany.* Aldershot, England: Dartmouth, 1993.

Papadakis, Elim. *The Green Movement in West Germany.* London: Croom Helm, 1984.

Paterson, William E. "The Christian Union Parties." In *West German Politics in the Mid-Eighties: Crisis and Continuity,* ed. H. G. Peter Wallach and George K. Romoser. New York: Praeger, 1985.

Phillips, Ann L. "Socialism with a New Face? The PDS in Search of Reform." *East European Politics and Societies* 8, no. 3 (Fall 1994):495–530.

Poguntke, Thomas, and Rüdiger Schmitt-Beck. "Still the Same with a New Name? Bündnis 90/Die Grünen After the Fusion. *German Politics* 3, no. 1 (April 1994):91–110.

Pridham, Geoffrey. *Christian Democracy in Western Germany: The CDU/CSU in Government and Opposition, 1945–1976.* London: Croom Helm, 1977.

Prittie, Terence. *Willy Brandt: Portrait of a Statesman.* New York: Schocken, 1974.

Richter, Michaela W. "Exiting the GDR: Political Movements and Parties Between Democratization and Westernization." In *German Unification: Process and Outcomes,* ed. M. Donald Hancock and Helga A. Welsh. Boulder: Westview Press, 1994.

Sartori, Giovanni. *Parties and Party Systems: A Framework for Analysis.* Cambridge: Cambridge University Press, 1976.

Schellenger, Harold K., Jr. *The SPD in the Bonn Republic: A Socialist Party Modernizes.* The Hague: Martinus Nijhoff, 1968.

Smith, Gordon. *Democracy in Western Germany: Parties and Politics in the Federal Republic.* 3d ed. Aldershot, England: Gower, 1986.

Smith, Gordon, William Paterson, Peter Merkl, and Stephen Padgett, eds. *Developments in German Politics.* Basingstoke, England: Macmillan, 1992.

Søe, Christian. "The Free Democratic Party." In *West German Politics in the Mid-Eighties: Crisis and Continuity,* ed. H. G. Peter Wallach and George K. Romoser. New York: Praeger, 1985.

―――. "Unity and Victory for the German Liberals." In *The New Germany Votes: Unification and the Creation of a New German Party System,* ed. Russell J. Dalton. Providence, R.I.: Berg, 1993.

Stöss, Richard, ed. *Parteien-Handbuch: Die Parteien der Bundesrepublik Deutschland, 1945–1980.* 2 vols. Opladen: Westdeutscher Verlag, 1983.

Tempel, Karl G. *Die Parteien in der Bundesrepublik Deutschland und die Rolle der Parteien in der DDR.* Opladen: Leske und Budrich, 1987.

Thompson, Wayne C. *The Political Odyssey of Herbert Wehner.* Boulder: Westview Press, 1993.

Turner, Henry Ashby Jr. *The Two Germanies Since 1945.* New Haven: Yale University Press, 1987.

Veen, Hans-Joachim, Norbert Lepszy, and Peter Mnich. *The Republikaner Party in Germany: Right-Wing Menace or Protest Catchall?* Westport, Conn.: Praeger, 1993.

Wallach, H. G. Peter, and George K. Romoser, eds. *West German Politics in the Mid-Eighties: Crisis and Continuity.* New York: Praeger, 1985.

Weber, Hermann. "The Socialist Unity Party." In *Honecker's Germany,* ed. David Childs. London: Allen and Unwin, 1985.

Wolinetz, Steven B., ed. *Parties and Party Systems in Liberal Democracies.* London: Routledge, 1988.

Young, Brigitte. "The German Political Party System and the Contagion from the Right." *German Politics and Society* 13, no. 1 (Spring 1995):62–78.

About the Book and Author

THIS COMPREHENSIVE text provides a detailed overview of the party system and politics of one of the most powerful states in the international arena. Noted scholar Gerard Braunthal surveys the parties in the Federal Republic of Germany and in the German Democratic Republic after World War II and in united Germany since 1990. By illustrating the central decisionmaking and stabilizing role the parties have played and continue to play in the political sphere, Braunthal's pioneering book fills a crucial gap in the study of German politics for scholars and students alike.

Gerard Braunthal is professor emeritus of political science at the University of Massachusetts–Amherst.

Index